THE ORDINATION OF A TREE

The Ordination
of a Tree

The Thai Buddhist Environmental Movement

SUSAN M. DARLINGTON

Cover photo: Informal tree ordination in Nan Province, performed by Phrakhru Wiboon Nanthakit. Credit: Susan M. Darlington.

Publication of this work has been supported by the Association for Asian Studies First Book Subvention Program, and by faculty development grants from Hampshire College.

Published by State University of New York Press, Albany

For information, contact State University of New York Press, Albany, NY
www.sunypress.edu

Production by Ryan Morris
Marketing by Anne M. Valentine

Library of Congress Cataloging-in-Publication Data
Darlington, Susan M.
The ordination of a tree : the Thai Buddhist environmental movement /
  Susan M. Darlington.
pages cm
Includes bibliographical references and index.
ISBN 978-1-4384-4465-9 (hardcover : alk. paper)
1. Environmentalism—Religious aspects—Buddhism. 2. Environmentalism—Thailand.
I. Title.
BQ4570.E58D37 2012
294.3'37709593—dc23
                                                                    2012000339

10 9 8 7 6 5 4 3 2 1

In memory of
Luang Pu Phuttapoj Waraporn,
with eternal gratitude

Contents

Illustrations

Gallery of color photographs follows page 166. All photographs taken by Susan M. Darlington unless otherwise noted.

Plate 1. Sacred tree at Wat Chedi Luang, Chiang Mai

Plate 2. Informal tree ordination in Nan Province, performed by Phrakhru Wiboon Nanthakit

Plate 3. Formal tree ordination in Nan Province, 1991

Plate 4. Miss Thailand Universe 2010 contestants performing a tree ordination. Photo provided by Bangkok Broadcasting & T.V. Co., Ltd. with watermark. Copyright 2010

Plate 5. Phrakhru Pitak Nanthakhun

Plate 6. Deforestation in Nan Province

Plate 7. Accepting seedling donations at *pha pa ton mai* ceremony and tree ordination in Nan Province, 1991

Plate 8. Celebration of Phrakhru Pitak Nanthakhun's ecclesiastical promotion and environmental award at *suep chata* ceremony for the Nan River, 1993

Plate 9. Monks chanting at a tree ordination holding the *sai sincana,* or sacred cord, connecting them to water, the Buddha image, and the tree being consecrated

Plate 10. Spirit shrine behind ordained tree in Phrakhru Pitak's village

Plate 11. Skit enacting blame for deforestation on government policies, performed as part of tree ordination in Nan Province, 1991

Acknowledgments

THIS BOOK HAS BEEN a long time in the making. I owe a great many people gratitude for their help and support along the way, most importantly the monks who gave me their time, shared their stories, and were infinitely patient with me. First and foremost, this project would not have happened at all were it not for Luang Pu Phuttapoj Waraporn (Chan Kusalo). His willingness to let me research the work of the Foundation for Education and Development of Rural Areas (FEDRA) at Wat Pa Darabhirom in Chiang Mai gave me a start on understanding the engaged Buddhist monks in Thailand. Luang Pu shared his wisdom, insights, and humor with me for the two years of my dissertation research, and every time I visited him over the more than twenty years since. I am only one of many people who mourned his passing in 2008, but he left us all with tremendous gifts. I hope this book gives back at least some of what he gave to me.

Phrakhru Pitak Nanthakhun and Phra Somkit Jaranathammo, both of Nan Province, welcomed me into my research on environmental monks in the early 1990s. They patiently put up with my endless questions, and invited me to participate in various rituals, events, seminars, and conferences. As with Luang Pu Phuttapoj, I am honored to count them among my most important teachers. I hope I have interpreted their ideas and words correctly, and that they will forgive any mistakes.

I visited Phra Paisal Visalo at his forest meditation center in Chaiyaphum for several days in 1992, during which he graciously allowed me to interview him at great length. Several years later, he granted me another interview. From him, I gained sharp, critical insights into both the social problems activist monks attempt to deal with and the challenges within the sangha itself. Several other monks also gave me their time and thoughts through interviews and at seminars. These included Phrakhru Manas Nathiphitak, Achan Pongsak Techadhammo, Phra Prajak Khuttajitto, the late Phra Phothirangsri, the late Phrakhru Saokham, Luang Pho Nan (Phrakhru Phiphitprachanat), Phra Maha Chan Khunwuttho, Santikaro Bhikkhu, Phra Sunthorn Yannitsaro, Phra Maha Boonchuay Siridharo, Phra Kittisak Kittisophano, and Phrakhru Wiboon Nanthakit, among others. To each of these revered monks, I convey my humble thanks, grateful for what they each taught me. They are only a few of many activist monks who take risks every day to share the dhamma and help end suffering in light of contemporary social issues. My goal and hope are to help a larger world understand their work, their interpretations of the dhamma, and the contexts within which they practice.

Beyond the monks, many lay people in Thailand made this work possible. In many ways, this project was collaborative because of the degree of assistance and exchange of ideas I had with some of my Thai colleagues. Pipob Udomittipong helped me at every stage of my research since the early 1990s. Several times he and his wife, Buachan, opened their home to me, and traveled with me from Chiang Mai to Nan. While the ideas here are ultimately my own, I benefited greatly from Pipob's insights and experience.

In Nan, Samruay Phadphon became a true friend and guide. He and Bunmee, his wonderful wife, invited me to live with them in the city while I was undertaking my primary research. Their home became my refuge and base, and Samruay and I would talk about politics and environmental issues well into the night. Their first two children, Bow and Rain, kept things in perspective for me with their humor and play.

Others in Nan generously helped me negotiate the place and politics surrounding environmentalism and Buddhism. Achan Prateep Insang, Aeng, and the staff at Hak Muang Nan all contributed significantly to my understanding of the province, its culture and way of life, and the problems it faces. The family I stayed with and the headman in the village where I focused my research deserve special thanks for their hospitality and patience.

One should consider one's self fortunate to have a good mentor. By that standard, I am doubly blessed. Don Swearer, the teacher I never had as an undergraduate or graduate student, has guided and advised me over the years since we first met in Chiang Mai. Sulak Sivaraksa has been a constant source of support and insight, as well as helping me with numerous contacts that made my research possible. I learned from both Achan Don and Achan Sulak important lessons surrounding not only the content of my research, but the worlds of academia and activism respectively. I hope I have lived up to their expectations and models, and continually thank them for being there.

The anthropologists at Chiang Mai University offered support and even sponsored some of my research trips. In particular, I am grateful for guidance and feedback from Anan Ganajapan, Sharlardchai Ramitanondh, and Chayan Vaddhanaphuti.

Friends and colleagues across Thailand, the United States, and elsewhere provided insights, assistance, and support, including Vasana Phethay, my research assistant. Vasana put up with many challenges and difficulties in dealing with a *farang* researcher, taking on numerous arduous and sometimes boring tasks critical to the project. Yoko Hayami, Nina Kammerer, Patricia Symonds, Debbie Wong, and Mary Beth Mills were all in the field at the same times I was at various points, offering friendship, laughter, and advice. Nancy Eberhardt and Margaret Sarkissian read early drafts of parts of the book during our "Southeast Asian play group" when Nancy and I were both on sabbatical and writing in Amherst in 1999 to 2000. Others in Thailand who mattered and helped include Lee Chatametikool, Peter Halford and Sei Sei, Panom and Petchara Meesuk, Vira Somboon, the staff at TICD in the early 1990s, Katie Redford and Ka Sa Wa, the late Sam Kalayana, Anan Wiriyapinij, Geoff Walton, and Varong Israsena and family. I'm grateful to Hank Delcore, Charlie Hallisley, Abe Zablocki, Betsy Hartmann, Bob Rakoff, Anne Downes, Jay Garfield, Len Glick, Stana Wheeler, Thongchai Winichakul, Katherine Bowie, Mike Cullinane, Mogi Roulet, Jennifer Hamilton, Kate Gillogly, Les Sponsel, Aaron Berman, Chyrell George, Emily Gallivan, Paula Green, and Peter Gregory for support, encouragement, and various kinds of advice at different stages of my project.

Three people read most or all of the manuscript and provided invaluable feedback. Susanne Mrozik brought extensive knowledge of Theravada Buddhism to bear, and thought through crucial aspects of my argument with me. Stephanie Levin read closely for grammatical sense, and asked critical questions that helped me clarify key points and make the book more accessible to a general audience. Bob Darlington read for clarity, punctuation, and general encouragement. While the final decisions on the book are all mine, I credit them with improving it significantly and helping me get it finished.

I owe a great deal to my late first husband, Joe, and his family. Joe accompanied me during much of my research in Nan in the early 1990s, and his family welcomed me into their home on the Burma border when we needed to step back from my research and work on things of concern for him. Although he passed away in 1995, his family remains mine, and they never fail to make me feel at home on every visit to Thailand.

Long-term research cannot occur without financial support. I am appreciative of the many sources of funding I received over the life of this project, including the following major grants: The Fulbright Commission (1986–88); the Social Science Research Council (1991–93); the National Endowment for the Humanities (1999–2000); and the Marion and Jasper Whiting Foundation Fellowship (2006). I received fellowships for several academics seminars, which helped me refine my ideas: NEH Seminar Fellow (funded by Social Science Research Council; 1992); Salzburg Seminar Presidential Fellow (1995); United States Institute of Peace Fellow (1996); Salzburg Seminar Freeman Foundation Fellow (1998); and the University of Massachusetts-Amherst Office of Faculty Development Online Writing Fellow (2009). The Association for Asian Studies awarded me a first book subvention grant to assist with publishing the photographs in color. I received smaller, but nevertheless significant support from various faculty development grants at Hampshire College, including from the Jerome Lyle Rappaport Faculty Recognition Award, the Leo Model Foundation Endowment, the Martha Sharp Joukowsky Endowment for Faculty Development, the MacArthur Foundation, and the Christian A. Johnson Endeavor Foundation for Faculty Development. The deans and administrators at Hampshire have been supportive of my work from the beginning, providing me with both time and funds to conduct shorter research trips, attend conferences to present my work, and develop new courses that include aspects of my research, allowing me to further explore my ideas and conclusions with the creative and critical students at the college.

Short parts of the book were previously published in journal articles or book chapters. All of these have been revised and updated for this context. These include: "The Ordination of a Tree: The Buddhist Ecology Movement in Thailand," *Ethnology* 37, no. 1 (1998): 1–15 in chapter 3; "Buddhism and Development: The Ecology Monks of Thailand," in *Action Dharma: New Studies in Engaged Buddhism,* ed. C. Queen, C. Prebish, and D. Keown, (London: RoutledgeCurzon Press, 2003) in chapters 4 and 6; "Practical Spirituality and Community Forests: Monks, Ritual, and Radical Conservatism in Thailand," in *Nature in the Global South: Environmental Projects in South and Southeast Asia,* ed. P. Greenough and A. L. Tsing (Durham and London: Duke University Press, 2003) in chapter 2; "The Spirit(s) of Conservation in Buddhist Thailand," in *Nature across Cultures,* ed. H. Selin (Dordrecht:

Kluwer Academic Publishers, 2003) in chapter 3; "The Good Buddha and the Fierce Spirits: Protecting the Northern Thai Forest," *Contemporary Buddhism* 8, no. 2 (2007): 169–185 in chapters 3 and 7; and "Translating Modernity: Buddhist Response to the Thai Environmental Crisis," in *Trans-Buddhism: Transmission, Translation, and Transformation,* ed. A. Zablocki, J. Garfield, and N. Bhushan (Amherst: University of Massachusetts Press, 2009) in chapters 3, 5, and 7.

All of the photographs in the book were taken by me, with the exception of the Miss Thailand Universe 2010 beauty contest (Plate 4). I gratefully acknowledge Bangkok Broadcasting & T.V. Co., Ltd. (Channel 7), the sponsors of Miss Thailand Universe, for permission to use this photograph. In typical Thai fashion, they sent the photo with the official watermark of the contest as evidence of their permission for me to reprint it.

Finally, none of this project could have been done without the love and support of my family and close friends. Although she did not have anything directly to do with this project, Janet Hentschel made life easier to bear, always supporting me through the challenges and encouraging me with the joys of life.

My parents, Jeanne and Bob Darlington, first let me study in Thailand in 1975 as a high school exchange student, which began my love for the place and the people. They have been there for me throughout the ups and downs of my work and life. My sisters, Barbara Ito and Nancy Darlington, challenge me to do my best work, while keeping everything in perspective with a strong sense of humor. If it wasn't for Barb, I may never have found anthropology and been launched on my career path. Nancy continually teaches me the importance of balance and prioritizing the things that really matter.

Jeff Hagen, my husband and life partner, is the anchor in my life. He has patiently put up with my research trips, conferences, and fretting about this project. He is always there, and helps me keep my life in balance. I couldn't ask for a better partner.

Note on Language and Names

There is no one way to transliterate the Thai language. I have followed the Royal Thai General System of Transcription (RTGS), which does not use diacritics to mark tones nor differentiate vowel length. Despite the problems with this system, it remains the simplest and most straightforward one available. I have diverged from RTGS occasionally, mostly for names which are well known or if a person transcribes his or her name differently.

Monks are usually referred to by their title (*Phra* and *Phrakhru* being the most common) or terms of respect (*Luang Pi, Luang Pho, Luang Pu,* or *Luang Ta,* meaning respected older brother, father, or grandfather [two versions]) and their given name. To make the language less cumbersome, I sometimes use only the given name. I mean no disrespect by this, only to make the text more accessible for those less familiar with Thai and Buddhist customs.

As monks are public figures, and these monks in particular are well known, I decided to use their real names. This decision was not made lightly, and involved a conversation with some of the monks. Most lay people's names and village names have been changed, except for when citing public people or authors, in order to protect their privacy.

I have followed convention for Thai names. Professionally, Thais go by their given names rather than family names. I respect this practice in citations, bibliographic references, and when I refer to Thais in the text (for example, Sulak Sivaraksa is referring to as Sulak rather than Sivaraksa).

1

The Framework

Only the genuine Buddhists (those who have Dhamma and know the Buddha) can conserve Nature, while those who are Buddhists in name alone cannot do it. True Buddhists are able to conserve the deeper Nature, that is, the mental Nature. Non-genuine Buddhists can't conserve Nature, even the material kind. When the mental Nature is well conserved, the outer material Nature will be able to conserve itself.

—Buddhadasa Bhikkhu[1]

THE IMAGE of ordaining a tree sparks strong reactions. A scholarly debate surrounds the degree to which Buddhism is inherently environmental, but that debate remains primarily abstract: whether the Buddha raised concerns for the suffering of the natural world or focused primarily on humans; whether Buddhist scriptures encompass an environmental ethics; and what Buddhist concepts of nature are (Harris 1991; Holder 2007; Schmithausen 1997). The idea of wrapping a tree in a monk's orange robes in order to preserve the forest goes beyond these debates. The question of whether a tree can even be ordained because that status is reserved solely for humans aside (see Blum 2009; Darlington 2009), the act raises issues of politics, economics, inequalities, and power. What can religion offer these situations? In Thailand, Buddhism is a lived religion, one that responds to ever-changing circumstances and a variety of agendas. How it is interpreted and acted upon impacts not only how people perceive the world and their place within it, but their social responsibilities as well. Ordaining a tree is a radical, provocative, and controversial act that challenges people to take responsibility—for themselves, the society, and the natural environment.

Environmentalism captured the Thai imagination in the latter half of the twentieth century. While the issues involved ranged from urban pollution to hydroelectric dams to resource depletion, nothing seemed to occupy the growing environmental movement more than deforestation. What happens to trees is part of a much larger, complex problem, but trees matter.[2] They are tangible reminders of the power of the natural world, homes for not only birds, monkeys, and tigers, but, in the Thai world, spirits as well. And they symbolize the predominant religion in the country, Buddhism, because of the Buddha's intimate relationship with trees: He was born in Lumbini grove, enlightened under a bodhi tree, and physically passed (*parinibbana*, Pali) under a grove of sal trees. Not all trees are sacred, but they have come to embody the debates, struggles, successes, and failures of environmentalism in Thailand, particularly the efforts of a small number of Buddhist monks engaged in conserving forests, protecting wildlife, and changing the imbalance of negative effects of resource degradation and livelihood choices.

Five images of sacred trees encapsulate the evolution of what has become a Buddhist environmental movement in Thailand. The first is of the numerous trees with colorful cloths tied around their trunks (Plate 1). They are usually found in temple compounds but exist quietly in other auspicious sites across the country. Little notice is taken of them as Thai Buddhists proceed about their daily lives. They are just there.

The second image occurs in a dark forest (Plate 2). A Buddhist monk reaches around a moderately sized tree, tying an old orange robe with no fanfare. He utters a quiet incantation, but not loud enough for observers to hear. Nearby a small number of lay villagers do the same, marking trees throughout the forest as valuable to someone.

Far more conscious and conspicuous is the image of twenty monks seated near a large tree in the mountains of Nan Province. The monks chant, connected with each other and the tree by a white thread that conveys sanctity from the words to the tree. Shortly thereafter two monks wrap a tightly twisted orange robe around the wide circumference of the tree (Plate 3). The act is documented by multiple photographers, and witnessed by more than two hundred people—villagers, nongovernmental workers, and academics. A sign nailed to the tree reads, "*Tham lai pa khue tham lai chat,*" which can be translated as "To harm the forest is to harm life," or alternatively, "To harm the forest is to harm one's future lives," or "the nation" (Darlington 1998, 10).

Henry Delcore provides the fourth image through his description below, the setting of a tree ordination performed in 1996:

The focus of the ritual space was the altar at the front of the clearing, a tiered structure of carved wood tables four feet wide and five feet tall, the lower levels occupied by candles, flowers and incense, the top level by a foot-tall Buddha image. To the right of the altar stood an easel with a photo portrait of the King, set about level with the Buddha image. To the left of the altar was a folding table with the microphone for the public address system, where speakers stood to address the crowd later in the day. Directly to the right of the altar were chairs for the monks, who had not yet arrived. Eventually, another cluster of chairs formed near the monk section and would be occupied by the local officials and other honored guests in attendance; the villagers sat on mats on the ground. . . . Each ordination made use of a primary cloth marked by the kanchanaphisek symbol [the seal of the current Chakri Dynasty], which was tied to the "mother tree," the largest tree in the area. A large number of smaller, unmarked cloths, all the saffron color of monks' robes, were also tied by participants to trees in the area. A saay sin—a white string used in many Thai rituals to symbolically bind together the khwan—had been tied to the Buddha image on the altar, and ran around the entire clearing area, encompassing the participants. (Khwan is a kind of soul stuff possessed by both animate and inanimate entities.) Over the altar, a twenty foot long banner announced the formal title of the forest ordination program: "Program for the Community Forest Ordination of 50 Million Trees in Honor of the King's Golden Jubilee." (Delcore 2004b, 11–12)

The last image is the most recent, although forms of all the others continue to this day. Three beautiful, young Thai women pose holding a monk's robe around a large tree (Plate 4). Behind them a few other wrapped trees can be seen, but no other context identifies the place or the smiling women. The caption of this newspaper photograph reveals the women as contestants in the 2010 Miss Thailand Universe contest in Kamphaeng Phet Province ("Beauty Contestants Ordain Tree" 2010).[3]

All five images represent tree ordinations in Thailand. All but the first occurred since the late 1980s. The tree ordination—the ritual described in all but the first image—is the quintessential symbol of the Thai Buddhist environmental movement. Since the late 1980s a small number of monks have performed these rituals in which they consecrate a tree and the surrounding forest to bring attention to environmental problems, especially concerning

the forests and water, that make life difficult for Thai villagers, and by implication, for the nation as a whole. The rituals and the trees wrapped in orange
robes remind villagers of their dependence on the forest for their livelihoods—food, materials for daily life, and water. As monks depend on the
laity for their material needs, so too the forest depends on the people who
live around it for preservation. People can either protect the forest or cut it
down. Monks concerned with the consequences of the latter use the image of
ordained trees to encourage people to do the former.

The movement is not about trees per se, but the monks and the people
with whom they live and work who must deal with the direct consequences
of environmental destruction. In fact, the monk credited with performing
the first tree ordination did not intend to ordain a tree. He performed a
ritual to consecrate a forest and seedlings for reforestation to raise awareness
of people's dependence on them and to object to deforestation occurring
due to logging. The villagers who participated referred to the seedlings as
"ordained trees" (ton mai buat), thereby coining the term that has come to
identify a broader movement. Buddhist environmentalism is only one aspect
of a larger, vibrant environmental movement in Thailand comprised of many
interpretations and goals, a movement that Hirsch (1996, 15–16) describes
as "a multi-faceted discourse that deals with key social, economic and political issues, including questions of control over resources by empowered and
disempowered groups."

The different manifestations of the "ordained tree" in the images above
represent change in the forms, meanings, and control of the Buddhist environmental movement. They illustrate a general progression from an understated belief in spirits and honoring of the Buddha to ritual and symbolic
invocation of the Buddha's teachings to protect the forest and the humans
who depend on its resources, often in a manner that criticizes the direction
of state-led economic development. The ritual eventually became associated
with the king and the state, and even incorporated within popular culture,
limiting the sanctity of the ritual in some cases while claiming its moral
implications. At the same time, environmental monks continued to perform
tree ordinations for their own, non-state projects. Some incorporated new
approaches or shifted their focus to a more local rather than national level,
countering the appropriation of their symbolic action. Behind these images
lies a set of interrelated and contested discourses: of how Buddhism can and
should be used in the modern, social world; of the goals of environmentalism
and the relationship between humans and the natural world; of the meaning of "development," and the related tensions between material growth and

spiritual progress as measures of improving the lives of Thai citizens;[4] of concepts of power and knowledge, and the construction and appropriation of new forms of knowledge, including interpretations of Buddhism itself.

This book is the story of the Thai Buddhist environmental movement, the monks involved, and the debated meanings underlying their actions. I look at the movement historically to place it into its larger context of socially engaged Buddhism in Thailand as monks responded to social, political, and economic changes that impacted people's perceptions and practice of the religion. Socially engaged Buddhism, a phrase coined by the Vietnamese monk Thich Nhat Hanh, refers to the active use of the religion and its teachings to address social issues, such as violence and war, economic development and inequalities, gender issues, and environmental degradation. I witnessed the rise of environmental Buddhism in Thailand in connection with other forms of socially engaged Buddhism.

Although a few monks first explicitly engaged in environmental issues in the 1980s, monks have been involved in social and political issues in diverse ways throughout Thai history. The sangha (the order of monks) formed one-third of the triad of Buddhist society—the sangha, the monarchy, and the laity. In Theravada Buddhist societies in particular the sangha and the monarchy supported and legitimated each other. Some monks challenged this system, either by removing themselves from the influence and control of the king to practice an austere lifestyle in remote forests, or, in the case of a small number of millenarian monks in Northeast Thailand and Burma, leading unsuccessful uprisings against the state (Ishii 1975; Keyes 1977). Other monks have been used by the state to promote its agendas, such as the forest monks in the early twentieth century who enabled the central state in Bangkok to expand its influence into peripheral regions, especially in the Northeast (Tambiah 1996, 1984; Kamala 1997; J. Taylor 1993a). In the 1960s, Field Marshal Sarit Thanarat created Buddhist community development and missionary programs, Thammathud and Thammacharik, to push his economic development ideas and concepts of national identity into remote and border regions through the participation of monks (Ishii 1986, 115).

The monks with whom I am concerned here fall into another category of social activism. They do not support the state's objectives, and usually criticize the negative impacts of many state policies on rural people.[5] In particular, as I conducted my initial research on the rural development work of a high-ranking monk in northern Thailand in the mid-1980s, I realized the links between independent "development monks" (*phra nak phatthana*) and the criticisms of state-led development and modernization that these monks articulated, with the "environmental monks" (*phra nak anuraksa thamachat*), those monks who focused on the effects of environmental changes (human-made) on people's lives. Both groups—even as the label "group" may be a misnomer because of the fluidity of these movements—took on political issues surrounding the direction of Thai society and economy. They did not aim to engage in politics directly, with a couple of exceptions, but through their interpretations of the causes of suffering faced by the lay people they served they saw it as their responsibility as monks to raise questions and challenge the power of political and business interests. They struggled against the power of greed, anger, and ignorance (the root evils in Buddhist teachings), but also the dominant social views and agendas (i.e., concepts of consumption and accumulation) grounded in those attitudes. Ultimately, development and environmental monks use and reframe religious practice and interpretations to legitimate not the government, but local people—those who usually have no power.

Engaged Buddhism and the Environment

The main goal of Buddhism is to relieve suffering. Suffering (*dukkha*, Pali) has a specific meaning in Buddhism. The leading Thai scholar monk, P. A. Payutto, defines dukkha as "suffering; misery; woe; pain; ill; sorrow; trouble; discomfort; unsatisfactoriness; problematic situation; stress; conflict" (1985, 380–81). The concept lies at the heart of the Four Noble Truths, a central set of Buddhist principles: There is suffering; There is a cause of suffering; There is a cessation of suffering; The path to the cessation of suffering is the Eightfold Path (Payutto 1985, 181).[6] The philosophical concept involves mental dissatisfaction as much as physical pain and the attachment to a concept of self. The distinctions between philosophical Buddhism and socially engaged Buddhism lie in how suffering is interpreted and the actions taken to relieve it. Buddhists have always addressed suffering as a philosophical, spiritual, and metaphysical state of being; socially engaged Buddhists add to this list social, political, and economic forms of suffering. In addition to the philosophical extinction of suffering (*nibbana*, Pali, or "enlightenment"), engaged Buddhists work to end suffering in the here and now, targeting the social, political factors that affect people's lives, especially those who have little or no power in society. They see social justice as crucial to being Buddhists.[7]

The term *engaged Buddhism* is attributed to Thich Nhat Hanh. During the war in Vietnam in the 1960s, he used Buddhist principles to work for social justice and peace. The concept of engaged Buddhism as a means of responding to modern social problems emerged concurrently in many Buddhist societies in the mid-twentieth century. Initially, activists who took a Buddhist approach focused on local issues and communities. Globalization not only brought capitalism and multinational business to Buddhist countries but also introduced alternative ideas intended to help people oppose dominant concepts of large-scale economic development and rapid growth. Buddhists concerned with social issues in different nations began to support each other as part of this process. In 1989, the Thai social activist Sulak Sivaraksa founded the International Network of Engaged Buddhists (INEB), a nonprofit organization that brings together Buddhists from around the world concerned with social justice. Information and ideas exchanged at INEB conferences and through the journal, *Seeds of Peace,* sparked new actions on local levels. The actions of engaged Buddhists, whose work is grounded in Buddhist philosophy, are contributing to a rethinking of the application of Buddhism in the modern world.

Among the many foci of engaged Buddhists is concern for the natural environment and the impact of its destruction on all forms of life. Thai environmental monks did not invent the idea of using Buddhism to deal with environmental issues. Buddhists across Asia and America point to scriptures that document reverence for nature and ground ecological activism in Buddhist teachings. His Holiness the Dalai Lama included environmental issues in his call to make Tibet a zone of peace; the Korean nun Jiyul Sunim fought the destruction of a sacred mountain to build a railway tunnel; and American Buddhists draw from different forms of Buddhism to express concerns about, and responsibility for, nuclear waste, deforestation, and water usage, to name only a few cases (for more examples, see Kaza and Kraft 2000; Tucker and Williams 1997). Beyond the Buddhist world, a movement linking religions of all kinds with ecology has been growing worldwide over the past several decades.[8]

Most of the literature on Buddhism and environmentalism focuses on the philosophical issues underlying this relationship. Some of it criticizes any claims to authenticity in the Buddhist scriptures or early Buddhism (Harris 1991, 1994, 1995, 1997; Schmithausen 1997). Others counter these critics through close documentation of the philosophical underpinnings of environmental concepts in Buddhism (Holder 2007; Swearer 1997). The irony is that most of this literature remains abstract. Socially engaged Buddhism is ultimately about relieving suffering in *this* world. Yet scholars of engaged Buddhism often idealize or silence local variations and the messiness of the application of Buddhist principles to contemporary problems in their efforts to justify engaged Buddhism as an authentic form of Buddhism. Buddhism is a lived religion, however, one that has been adapted throughout its history to multiple contexts and new issues. Environmental Buddhism is one of many examples of this process.

The goals of environmental Buddhism, based on both the ecological concept of interconnectedness found in deep ecology (Devall 2000; Halifax 1990; Macy 2000) and the Buddhist concept of dependent co-arising (*paticca samuppada,* Pali), emphasize modern, scientific methods and ancient religious principles.[9] In this way, Thai environmental monks are neither "modern" nor "traditional." The monks' interpretations of religion and science, and tradition and modernity, do not fall into clear-cut categories, but rather represent a creative blend of approaches appropriate for a changing world. Their example complicates and highlights the tensions inherent in the environmental crisis itself, and the questions facing Thai society as it attempts to deal with the crisis. The presence of these monks challenges Thais at all levels of society to confront what it means to be modern or traditional, local or global, Thai, and even what it means to be Buddhist.

Sangha, Politics, and Environment

The environmental crisis to which these monks are responding is the result of Thai society buying into global capitalism and rapid economic and industrial growth. The monks' response takes an ideological stance that criticizes this form of modernization, arguing that capitalism and consumerism are pulling people away from spiritual practice. Capitalism, they argue, emphasizes greed, ignorance, and anger. The monks call for a return to religious values as a guide for living simply and purely, and an emphasis on community-level society in which people care for each other and are sensitive to the impacts of their actions on others, including the natural world. In this way, they create an environmentalism distinct from that in the West, which tends to emphasize separation of people and the natural environment.[10]

In an article on Thai civic religion, Frank Reynolds (1994) describes the imaginative-symbolic and the practical, programmatic discourses that together form the basis of Thai legal culture. He frames these discourses within the concepts of *chat* (nation, including the people), *satsana* (religion), and *mahakesat* (kingship), the three-part formula of Thai civic religion since the early twentieth century. He examines how various actors in social, legal conflicts use the rhetoric of these concepts to build their arguments. Reynolds points out two main strands in modern Thai Buddhism and how they intersect with Thai civic religion:

> The first is basically conservative in that those involved are generally in concert with the mainstream interpretation of Thai civic religion and with the current patterns of Thai politics and law. The second strand is more radical in that the beliefs and practices of those involved have produced tensions within the status quo and conflicts with the powers that be. (Reynolds 1994, 445)

Reynolds places engaged Buddhists within the second, smaller strand because of their "anti-establishment" perspective (ibid., 449).

I agree with Reynolds that engaged Buddhists in Thailand, especially monks involved in environmental work, tend to challenge the "status quo" and the "powers that be," including the state. The relationship between environmental monks and the state, however, is not static, shifting as the two respond and adapt to each other. At times, environmental monks such as Phra Prajak Khuttajitto embody criticism of the state and its agenda.[11] Other times, these monks negotiate with the state, finding cooperation and collaborations that place people rather than politics at the center of their actions.

Environmentalism has become a major site of contestation in Thailand since the mid-1980s. The state, corporations, nongovernmental organizations (NGOs), people's organizations, and monks all vie for the moral high ground to control forms of development, the definition of environmental problems, and the land. Forsythe and Walker (2008, 25–26) linked the production of environmental knowledge with the politics of state making through the use of "environmental narratives."[12] With echoes of William Cronon's (1996) critique of a wilderness approach to environmentalism, they argue that two main narratives dominate Thai discourse about the major environmental issue, the forest: One emphasizes an image of the forest as "wild," needing to be protected from people; The other prioritizes "local knowledge" of people living in the highlands for taking care of and conserving the forest. Both, they claim, "serve important political functions by enabling the Thai state to increase its control over resources and people, and by providing many of the ground rules within which environmental debate takes place and diverse social actors negotiate with the state" (Forsythe and Walker 2008, 18). Certainly the shifting engagement of environmental monks with the state falls into this description.

Yet the case of environmental monks is more complex than Forsythe and Walker's framework would allow. James Scott's concept of "hidden transcripts" may be more accurate in describing the monks' evolving relationship with the state. He argues that "every subordinate group creates, out of its ordeal, a 'hidden transcript' that represents a critique of power spoken behind the backs of the dominant" (Scott 1990, xii). Since the 1980s, these monks have both openly and quietly negotiated with and challenged the dominance of urban elite, business, and the state in environmental affairs through rituals, seminars, networking, and even public protests, all contributing to the construction of a new knowledge of Buddhism in society. On one level, they acquiesce to the state's authority, for example, inviting government officials to play key roles in public rituals such as tree ordinations that promote forest conservation. On another, the monks quietly use the officials' participation in these rituals to legitimize the involvement of the sangha in environmental issues and their version of environmental knowledge that usually supports local people's control of the forest, subtly criticizing state policy in the process.[13] Here we can see a version of Scott's hidden transcripts at work, albeit one in which a higher group (the sangha) speaks for a subordinate one (rural farmers).

The case of environmental monks illustrates the complexities of the connections between religion and environmentalism, and the challenges faced by monks who believe that engaging in social problems is a responsibility of the sangha. "*Phra nak anurak thamachat*," the term applied informally to these monks, literally translates as "monks who conserve nature." I loosely translate the term as "environmental monks" rather than "conservation monks" because, as with environmentalism more generally, their activities place them within political debates. The term *environmental* embodies political debate and activism, while *conservation* conveys a more static, less political goal, one focused primarily on a concept of the natural environment separate from humans. These monks do not merely conserve nature, nor do they have a deep knowledge of the science of ecology. Their actions, aimed primarily at relieving the suffering of rural people, challenge the political and economic powers they believe encourage material development, consumption, and greed, ultimately resulting in suffering.[14]

While these monks work with environmental and development NGOs and challenge people with political, economic, and social power through their use of religion, they also seek to redefine the issues at stake. Aware of economic and social inequities, they frame the debates—about whether people can live in and care for the forest, for example—in Buddhist terms, placing the relief of suffering at the center of their projects. Their actions serve to educate and motivate rural people to engage in conservation activities. More significantly, they add a moral element to environmental debates. Although they face risks and some have evoked strong criticism, through the exchange of experiences, philosophical interpretations, and the invention of new rituals, these monks have constructed a new knowledge of the spiritual and moral aspects of environmentalism.

Evolution of Buddhist Environmental Knowledge

Within a decade of the performance of the first tree ordination, this knowledge entered mainstream vocabulary. Initially, the sangha hierarchy and members of the urban middle class criticized tree ordination rituals as not being true Buddhism; people were shocked and even outraged that monks would initiate trees into the sangha, a status reserved for humans. Misunderstanding the purpose of the rituals, some critics saw tree ordinations as violating the Vinaya, the disciplinary rules monks observe, since only humans can be ordained. While the rituals are not ordinations in a formal sense, the image of sanctifying trees and the forest through the ritual gained national (and international) attention, raising awareness about the difficulties people dependent on the forest face. The shock value of using ritual to highlight social problems and challenge social power provided environmental monks with an effective tool to meet their goals.

Since the first tree ordination performed for forest conservation in 1988 the rituals have become increasingly accepted and popular across Thailand. The best example of the impact and popularity of tree ordinations came in 1996–97. During that time, a coalition of nongovernmental, people's, and governmental organizations initiated a program to ordain fifty million trees in honor of the fiftieth year of the king's reign (Tannenbaum 2000; Isager and Ivarsson 2002; Delcore 2004b). The image of the ordination described by Delcore above occurred as part of this program. It would appear that the environmental monks met their major objectives, at least in part. While threats to the forest still exist, the monks succeeded in raising awareness of deforestation. At the same time, they created a powerful, visible means of keeping Buddhism relevant in society, showing its applicability to dealing with social issues.

Yet the growing popularity of tree ordinations and their appropriation by mainstream society threaten their potential to effect change and help people deal with suffering. The contexts for the rituals have changed. Rather than pushing people to question modern, consumerist values as causes of environmental destruction and human suffering, such rituals are increasingly used to support national agendas and to undermine the power of the rural people whom environmental monks aim to help. The image of beauty contestants posed while wrapping robes around trees demonstrates the degree to which the ritual has been popularized and made into an expression of consumer culture, thereby removing it, at least in part, from its religious context.[15]

Environmental monks worked hard to gain acceptance by both the sangha and the laity, showing their work as grounded in Buddhist teachings. As their actions, particularly tree ordinations, became more widely accepted, these monks may have unwittingly undermined the effectiveness of their projects. Once accepted into the mainstream, the actions have become expected practice for many monks. They are performed frequently, often without educating the lay participants about environmental issues or a genuine commitment on the part of the sangha or the laity to follow up on the protection of the land and trees involved. Environmental monks are now often recognized for their work through ecclesiastical promotions and have considerable administrative responsibilities, leaving them little time to invest in conserving the forest or initiating new projects. Monks with whom I spoke in 2006 expressed this concern, saying they faced difficulties in maintaining the original intention behind the rituals and their environmental work. The necessities of obtaining funding for social change work often overrode their goals, leading to shifts in what they emphasized. For example, I was told that funders preferred projects directed at HIV/AIDs rather than building community forests. Even so, according to Phra Paisal Visalo, their work is still not fully supported by the laity (personal communication 10/6/2006). The challenge is to integrate their reinterpretations of Buddhist philosophy and practice with the expectations of Thai society.

Sources of Buddhist Environmentalism

Nature is *rupatham* [tangible], with several deeper levels of meaning. . . . Conserving nature is one means of conserving the deeper meaning of the religion (*namatham* [intangible]). (Phra Maha Chan Khunwuttho, interview 7/12/1991)

According to Phra Maha Chan Khunwuttho, an older monk from Khorat Province strongly influenced by the well-known philosopher monk Buddhadasa Bhikkhu, rituals are only tools of monks, one method of promoting environmentalism. More important for him are the Buddhist lessons underlying environmental activism. He sees nature as a means of teaching about and preserving the essence of Buddhism (what he calls *namatham,* or "intangible"), especially within a rapidly changing society. For Phra Maha Chan, Buddhist environmental activism serves two interrelated purposes: it helps to protect and preserve the natural environment with the goal of lessening the suffering that accompanies environmental destruction; and it supports and promotes the deeper meaning of the religion aimed at realizing enlightenment, or relief from suffering.

Incorporating Phra Maha Chan's approach with those of the activist monks (Phra Maha Chan sees himself more as a philosopher monk), it becomes clear that *rupatham,* in this case the tangible forms of Buddhist environmentalism, and namatham, its philosophical interpretations, exist in a dynamic, two-way relationship.[16] The philosophy supports and legitimizes activism by grounding it within religious and historical traditions. It supplies a conservative link with the Buddha's teachings that enables activists to innovate and challenge society from a sacred position. Buddhist activism, in turn, makes the philosophy relevant and applicable in the modern world. As Phra Somkit Jaranathamamo told me, the use of rituals and aspects of religious practice (including spirit beliefs) familiar to the lay people with whom activist monks work provides a context within which these monks can gradually adapt the religion—both popular practices and philosophical interpretations—to deal with new problems, including the environmental crisis.

The process of interpreting Buddhism to deal with environmental problems has been criticized by some Western scholars for either idealizing early Buddhists as having a conscious ecological ethic (Schmithausen 1997) or reading modern environmentalism into Buddhism without careful scriptural study (Harris 1991, 1994, 1995, 1997; Pedersen 1995). Buddhist environmentalists have, according to Ian Harris (1997), been overly influenced by a global environmental discourse leading them to argue for a Buddhist environmentalism that is not supported by either the texts or Buddhist history. For example, at the beginning of an article entitled, "Buddhism and the Discourse of Environmental Concern," Harris states,

> My central contention will be that, with one or two notable exceptions (Schmithausen springs to mind here), supporters of an

authentic Buddhist environmental ethic have tended toward a positive indifference to the history and complexity of the Buddhist tradition. In their praiseworthy desire to embrace such a "high profile"
cause, or, to put it more negatively, in their inability to check the
influence of a significant element of modern globalized discourse,
Buddhist environmentalists may be guilty of a *sacrificium intellectus*
very much out of line with the critical spirit that has played such a
major role in Buddhism from the time of the Buddha himself down
to the modern period. (Harris 1997, 378)

Perhaps Harris is right that a call for contemporary environmental activism cannot be supported through a strict philosophical interpretation of the
Buddha's original teachings. What I find interesting, however, is that many
contemporary Buddhists (including some learned monks) believe it *can*.
In addition, his criticisms do not take Buddhism into account as a living
religion that responds—and has throughout its long history—to different
and changing sociopolitical, cultural, and, I would argue, environmental
contexts. I examine Thai socially engaged monks' various interpretations of
Buddhist philosophy and teachings in their own terms, as social actors making conscious decisions about how they read, practice, and apply Buddhist
principles. Socially engaged monks are, in my view (and contrary to Harris's argument above), critically examining their tradition in light of contemporary situations and problems. Through their own agency, they have
aligned themselves with social and environmental activists, often taking on
controversial issues. Similarly, they articulate an environmental discourse in
terms meaningful to themselves and the local people with whom they work.
(While the Thai environmental movement has been somewhat influenced by
Western concepts of environment, most of the environmental monks with
whom I have spoken do not start from that perspective. Rather, they frame
their concepts of environment in terms of Buddhist ideas, even as these may
not align directly with more conservative interpretations of the scriptures.)
    Viewing Buddhism as a living and lived religion, with multiple forms,
interpretations, and practices, I take an ethnographic approach and follow
the lead of Thai people, particularly the villagers with whom I lived and
studied, in looking to environmental monks as sources of Buddhist environmentalism. These monks hold positions of influence, respect, and moral
authority among many Thai Buddhists in both cities and villages, thereby
providing insight into what the religion means to different people in changing contexts.

Socially engaged monks—including both development and environmental monks—must continually earn and defend their reputation and moral authority. There is not one exemplar "socially engaged monk" respected by all Thai Buddhists, nor is there a single, unified interpretation of Buddhism used by all activist monks to support their work. Their various interpretations show Buddhism as a lived religion, challenged and adapted by those who practice it to make it relevant to their daily lives and immediate situations (see McMahan 2008).

In the Field

Ethnographic fieldwork is not a value-free activity that results in hard facts. The knowledge gained and created in the process contributes to an evolution of understanding of the subject matter. In this case, my research with environmentalist monks contributed to the creation of the category of "environmental monk," in that my writing brought the activism of these monks to the world. I made certain monks famous internationally, such as Phrakhru Pitak Nanthakhun, because the idea of a tree ordination was as surprising and captivating for non-Thais and non-Buddhists as it initially was within Thailand (Darlington 1993, 1997, 1998, 2003a, 2003b, 2003c, 2007).

Shortly after the publication of my article "The Ordination of a Tree" in 1998, in which I detailed how tree ordinations occur, I began to receive inquiries from various researchers, reporters, and documentary makers about contacting Phrakhru Pitak. As far as I know, none have followed through in visiting Phrakhru Pitak in Nan Province, nor have they actually written about his work. But the form of the queries—asking about the work of environmental monks through questions about him specifically—demonstrated one unintentional outcome from my research. Phrakhru Pitak became a face of the movement for the world through my writing.

One purpose for writing this book is to correct the assumptions contained within such inquiries. First, despite expectations that such a movement could not last, the movement continues, including the performance of tree ordinations. The activities and foci have evolved and the emphases have expanded. The monks and their supporters no longer focus solely on forests, but consider the impacts of other kinds of environmental problems as well. They integrate other kinds of issues that affect the lives of the Thai people, such as development projects and HIV/AIDS. Their work remains vital and critical for addressing social issues and challenging the majority of

Thai society to enact Buddhist values in their daily lives rather than the values of consumption and economic growth.

Second, Phrakhru Pitak, while actively engaged in environmental and development efforts based on his interpretation of Buddhist principles and groundbreaking in his creative approaches to this work, is only one of a number of innovative monks doing this work. They all take risks in the process, ranging from close scrutiny by both the sangha hierarchy and the lay society, to the arrests in 1991 that ultimately ended Phra Prajak Khuttajitto's radical participation in the movement, to the assassination of Phra Supoj Suvacano in 2005 in a conflict over land use (see chapter 7). All these monks contribute to the progress of environmental awareness, the understanding of the negative impacts of certain kinds of economic development, and the rethinking of Buddhism in society. Even though I focus on particular monks, including a chapter on Phrakhru Pitak's story (chapter 2), readers should realize that these monks are representatives of a larger, and evolving, movement.

Third, despite all they have accomplished, these monks are not flawless heroes. It is easy to idealize them and perceive them as the leaders of a valiant fight against the evils of capitalism and globalization. As monks, they occupy a revered status in Thai society, but not one that is above criticism. In my writing I try to balance my respect for these monks and their work, and the obligations I owe them for allowing me to witness their efforts, with the realities and challenges they face daily. They each negotiate many pressures—from the sangha, the laity, the government, the media, and researchers like me—and make compromises along the way. As a small minority of the sangha in Thailand, they do not represent all of Thai Buddhism, and some Thais criticize them for going beyond the "norm" of expected behavior for monks. At the same time, their successes and efforts have created new norms of expectation. My goal is to shed insight into the processes through which these monks maneuvered, and to understand the anticipated and unintended consequences of their decisions and actions on both Buddhism and the environmental movement in Thailand.

My path to Phrakhru Pitak, Phra Somkit, and Luang Pu Phuttapoj Waraporn, the three monks with whom I have studied most closely, illustrates the somewhat random nature of ethnographic fieldwork. It is important to understand both who they are and how I came to work with them, placing both their work and mine within the broader contexts of Buddhist environmentalism in Thailand and the anthropological study of this movement. I chose to work with these monks because of the innovative nature of their work, and because I had introductions and connections to them.

I could easily have chosen other monks in other regions of Thailand, and I encourage future researchers to do so to flesh out our understandings of engaged Buddhism in Thailand, the influence of Buddhist thinkers on environmental and development issues, and the ways in which Buddhism is evolving through both the work and ideas of these monks and the responses of others, lay and religious, to them.

My introduction to engaged Buddhism in Thailand came from Vira Somboon, then a graduate student of political philosophy at the University of Michigan who was one of my Thai language teachers. Vira had ordained for a year as a monk with Buddhadasa Bhikkhu, one of Thailand's preeminent Buddhist philosophers and an engaged Buddhist leader. He gave me a book by Sulak Sivaraksa, a lay Buddhist leader and social critic, entitled *Religion and Development,* first published in 1976, and encouraged me to examine the work of monks undertaking alternative development initiatives based on Buddhist principles. The ideas of these two engaged Buddhist thinkers—Buddhadasa and Sulak—influenced my own approach to questions surrounding economic development and engaged Buddhism, even as I never met Buddhadasa and only met Achan Sulak[17] several years after I began my research. Their impact on engaged Buddhism in Thailand, particularly with monks involved in development and environmental activism, is pervasive even today, almost two decades after Buddhadasa passed away. Their work led me to study the alternative development promoted by Buddhist monks, even though the first monk with whom I studied, Luang Pu Phuttapoj Waraporn (Chan Kusalo),[18] was not directly influenced by either of them.

Inspired by Sulak's ideas, I began my research in 1986 in northern Thailand on monks undertaking rural economic development. Anan Ganajapan, an anthropologist at Chiang Mai University, directed me to Luang Pu Phuttapoj's organization, the Foundation for Education and Development of Rural Areas (FEDRA), just north of Chiang Mai city. Phuttapoj, aware of young villagers leaving for work in the cities as early as the 1970s, founded FEDRA in 1974 to support the livelihoods of farmers and give them the tools and knowledge to remain in the villages. His favorite saying, "spiritual and economic development must work together to solve problems" (*setthakhit kap chitchai tong kae panha phromkan*), captures his philosophical as well as practical approach. Phuttapoj was one of the first Thai monks to interpret Buddhism as the basis for dealing with poverty and its resulting suffering, challenging the material, consumer focus of government-led economic development.

I spent two years researching Luang Pu Phuttapoj's work, FEDRA's programs, and villagers' reactions to them. I learned about the challenges facing the minority of Thai monks who saw development work as central to their mission of relieving suffering. The predominant push in Thai society toward consumerism, measuring success and the "good life" through material goods, ran counter to the efforts of development monks and NGOs struggling to promote alternatives (Darlington 1990). During this research, I became aware of a few monks incorporating environmental concerns with their development work.

I returned to begin this next project—really a continuation of the original research—in 1991, again starting in Chiang Mai. Many of the anthropologists at Chiang Mai University are social activists, combining their research with social criticism and efforts to promote social and economic justice. By 1991, a national movement had emerged advocating for legal recognition of community forests. Although the definition of "community forest" was debated, the common element in the activists' movement emphasized the agency of local people whose lives depended on the forests. Recognizing the critical position of monks in village life, the NGOs and academics in the community forest movement reached out to support the emerging Buddhist environmental movement. Through Anan Ganajapan and the community forestry project of a coalition of academics and NGOs, I met Sakchai Parnthep, an activist from Nan Province who worked closely with Phrakhru Pitak Nanthakhun. Traveling to Nan and participating in a tree ordination supported by Northern Thai NGOs and academics, coordinated by Sakchai and other local NGO workers, and sponsored by Phrakhru Pitak, initiated me into the Buddhist environmental movement and set me up for fieldwork in Nan.

My research with environmental monks, unlike my initial study of FEDRA, was multisited. While based in Nan and focusing on Phrakhru Pitak's projects, I traveled across Thailand to visit other monks engaged in environmental and development projects. In the early 1990s, NGOs coordinated numerous seminars for environmental monks, sometimes as many as twenty a year. I attended several of these seminars, further expanding my exposure to different monks' work. In 1992–93, I concentrated on this project, balancing my time between Nan, where I primarily stayed in Phrakhru Pitak's home village, visiting other monks, and observing environmental seminars. I gained a sense of how villagers reacted to these projects in Nan, but mostly I focused on the ways in which monks implemented their projects and how they used Buddhist principles in the process.

I discovered that most of the activist monks did not articulate strong philosophical statements for their approaches. They used simplified explanations, aimed at getting local people committed to their projects. An extensive literature on Buddhism and ecology explores the scriptural connections, as discussed above. I was more concerned with how the monks on the ground interpreted them for practical applications, the challenges they faced, and the potential of their projects for long-term impact.

As a white, middle-class woman from the United States, I found interacting with monks different from the experiences of my Thai colleagues, male and female. First, I needed to be circumspect in my dealings with the monks, especially after a series of sex scandals rocked the Thai sangha in the early 1990s. All my encounters with monks had to be in public, or at least where anyone could listen in or witness our engagements. The fact that I was a foreigner mediated this challenge. I was often seen in a different category from Thai women. Monks and lay people alike assumed I had limited knowledge of either Buddhism or Thai society, and therefore excused mistakes in my behavior. People took the time to explain obvious details to me, often as if speaking to a child. In reality, I was a child in relation to their lives and knowledge, and I appreciated their patience in teaching me.

This exceptional category gave me access to particular settings. The Buddhist environmental movement is primarily a site for monks and men. The only women involved are a few NGO workers, who mostly focus on villagers, and academics. I never met any female monastics engaged in the movement, beyond providing logistical support. This case highlights the gender imbalances in Thai Buddhism. Until recently the only religious option for Thai women was to become *mae chi*. Mae chi are not fully ordained, and Thais hold relatively little respect for them.[19] The predominant female academic promoting Buddhist environmentalism during the 1990s was Chatsumarn Kabilsingh. In 2003, she ordained as a *bhikkhuni* (fully ordained nun) in Sri Lanka, where female ordination had recently been revived (Mrozik, 2009). With her struggles to gain acceptance for female ordination in Thailand, she currently pays less attention to environmental issues than she did in the 1990s.

In 1992, I observed a small seminar on the problems faced by activist monks, including relations with women. Twenty monks participated, supported by three lay NGO workers. The only other women there were three mae chi who did not participate in the seminar but cooked for the participants. The monks allowed me to listen into all their discussions except those explicitly concerning women. One older monk expressed some hesitations about my presence until I articulated what I was learning from them and the value of understanding their perspectives on their work, and promised to help explain their efforts to a larger audience.

As I did many times during my research, I needed to explain my position and project in order to gain access to key actors and events in the movement. The consequence of repeatedly explaining myself was that people responded to and engaged in discussion of my ideas and understandings. In this way, I tested my ideas with my informants, leading to greater complexity and confidence in my insights.

Over time I gained a broader perspective on the movement and its intersections with environmental and other social issues in Thailand. Environmental monks, despite the label, are concerned with problems beyond those affecting natural resources. Environmentalism in its very essence is political, as environmental activists must deal with broader social, economic, and policy issues that all impact the natural environment.[20] The monks' primary concern, relieving the suffering of, in this case, rural villagers, must incorporate problems of poverty and debt, conflict with developers, seed companies, and plantation owners, and awareness of the effects of government policies. In the early 1990s, much of Thai society debated forest policy, including the adoption of a Community Forestry Bill. In the 2000s, focus shifted to prioritize HIV/AIDS issues. Since the coup in 2006 that ousted Prime Minister Thaksin Shinawatra, the main crisis facing Thailand surrounds the government as different factions protest, stop government and economic dealings, and fight over who should run the nation and the meaning of democracy. People who have spoken out against the current government or political system have been charged with lese majesté, effectively silencing open dialogue about politics or society. Few other concerns compete for national media attention. Yet the engaged Buddhist monks quietly continue their efforts to improve the lives of rural people, still performing tree ordinations and other rituals and programs even while they are pushed in other directions due to funding opportunities and political debates.

The Structure of the Book

This book aims to present the work of environmental and development monks over time. While the focus is on environmental issues, these cannot be separated from development agendas and efforts, both in terms of the economic priorities of government policies and the alternative approaches advocated by development monks and NGOs. Environmental concerns arose from the effects of both kinds of development agendas. I look at how the Buddhist environmental movement emerged from the work of independent development monks, and how they continue to integrate alternative development approaches. Mostly I tell stories, stories of individual monks who make social activism a central aspect of their practice as monks.

In chapter 2, I tell the story of Phrakhru Pitak Nanthakhun, yet I could easily have chosen any other activist monk to highlight. I describe his life, his village, and the particular situation in which he operates. Phrakhru Pitak's story puts faces on some of the people involved in the movement: monks, villagers, NGO workers, and government officials. The chapter places the reader into the setting, showing the problems villagers face, and the circumstances that led to Pitak's decisions to ordain and to engage in environmental conservation. Fox (1991) argues that life histories provide insight into how individuals negotiate and overcome broader historical, political, and cultural contexts that affect them. They allow us to see people as agents working through larger pressures and making conscious choices. Phrakhru Pitak's history illustrates how one monk encountered, understood, and translated the outside influences on his life and those of other villagers in an effort to improve their lives.

Studying a social movement such as Buddhist environmentalism, it is easy to think in the abstract, regarding the movement as an entity in itself buffeted by outside forces. The "movement" pushes back, interprets philosophy, and reacts to social conditions. Yet we must never forget that movements are made up of individuals, each with their own backgrounds and each making their own choices. They talk among themselves, debate issues and approaches, and sometimes disagree, or create conscious collective decisions. Even then, individuals are the actors who put these decisions into practice, who deal with the unexpected and the challenges that arise as a result. Telling Phrakhru Pitak's story provides a window into how one monk responded, and reminds us that each monk has his own story to tell.

At the same time, such movements are not merely random collections of individuals. A whole does emerge as the monks inclined to deal with social issues begin to enact their visions, respond to social and political forces, and collectively develop an approach. The rest of the book critically examines the process through which both development and environmental monks emerged as a social movement in Thailand, and the forces that influenced them.

What distinguishes environmental monks from other environmentalists the most is their use of ritual to give their work spiritual meaning and build moral commitment among their followers. Chapter 3, "The Rituals," unpacks the rituals they use, examining how they evolved, their growing popularity among the laity, and their local effectiveness. While tree ordinations are the preeminent ritual associated with Buddhist environmentalism (symbolizing both the movement and the moral imperatives behind it), some monks perform long-life ceremonies for waterways, or use local spirit beliefs to engage lay people's concepts of the forest and nature. Central to this process is how the monks read their targeted audiences. They adjust the form of their message to meet the needs and spiritual, as well as sociopolitical, levels of different segments of society, from villagers to the sangha hierarchy to state officials. They are enacting an example of *upaya,* or skillful means—teaching people in ways appropriate to their ability to grasp the lessons.

Rituals can be seen as a form of public performance. Anthropologist Diana Taylor (2002) analyzes protests as performances, demonstrating how children of the disappeared during Argentina's "Dirty War" publicly shamed the military and government agents responsible. They used theatrical and ritualistic techniques to gain attention and make people remember crimes that occurred one to two decades earlier. Elsewhere, Taylor (2009, 25) describes a performance's audience as "witnesses" to a traumatic event. Theater reveals an event, pulls the audience in, and shares the emotions and meanings with them. No longer can they claim ignorance. The goal is to provoke responsibility and empathy—even sympathy—on the part of the audience. Similarly, tree ordinations in Thailand are performances, designed not to invoke traumatic memories but to gain people's commitment to the more mundane projects the rituals introduce. Through participation in a ritual, people publicly demonstrate their involvement in the project, taking oaths and making merit. Simply through their presence and engagement, the audience acknowledges the power imbalances that led to the need for the ritual in the first place. In rituals such as the long-life ceremony performed for the Nan River, Phrakhru Pitak engaged public and military officials, even making them actors in the drama that told of the urgency of protecting the river.

Diana Taylor equates performances with history in Mexico, as people in Tepoztlán conduct a festival and ritual that challenge colonial and governmental versions of history and make claims about human rights and land rights. In that case, she argues, "[t]he physical mechanics of staging can also keep alive an organizational infrastructure, a practice or know-how, an episteme, and a politics that goes beyond the explicit topic" (Taylor 2006, 68). Thai environmental monks are not retelling or rethinking history, but social hierarchies and power. Although eventually some tree ordinations served to reinforce social hierarchies (Delcore 2004b), initially they served to empower rural farmers to lay claim to their forests and land use. These rituals are embodied actions, ones that validate villagers' knowledge and abilities, especially against broader social structures that usually devalue or create idealized images of village life. Although not explicitly political, the underlying motivations for performing these rituals in the first place are political.

Tree ordinations in particular shocked the broader public. Trees are not human, and although the monks do not claim actually to be turning them into *bhikkhu,* or fully ordained monks, as a performance the rites lead people to perceive them as such. One of the criticisms of tree ordinations is that they challenge what people consider sacred—placing trees on the same level as monks goes against the sacred and social hierarchy in place. Members of the media, the government, the sangha hierarchy, and even some mainstream monks accuse environmental monks of stepping beyond appropriate boundaries, manipulating the public through changing sacred relations, thereby challenging power relations. Like Argentina's Mothers of the Disappeared, a key aim of tree ordinations is to gain attention. If people are not watching—and witnessing—the performances are ineffectual. Tree ordinations captured the Thai imagination, pulled people in, and sparked lively debates about their appropriateness, and the social, economic, and political circumstances that led to their performance.

Chapter 4, "The Precedents," looks at the history of development in Thailand and the place of monks within it, setting the stage for the emergence of environmental monks and their use of ritual. In the 1970s and 1980s, Thai society struggled with the impacts of the rapid economic development policies initiated in the 1960s. Debates arose surrounding the consequences of these policies and whether they truly benefited rural people and the future of the nation. Monks such as Luang Pu Phuttapoj Waraporn witnessed the negative effects on villagers of the nation's push to modernize, and established organizations such as FEDRA as an alternative form of development. The case illustrates the manner in which a small number of monks began, and continue, to challenge state-led development policies.

The philosophical interpretations and development activities of these monks contributed to the gradual coalition of engaged monks in the Buddhist environmental movement. Environmentalism and approaches to development cannot be separated, as the latter affects both the environmental problems that emerge and the ways people deal with them. Whether a given monk is labeled a "development" or an "environmental" monk depends more on where he places his emphasis in describing social issues rather than any clear boundaries between these somewhat artificial categories.

Chapter 5, "The Grassroots," follows the emergence of environmental monks from the work of development monks, paralleling the rise of the environmental movement in Thailand. As the latter incorporates considerable variation in terms of issues emphasized and philosophical approaches (such as whether forests benefit most from removing or leaving the people who live in them), so does the Buddhist environmental movement.[21] Most environmental monks work locally, engaging in and supporting concrete actions with local people. Projects they run or support range from forest and wildlife conservation and water preservation to promoting integrated agriculture.[22] They see links between forms of agriculture and people's livelihoods, recognizing the debt that results from cash and mono-cropping. Several monks encourage farmers to shift from cash cropping to a form of sustainable agriculture—growing first to feed themselves, only selling any surplus. The grassroots efforts of these monks reflect their close connections with rural people, and the rural backgrounds from which many of these monks come. Regardless of the philosophical debates surrounding whether environmentalism is inherent or authentic in Buddhism, these monks emphasize empirical actions that can literally end people's suffering in the here and now. Some monks have engaged in protests against large-scale development projects such as dams. In fact, participating in such protests initially brought monks into the public eye in relation to environmental issues, even before they began to perform tree ordinations.

Chapter 6, "The Movement," examines the process through which individual monks performing rituals and enacting environmental projects came together to form a loose movement. While the work of a single monk may be effective in his local community, the impact of monks sharing ideas, methods, and encouraging each other—together with the support of NGOs and academics—increased the effectiveness of their work in society. In the early 1990s, NGOs such as the Thai Interreligious Commission for Development (TICD) and Wildlife Fund Thailand (WFT, an affiliate of World Wildlife Fund) sponsored numerous seminars for environmental monks to share their experiences, ideas, and challenges. TICD helped establish *Sekhiyadhamma*, an informal network of activist monks that sponsored many of these seminars, and produced a regular newsletter and Web site for monks concerned with promoting social justice grounded in Buddhist teachings. Currently, monks rather than TICD run Sekhiyadhamma. Activist monks in some regions, notably Khorat (Nakhorn Ratchasima Province) in the northeast, Surat Thani in the south, and the Northern Development Monks Network based in Chiang Mai created provincial and regional networks to collaborate on projects and validate their work.

Although activist monks periodically come together to share experiences, discuss challenges, and gather ideas and support for their work, they have not developed a common platform. Most tend to favor working with local people, seeing them as the proper stewards of the environment in which they live. A minority, such as Achan Pongsak Techadhammo, founder of Dhammanaat Foundation in Chiang Mai Province and one of the better-known and more controversial environmental monks, stands with those who hold nature as wilderness, something that should be kept pristine from human presence. In particular, Achan Pongsak pushed for the removal of Hmong people, one of the ethnic minorities in northern Thailand, from the watershed above his meditation center and the ethnic Thai villages with which he worked (Lohmann 1999, 2000; Paiboon 2003; Pinkaew 2001; Renard 1994; Suphaphan 1991). Many environmental monks in the north work with the ethnic minorities in their areas, and some criticized Achan Pongsak's approach because of his treatment of the Hmong people. The debate over people in the forest runs throughout the Thai environmental movement, and monks each bring their own perspectives and experiences to bear in their projects and criticisms of government policies.

Environmental monks use the rituals to engage social and political powers. Phrakhru Pitak, for example, learned from the arrests of Phra Prajak in 1991 and invited government officials to attend rituals he conducted. Their participation publicly displayed support for the projects, countering possible future criticisms. Some monks engage in far more overtly political and antigovernment activities, joining public protests of specific government programs such as the proposed cable car up Chiang Mai's sacred mountain Doi Suthep or the Pak Mun Dam in the northeast. In chapter 7, "The Challenges," I analyze the struggles monks face through their public and political involvements. The risks range from criticism in the media and being passed over for ecclesiastical promotion to arrest, death threats, and even assassination. Even as tree ordinations gained popular support and people came to expect rural, and especially forest, monks to protect the forest, environmental monks still threatened major powers in Thai society—perhaps even more so because of their growing popularity. Yet after Phra Supoj's murder in 2005, public response was lacking. The case was mishandled in numerous ways, including the intimidation of witnesses and loss of evidence (Budsarakham 2005). Ironically, the case also demonstrated the effectiveness of environmental monks and their acceptance as part of the mainstream environmental movement. In the few years surrounding Phra Supoj's death, several other prominent environmental and human rights activists were killed (eighteen between 2001 and 2005; Haberkorn 2005). Those who benefitted from control of natural resources and the silent acquiescence of local people clearly feared the effectiveness of leading environmentalists, including monks.

Looking Forward

In the process of speaking out publicly and visibly supporting each other, environmental monks constructed a new knowledge—of Buddhism and of environmentalism—for Thai society. They demonstrated that despite the criticisms, arrests, and threats, their engagement in such worldly concerns as the condition of the environment and how it affected the lives of villagers fits within the purview of a monk's responsibility. Under close scrutiny by the sangha hierarchy and the public, they attempted to live exemplary lives, acting as moral guardians against powerful forces that affect villagers' lives and society. While the government pursues its agenda of economic growth, businesses seek greater profits, and people fight over politics on the streets of Bangkok, engaged Buddhist monks continue their efforts on the ground in the places they live. They remain willing to point out the increased debts of farmers that result from capitalist agriculture, to identify the sources of poverty within the state that supposedly carries the mandate to care for its citizens. Beyond the criticisms, these monks take concrete actions to improve villagers' lives, challenging the effects of globalization, state policies, and market forces through grassroots projects.

The success of environmental monks' programs is hard to measure in empirical terms. One could assess the level of debt of farmers before and after community forests have been consecrated, or how much households spend on food after incorporating the produce from new integrated, organic farms or fish from sanctuaries in nearby rivers. As far as I know, no one has conducted such studies. These figures would not reflect the full impact of the work of development and environmental monks, however. The changes have occurred on a more abstract level, in the growing acceptance of framing livelihood decisions in Buddhist terms even while some argue that Thailand is becoming increasingly secularized. Another indication is the efforts by state and corporate agents to appropriate key elements of the movement, particularly tree ordinations, to support their own agendas.

Although engaged monks still make up only a small fraction of the total Thai sangha, a percentage that is impossible to determine because there is no official category for "development monk" or "environmental monk" in sangha accounting, the public no longer sees them as oddities or renegade monks. When I began my fieldwork in the mid-1980s with Luang Pu Phuttapoj, people in Chiang Mai were familiar with him more because of his high ecclesiastical rank and the belief that he was a potent "field of merit"[23] than because of his development work. By the early 1990s, development monks were more familiar to the public, but few people had any sense of what environmental monks did. Tree ordinations captured people's imagination because of the radical idea of performing rituals for nature and the misconception that trees were actually being ordained. Members of the sangha and laity alike called for monks conducting tree ordinations to be derobed because of their unorthodox behavior. Yet as early as 1991, Phrakhru Manas Nathiphitak, the monk credited with performing the first tree ordination, quipped at an NGO conference that the nation was "going crazy" for tree ordinations, as the governor of Chiang Mai used the rite to determine the fate of old rubber trees lining the road between Chiang Mai city and Lamphun (conference presentation, 8/4/1991). By the mid-1990s, tree ordinations became increasingly accepted as a way to demonstrate public concern for the environment.

In 1996–97, the project to ordain fifty million trees in honor of the king's fiftieth year of reign marked a sharp shift in how Thai society perceived tree ordinations and the Buddhist environmental movement. I agree with the analyses of this project by several anthropologists that in the process the state appropriated the medium of tree ordinations for its own purposes (Delcore 2004b; Isager and Ivarsson 2002; Tannenbaum 2000), to some degree undermining the effectiveness of environmental monks' criticism of state-led development (Darlington 2007). The incorporation of a tree ordination as part of a beauty contest in 2010 further dilutes the moral and political impact of the rituals on a national level, even while indicating the degree to which they have entered popular culture and are used to define what it means to be "Thai."

The monks concerned with social issues and social justice have continued to adapt to both threats and appropriation of their ideas. Chapter 8, "The Future," examines how they adjust their approaches, seeking new alliances and creating new projects, with their primary goal still focused on relieving suffering. Subjects on rural development and environmentalism have been incorporated into the curricula of the Buddhist universities, and the laity has come to expect monks to engage in such issues. Some of the organizations that support engaged Buddhist monks, such as the Spirit in Education Movement (SEM) founded by Sulak Sivaraksa, now reach out to the sangha in neighboring countries to promote similar movements. Buddhist development and environmental movements are emerging in Cambodia, Laos, and even Burma, further demonstrating the potential of Buddhist thought as a means of promoting social justice and social change.

Environmental monks in Thailand serve as a model for Buddhists worldwide. They demonstrate the relevancy of the core values of Buddhism for dealing with modern problems, and the flexibility of methods in the process. Tree ordinations, even as the perception of them in Thai society has changed, still embody the values and goals of monks determined to end environmental degradation, promote social justice, and relieve suffering, all grounded in their interpretations of Buddhist teachings.

While focused on the actions and interpretations of a specific group of monks, this case provides insights into religious change. Environmental monks are inventing new ways of dealing with social problems, pushing the methods and meanings of socially engaged Buddhism into new realms. At the same time, they are part of a process in Thailand negotiating Buddhism's response to a world of growing consumption, exploitation, and globalization. Rachelle Scott (2009, 158) would probably see them as influenced by what she calls the "neo-Orientalists" in their criticism of Western materialism and its impact on Buddhism, and their idealization of Buddhism's simplicity. In her study of the Dhammakaya movement as an alternative to mainstream Thai Buddhism, she places engaged Buddhists among the dominant voices in articulating the place of religion in Thai society. This book examines the process through which socially engaged Buddhists in Thailand, particularly development and environmental monks, went from being seen as radical, alternative, inauthentic, and even crazy, existing on the periphery of Thai Buddhist practice, to becoming one of the predominant frames of authentic Thai Buddhist responses to modernity.

2

The Forest, The Village, and
The Ecology Monk

In the past, Nan's natural resources were so abundant that if you walked in the
forest you would trip. When you stood up, your mouth would be full of bamboo
shoots and your hands full of mushrooms. Looking back at what you tripped over,
you would see a python slithering away.

—Folk saying in Nan Province[1]

I FIRST TRAVELED to Nan Province in the far east of northern Thailand
in July 1991. Two weeks earlier at a nongovernment organization (NGO)
meeting at Chiang Mai University I had met Sakchai Parnthep, who ran his
own NGO to conserve indigenous seeds of Nan and worked closely with
Phrakhru Pitak Nanthakhun on his environmental programs. Sakchai, in his
early thirties, idealistic and dedicated to preserving Nan's culture and natural
environment, was in Chiang Mai seeking support for Phrakhru Pitak's second tree ordination, this time to sanctify a community forest for ten villages.
He invited me, along with all the NGO workers present at the meeting, to
participate, and even offered to let me stay with his family in Nan city for a
few days.

On July 8, I boarded a bus for a six-hour ride from Chiang Mai to Nan
to meet Phrakhru Pitak Nanthakhum (see Plate 5) and to join in the tree
ordination. As the crow flies, Nan is only about 200 kilometers (~120 miles)
from Chiang Mai, but it is impossible to travel that route directly. The bus
winds its way southeast through Lamphun, Lampang, and Phrae provinces
where the mountains are lower and more passable, before heading north
again to Nan.

Through Lamphun, Lampang, and Phrae the road is relatively flat, stretching past wet rice paddy fields and small villages. Nearing Nan, the road begins to climb and twist. I grew to dread this bus trip over the next few years; the rises, drops, and sharp turns made my stomach churn, especially if I got stuck toward the back of the bus.

The scenery was spectacular, however. On that first trip I was glued to the window gazing in awe at the broad vistas across the mountains and valleys of the province. Nan is one of the most mountainous provinces of northern Thailand. Its small area of 11,472 km^2 is tucked between the Thai provinces of Phrae to the south and southwest, Phayao to the northwest and Chiang Rai to the north, and northern Laos to the east. With a population of only a little more than five hundred thousand, Nan has a low population density, which emphasizes the sense of wilderness of the mountains even more.

Compared with Chiang Mai, Nan retains a backwater feel. Relatively few foreign tourists visit, and few Thais from other provinces have ever been there. Despite its contemporary remoteness, the province has a rich history. Its first recorded king dates to the fourteenth century. Over the centuries, the principality of Nan came under the suzerainty of Phayao, Sukhothai, Phitsanulok, Chiang Mai, Burma, and Bangkok. Nan nevertheless preserved its own identity and pride, claiming both a strong tradition of spirit lords who helped protect the region from invading armies early on and enforced morality among its rulers (Wyatt 1994, 1079), and a reliquary "believed to enshrine a relic of the Buddha's mortal remains" (Wyatt 1994, 1080) that became one of twelve major pilgrimage sites for northern Thailand (Keyes 1975). The people of Nan remain proud of their distinct past, maintaining an emotional affiliation with the semi-independent principality of historical Nan that is much stronger than that with the modern Thai state. As the history of Dok Dang Village that follows shows, the province—and its natural resources—has been pulled rapidly and firmly into the nation-state and its economy over the past century, a pattern typical of locations across Thailand.

Watching the mountains roll by as the bus made its way to the capital city, I gradually realized why the views were so stunning. Few trees blocked my sight. The hills were green from the rainy season growth of cash crops, mostly feed corn grown in near vertical fields on every slope. Occasionally I would see a reservoir or stream, the banks of which were brown from low water levels, despite recent rain. Small villages and wet rice paddies filled the valleys, but Nan Province is mostly mountains. The historical subsistence agriculture of its people, who include Northern Thais, Lao, and Tai Lue living predominantly in the lower and mid-range altitudes, and Hmong,

Yao (Mien), Htin, Khmu, and Malbri[2] in the highlands, was swidden, or slash-and-burn, dry-rice farming on the mountainsides. Today most people grow feed corn, green beans, cassava, and other cash crops to sell, and buy their daily rice and vegetables. Some still grow rice to eat, but it usually is not enough to last from one harvest to the next. The province is famous for mandarin oranges, the orchards of which have replaced large areas of forest. The exploitation of timber and the search for agricultural land have nearly destroyed the province's forests as the economy shifted from subsistence to a monetary base. By the time I reached Nan city, a small, provincial capital of about thirty thousand,[3] my impressions of the province as hit hard by deforestation and related environmental degradation were set (Plate 6).

I soon learned that Phrakhru Pitak, Sakchai, and other NGO workers in Nan, as well as people from the monk's home village, Dok Dang, shared my concerns about the province's natural resources. Their worries were based on lives watching the forest diminish and daily struggles to eke out a living from its depleted resources. Their creative responses and efforts to deal with the problems of deforestation through the use of Buddhism and local culture led me to choose Dok Dang and the work of Phrakhru Pitak as the focus of my research on environmental monks.

The history of Dok Dang Village and Pitak's experiences growing up there serve as a microcosm of the economic change Thailand has undergone over the past century, and the problems and potentials it created for the Thai people. This case sheds insight into what motivates and influences environmental monks. Pitak's case goes beyond an individual Thai Buddhist monk responding to particular situations, constraints, and cultural and religious influences. He innovates. He reflects on his experiences and those of his relatives, the pressures they feel to live certain kinds of lives, and the potential futures they face. In the process, he draws from cultural experiments by other monks and creates his own approaches. His efforts have become famous across Thailand, impacting the shape and direction of Buddhist environmentalism and Thai environmentalism more generally, even as his work is informed by the actions of others and the sociopolitical and religious contexts in which he lives. His experiences reinforce the need to understand individual stories of agency and how choices are made within broader sociopolitical contexts.

Following Delcore (2004a) and Fox (1991), I approach life history as a way of showing how individuals work within, negotiate, and transcend the broader historical, political, and cultural contexts within which they live. Delcore tells the story of a Northern Thai farmer, Berm, who lived and worked within a context of rapid development. As Delcore (2004a, 33) comments, "Far from a benighted victim of the discursive straitjacket of development, Berm emerged as an influential local figure who appropriated Thai development for personal and political projects that engaged yet also transcended the discourse and material process of development identified by poststructuralist analysts." Growing up and working during the same process of development, facing similar constraints, pressures, and cultural factors, including gender, class, and local politics, Phrakhru Pitak also draws from his experiences and acts under his own volition and agency in creating his responses to the difficult situations facing the villagers of Dok Dang and Nan Province more generally (Delcore 2000, 154). He integrates ideas coming from outside Nan—ideas of environmentalism and socially engaged Buddhism (from both national and transnational contexts)—and translates and transforms them into a form that speaks to villagers, local and provincial leaders, and activists across the nation. Environmental, social, and political conditions have changed, and he and other activist monks have continually adapted to and affected the direction of this change. His story—especially in the context of the history of Dok Dang Village—puts a face on the process of experimentation, creativity, and change in which environmental monks engage.

From Forest to Village

Dok Dang sits high in the mountains north of Nan city. Most of its houses are spread out for two kilometers along the twisty, narrow road that runs from the city to a district town.[4] The land drops sharply down away from the road within a couple of hundred meters; in some places the houses, built only a few meters from the road, are cantilevered over the edge of the descending hillside.

The earliest stories about the village were usually told by *Ui* Lek,[5] a village elder in his mid-eighties when I met him in 1992. Ui Lek and two of his brothers, including Phrakhru Pitak's father, were among the first to migrate to what is now Dok Dang. They came in the 1930s looking for agricultural land, clearing dry rice fields in the forest for their families, and as merchants, joining others who passed through on their way to sell forest products in Nan city.[6] As the number of families that migrated into the mountainous forest grew, they initially lived scattered through the forest, moving homes and fields as needed. Dok Dang only became a unified village in 1959, when the local provincial authorities settled the families along the forest path to the city (Delcore 2000, 167).

Ui Lek described the forest when he first arrived as follows:

> In the past, this was a deep, cool forest. There were many wild animals, not like today. There used to be teak forests, not like the forest now. At first you could go to the forest to collect mushrooms, but you couldn't go far. The trunks of bamboo trees were as thick as your arm. Wherever anyone went [to live] they had to clear the forest, until it became what you see today. (Interview, 4/3/93)

The people of Dok Dang came as immigrants from other areas, mostly northern Laos or neighboring villages.[7] They included ethnic Lao, Northern Thai, and Khmu. They moved in search of land to farm, pushed into the mountains as the good rice paddy land was already claimed in the lowlands. "This was a vast forest," one grandmother, who herself moved to Dok Dang in 1954, told me. "Whoever cleared the land could claim it." The migrants believed that land empty of settlers was free for the taking, waiting to be tamed.[8]

The migrants brought with them a belief system that included Buddhist teachings, Brahmanic rites, and spirit beliefs. While scholars tend to categorize these aspects of rural Thai religion separately, for the villagers they work together in a single, syncretic system (Kirsch 1977). Particularly relevant here were the villagers' beliefs in the spirits that occupied the forest. Before land could be cleared or plowed, the farmers made offerings to the spirits that lived in the trees, streams, and forest. Without their concurrence, the villagers could not safely cut the trees or make changes to the natural environment. Offending the spirits resulted in accidents, illness, or even death. The area of Dok Dang was equated with a village guardian spirit, one of the named "spirit lords" with lineages and influence across northern Thailand (Shalardchai 1984). Villagers informed him of all significant life events (births, marriages, deaths, etc.) and changes in the village.[9]

The settlers cleared the forest to grow food, mostly upland rice, using swidden agricultural techniques. They worked the land for three to five years, rotating their fields and houses as the land wore out, and allowing used land to regenerate as it lay fallow. A small field could easily support a family, producing enough rice to last until the next harvest. The villagers described the soil as rich in nutrients and claimed no fertilizers were necessary.

The forest also provided food. People hunted for meat, gathered mushrooms, bamboo shoots, and other vegetables, and caught fish and crabs in the streams. Villagers sold forest products such as excess meat from hunting, hemp, leaves and bark for making saa paper, and grasses for brooms in the city. There they would buy supplies for their families—dried fish, spices, cloth, farm tools, etc.—and goods to sell to other villagers. Although only twenty-five kilometers, the trip from Dok Dang to the city took several hours walking single file along a narrow footpath through the forest. Ui Lek claimed the trip took two days, as they would sleep in a lowland village about halfway to town. He described the challenge of carrying his goods in two baskets, hung from either end of a bamboo pole on his shoulders, along this trail. It was not wide enough to walk easily with a wide load as branches continually caught the pole and baskets.

Even in the 1960s, when Phrakhru Pitak was a child, the forest supported the people who lived there. The community was poor in monetary terms, but could survive on the forest resources. Pitak described the abundance of the forest animals:

> During the day groups of langurs came into the village. We had to use sling shots and sticks to chase them out so they wouldn't eat all the betel nuts and roots we collected or the eggs in the chicken coops. There were so many forest animals, if you went into the forest you didn't need a gun to hunt the squirrels. You just bent tree branches to the ground and the squirrels came running out. They were noisy, calling all the time. You only needed a slingshot, not a gun, to hunt when I was a child. (Thai Interreligious Commision for Development n.d. [1993], 7; author's translation)

Today there is little room left for expansion. The houses are crowded together in five separate groupings along the road. The population of a little more than two hundred people is not growing as many younger people leave the village in search of work in the cities. Many eventually move back, but few new families have migrated into the village since the mid-1970s. One woman told me that new people would not be welcome anymore because the land could not support them.

The problem of overcrowding in Dok Dang—and its impact on the forest—was exacerbated when the central government under Field Marshal Sarit Thanarat (1958–1963) sped up economic development in the 1960s by promoting agricultural expansion for export and the use of natural resources for industrialization. These policies intensified the competition for arable land already occurring due to population pressures. For Dok Dang, this process meant yet more people moving up from the lowlands seeking either new farmland for cash crops or timber to sell. The villagers themselves, encouraged by the modern lifestyle promised in government economic development rhetoric, similarly turned toward the forest as a source of cash, gradually giving up their subsistence lifestyle. As more forest was cut for profit, it became harder for villagers to subsist on its resources. The number of animals declined and streams began to dry up.

Consequently, people cleared yet more forest to earn a living and pay off debts incurred through cash cropping. Farming for sale entailed significant initial investment in seeds, fertilizers, pesticides, and labor. When I moved into the village in 1992, farmers were complaining about the string bean crop. That was the first year many people planted beans to supplement or replace the feed corn crop that was introduced into the village in the 1970s. Both the local agricultural cooperative and the national agricultural bank encouraged villagers to grow corn and beans, even facilitating connections with the companies that promoted these cash crops. Most villagers borrowed heavily to plant cash crops and to buy food before their crops could be harvested and sold. Companies that brought in crop seeds gave farmers seeds, fertilizers, and pesticides. They expected that when they returned to buy the crops, their investment would be repaid before the farmers received any money for their crops. Farmers were locked into doing business with specific companies. Few villagers gained back their initial outlay, especially if weather conditions limited crop production. String bean production in 1992, for example, was significantly lower than people expected. The beans required intensive labor to harvest. That year the assistant headman died days before the bean crop was to be harvested, and many families missed the prime harvest time in order to attend his funeral. The beans they later harvested were too big by the company's standards for it to buy. Between dwindling corn and string bean crops, many farmers became caught in a cycle of debt followed by pressure to plant even more cash crops in order to pay it off. In 2006 Phrakhru Pitak responded to my question about the largest problem facing the people of Nan with one word: "debt."

The villagers also faced challenges due to concessions the national government granted to logging companies throughout the forest. Since the villagers did not have title to their land, they could do little to prevent major logging or the small-scale deforestation that followed. In 1998 Phrakhru Pitak recounted the impact of logging:

The cause of deforestation between 1969 and 1971 was the granting of concessions. Forest companies had cut down the large trees until they became hard to find, and then they pulled out. Smaller investors from nearby villages then came in to cut down the remaining trees for sale. In addition, sellers of firewood hired villagers from outside to cut down trees, both big and small, to use in tobacco curing houses and refugee camps,[10] until the forest that had previously provided such refreshing shade and fresh air was almost gone. (Webb 1998, 207)

From the late 1950s through the 1970s, national politics contributed to the deterioration of Nan's forests in another way. Responding to the autocratic rule of Field Marshal Sarit and subsequent right-wing governments, the Communist Party of Thailand gained momentum in its struggle against the central government. They operated guerrilla style, based in remote areas of northeast and northern Thailand, including the mountains of Nan.[11] The Thai military built roads and pushed economic development in these areas with the aims of simultaneously destroying the Communists' hiding places (the forest) and preventing villagers from either supporting or joining them due to dissatisfaction. The road through Dok Dang was built in 1968, during the height of the anti-Communist era. It not only eased the military's access to Communist bases (one of which was reputedly near where the village temple now stands) but also enabled still more lowlanders to move upland into the village's forest land. At the same time, farmers could more easily get their goods to the markets in Nan city, and middlemen could come to the village to buy cash crops and forest products.

Today, most of the people in Dok Dang earn a living through planting cash crops. They are heavily in debt, and often have to buy rice to eat as their upland rice fields have been converted to cash cropping. Every family raises chickens, and many also own a few head of cattle or a couple of pigs. The hillsides are too steep to allow large holdings of livestock or vast fields in any one place. The villagers still live from the forest as well, selling forest products in the city. Every afternoon and evening women sit together plaiting bamboo strips to sell to a hat manufacturer. Another middleman visits the village during mushroom season, buying what villagers collect. The former headman, who ran the village for twenty-two years, now sells medicinal herbs at a roadside stand.[12] In the past the villagers ate what the forest offered, selling only the surplus; today they sell what they find and buy much of their food in the district town market. A few villagers run small shops from their houses for vegetables, rice, and other basic necessities brought from the city market. Formally, most of these foods and goods were available from local resources. It was in the context of this changing history of a small forest village that Phrakhru Pitak grew up and formulated his ideas of development, the natural environment, and Buddhism.

Village Child to Ecology Monk

Shortly after I arrived in Nan city in 1991, Sakchai took me to Wat Aranyawat to meet Phrakhru Pitak Nanthakhun. The temple compound was full—of people and saplings—as they prepared for the upcoming tree ordination. Local nurseries and individuals, mostly middle-class people from the city, donated a couple of thousand saplings to be blessed, given out to villagers, and planted in deforested areas. Coupled with the tree ordination, Pitak adapted another traditional ceremony, *thot pha pa* ("giving of the forest robes") in which lay people give robes and other necessities to the sangha, as *thot pha pa ton mai,* or "giving of the forest robes and trees." In addition to the robes, saplings are given to the monks as symbols of the necessity of trees for life and the relationship of trees to the Buddha. In some ceremonies, such as those performed by Phrakhru Manas Nathiphitak in Phayao Province, the saplings are mostly the sacred bodhi tree, the tree under which the Buddha achieved enlightenment. In Nan, the saplings were varied, including many practical species such as fruit trees that could be economically productive without being cut down. I arrived two days before the actual rituals, as Pitak, the monks and novices at Wat Aranyawat, and workers from several NGOs in Nan were carrying out the final preparations for the ceremony (Plate 7).

Despite the hectic activities in the temple, Phrakhru Pitak took time to talk with me. He was serious as he told me what I later recognized as the formal explanation of his environmental work. Upstairs in the reception area of his residence, he sat still as he recited his brief history. He was eloquent and thorough, and somewhat intimidating due to the reserved nature of his manner and story. I later realized that even by 1991 Pitak had related this story multiple times, often for people such as his sangha superiors who were skeptical or critical of his social engagement. People from across Thailand (and across the world) asked him about his environmental work, especially the performance of tree ordinations. I heard the rehearsed version of his story, emphasizing the negative impacts of deforestation on villagers' lives and the value of Buddhist teachings for dealing with the resultant suffering.

Another event, which occurred two years later, illustrated a different side of the monk, one that showed his rural roots and close connections with villagers. I accompanied Phrakhru Pitak to a village in Santisuk District. He had received a national environmental award, and the crew of an educational children's television show wanted to film him teaching environmental lessons to village kids. He set up a slide show for the children, who packed the open building at the local *wat* (temple). The kids were restless and excited by the television cameras, and were slow to settle down. Pitak opened with slides of cartoon characters, telling funny stories of the misadventures of fictitious animals and villagers. Soon the kids were mesmerized, laughing and shouting answers to the monk's questions. Besides ecological lessons, moral ones were embedded in the stories, as he showed cartoon versions of Jataka tales, stories of the previous lives of the Buddha. Throughout the show, he integrated Buddhist teachings, the centrality of water in the children's lives, and the importance of caring for the forest and wildlife. I often witnessed the monk's skill in targeting his audience in seminars for environmental monks, to government meetings, to village presentations preparing for tree ordinations. He spoke to any audience with authority and confidence, but clearly enjoyed and related to rural people the most.

Phrakhru Pitak's work goes beyond slide shows and meetings. He works closely with NGO workers, villagers, and other monks to build an ongoing program that he adjusts with the changing social, religious, and political climate. Having grown up in Dok Dang and witnessed firsthand the negative effects of deforestation on the lives of the villagers, he was determined to develop and use his skills and his religion to make a difference. His approach is the result of both his personality and the historical context within which he lives. His life story offers insights into how one man draws from his cultural and historical setting to create innovative responses whose impact has extended far beyond the mountains of Nan.

Forest Childhood

Phrakhru Pitak was born Sanguan Phancha in 1958, the seventh of twelve children.[13] His father, ethnically Thai-Lao, supplemented his farming through hunting for food in the forest and selling excess meat in the city. His mother was Khmu, one of the smallest ethnic minorities in Thailand. His generation was the first born in Dok Dang.

Pitak's childhood was spent immersed in the forest environment. Growing up, he witnessed the impact of the changing economy on the people

around him and the forest resources, although he admits he did not understand the connections at the time. He noticed that over time it was harder
for him and his siblings to find crabs or fish in the streams. Water levels were
lower than they used to be and could not support as many fish. Even as a
child, Pitak began to think about the forest and people's dependence on and
exploitation of it.

The defining moment Pitak credits for his realization of both his concern
about the natural environment and his commitment to Buddhism occurred
when he accompanied his father on a hunting trip.

My father was a hunter and an upland farmer. I saw him kill animals
often, and I felt sorry for them. Once, he came across a group of
mountain lion cubs in the forest without their mother around. He
killed them all, strung them together, brought them home, and laid
them on the ground. I went up to them and touched them, and saw
that each one was dead. That night, the mother came around the
edges of the village and cried all night. I almost couldn't stand the
sound. Another time, I was with my father, and we came across a
group of langurs. My father told me to stay back a little and be very
still, but when they saw us, they started to flee. But there was one
that was slower than the others because it had a baby clinging to it.
My father shot and killed it, and it fell to the ground. We went over
to it, and the young one was still alive. My father went to kill it, but
I said, "Wait, don't. I'll take it home and raise it." So we went home
with it. My father skinned the mother, and lay the hide out on the
fence to dry. I put the young one in an old chicken coop. It cried
and cried, and wouldn't eat anything. I tried to give it bananas and
other fruit, but it wouldn't eat. Then I asked my mother for some
of her mother's milk, because she was nursing my younger sibling.
She squeezed some out into a bowl, but the langur didn't touch that
either. So after a few days, I decided to try to let it go. I opened
the cage and let it out, and it ran to the skin drying on the fence
and started hugging and kissing it, because it remembered. (Delcore
2000, 168)

The incident impacted Pitak profoundly. In the 1990s, more than thirty
years later, he frequently related the tale at seminars for activist monks and
other environmental events. The story illustrated his awareness of the suffering people inflict on other sentient beings, and their interconnections with
and responsibility toward them and the natural environment. He credited

the event with planting the seeds of Buddhism in his consciousness, as he recognized the relationship between its teachings and the causes of the baby langur's suffering. In reality, it was years later, after schooling and religious training as a novice, before Pitak began to articulate the connections between Buddhism and the environment that form the basis of his work today, and projected a Buddhist interpretation onto the baby langur incident.

Pitak was the only one of his siblings to attend school, as the others were either needed at home or had no interest in education. Although the government at the time mandated that every child complete at least the fourth level of elementary school, hardships made this impossible for many rural people. Some families needed their children at home to help with farming, and the girls often had to care for younger siblings. Some villages had no school, as was the case in Dok Dang. If children had to go to school in a different village, there were extra expenses. They often had to pay tuition as an outside student, or room and board to stay at or near the school. Although Pitak's family was poor, there were enough other children at home to enable him to go to school. His father drew on connections with the temple in a village down the mountain, and sent Pitak at the age of seven to live at the temple while attending school.

Pitak finished his public schooling with the fourth grade in 1972 but continued his studies as a novice at the temple where he lived. His decision to ordain in order to continue his schooling followed one of two strategies poor rural families with boys often choose to enable their sons to get an education. One option is to send a son to live at a temple while attending school. There, in exchange for helping with tasks around the temple, the boy receives room and board. A second option is for boys—sometimes as young as eight—to ordain as novices to receive a religious education in the *dhamma,* or teachings of the Buddha, as well as some secular topics at the temple itself.[14] Novices help around the temple and do not spend money on tuition, room, or board. In addition, they gain the social status of being a novice, a status that continues to give them privilege in lay life if they derobe. Many novices leave the sangha after schooling, but Pitak chose to remain in robes throughout his life.

Pitak did well in dhamma studies, easily passing the third level of religious examinations in four years. Since the temple school lacked sufficient teachers, the abbot asked him to teach the younger novices in the first level while he was studying the third level. Even as a novice, he distinguished himself as a quick learner and effective with people, both skills he uses today.

Return to the "Forest"

In 1975, at age seventeen and still a novice, Pitak was sent by the sangha authorities back to his home village to establish a temple. When he returned, having been away for years, Pitak noticed that much of the forest had been destroyed. People lacked sufficient water, and had difficulties finding enough food from the forest. They cleared land to expand their farms, especially to plant corn, exacerbating the situation. Logging, both legal and illegal, also contributed to much of the deforestation.

The headman, originally from another village, donated land to build the temple, and villagers began to cut wood for the building. Pitak eventually realized that he had become a tool for the headman's greed when the wood kept disappearing from the site and no temple was built. When he challenged the headman as to the whereabouts of the wood, the latter fled, and the novice unofficially became both headman and abbot for the village.[15]

Phrakhru Pitak's first formal deed as acting headman was to bring in teachers from the province's non–formal education program to help villagers learn to read and write. Of the three people who finished the program, two were Pitak's brothers; the older one was then elected as the new headman and the younger one became his assistant.

The experience of the stolen wood, the greed behind it, and the villagers' ignorance of ways to fight it, together with watching the forest (which he understood as the source of people's livelihood) disappear, all contributed to Phrakhru Pitak's growing interest in environmentalism. His apprehension increased when, in 1976, the government talked about granting a new logging concession to the Nan Timber Company in the area, which would increase the speed with which the forest was being cut down.

Given his concerns about the condition of the forest, Pitak's sermons included teachings about the relationship between people and nature, and human responsibility toward the latter. He promoted forest preservation, especially in watershed areas, and reforestation in denuded areas. As always, he took a middle way approach, encouraging villagers to learn to use forest resources sustainably while protecting the forest environment. Concerned because villagers did not hold legal title to their land, the monk encouraged them to plant seeds and saplings to regenerate the forest when they moved their fields. In other regions, the government had claimed such areas as abandoned and taken them over. Over the years Pitak helped the village improve its infrastructure, building a temple and a short road to it, a reservoir and wells, and establishing a local cooperative store. He advised the Village Youth Association, beginning his ongoing commitment to helping youth develop morally and gain a strong basis for a good life. He later continued this effort through a summer novice ordination program that supported poor rural boys from his district to become novices for two months to learn about the religion and environment.

Beyond the Village

Throughout this time Phrakhru Pitak progressed rapidly in his religious career. In 1978 at age twenty he was fully ordained as a monk. In 1979 he went to study in Nan city at Wat Aranyawat, becoming the assistant abbot there later that year. He received the ecclesiastical title of Phra Palat Sanguan. During his first year at Wat Aranyawat, he took the opportunity to train in the government-sponsored Thammathut program, which sent monks to missionize in politically sensitive and economically poor border provinces with the goal of strengthening people's ties with the state.

Phrakhru Pitak became abbot of Wat Aranyawat in 1983. He remained abbot of the village temple, too, as there were no other monks to take over, splitting his time between the two temples. To continue his informal education, he volunteered for another government-sponsored sangha program, Thammacharik. Similar to Thammathut, this program promoted rural development and integration into the Thai nation, but in this case the projects targeted minority mountain peoples. Through the program, monks worked with the Department of Public Welfare among mountain peoples to convert them from animism and to "develop" them (Tambiah 1976, 434–71). Phrakhru Pitak spent three days at Wat Sri Soda in Chiang Mai for Thammacharik training. During the two years he worked as a Thammacharik monk, he emphasized ending opium addiction among the mountain peoples of Nan Province.

Pitak continually looked for other ways to learn, recognizing experience as a form of education. Shortly after becoming abbot of Wat Aranyawat, he began to visit monks across the country known for their activism and use of Buddhism to promote social justice. He visited several self-proclaimed "development monks" (phra nak phatthana), observing their methods, discussing their interpretations of Buddhist teachings, and witnessing the results of their programs. Over the years he visited, among others, Buddhadasa

Bhikkhu, a famous scholar monk; Luang Pu Phuttapoj Waraporn at Wat Pa Dharabhirom in Chiang Mai, one of the first independent development monks who established the Foundation for Education and Development of Rural Areas (FEDRA) in the 1970s; Luang Pho Nan of Surin Province, a leading "development monk"; Phrakhru Manas Nathiphitak in Phayao Province, the monk credited with performing the first tree ordination with the purpose of conserving forests; and Phra Prajak Khuttajitto of Buriram Province in the northeast, who in the early 1990s became infamous for his challenges to government development schemes and his resulting arrests. Pitak valued the lessons taught by other monks, and drew from their experiences to develop his own approach to development and environmentalism.

In 1985, Phrakhru Pitak learned of another missionary monk program, Thammathayat, that was not government run. This program was based at Wat Chonprathan in Nonthaburi Province, a branch of Suan Mokh. Suan Mokh was the meditation and study center of Buddhadasa Bhikkhu, the influential philosopher monk whose interpretation of Buddhist principles encouraged Buddhist monks and lay people alike to work toward a socially and economically just society. Unlike Thammathut or Thammacharik, the Thammathayat program receives no budget from the Department of Religious Affairs, but depends on donations and the commitment of its member monks.

All three programs have similar goals of helping people live better lives through teaching Buddhism and promoting development programs. Thammacharik, however, offers participating monks only a few days of training before sending them out to a specific place for between ten to twenty days a month. Thammathayat provides two to three months of intensive training, first in Vipassana meditation, then preaching, and community development, before monks are sent to an area for which they are responsible for most of the year. Among other things, Pitak learned lecturing techniques, including the use of technology such as slide and video shows, an approach he continues to use effectively today. He participated in the fourth class to undergo Thammathayat training, returning to Nan Province to work. He encouraged other monks from Nan to join the program, and soon thereafter established the Thammathayat Center at Wat Aranyawat. Through the center, he encouraged monks in Nan to exchange ideas and support on social issues (Delcore 2000, 181).

As a result of his frequent travels in the mountains, first through Thammacharik then Thammathayat projects, Phrakhru Pitak further witnessed the negative ecological impacts of economic development throughout the province. Drawing on his exposure to the teachings of Buddhadasa and the experiences of other socially engaged monks, he preached an environmental ethic along with the Buddhist missionary work of both programs.

Environmental Activism

Phrakhru Pitak's first real struggle in the name of conservation came in 1986 when the provincial government, following a national trend, began a program to make Nan Province "green." This entailed putting the province's resources into planting commercial forests, especially eucalyptus trees, a non-native species, with the stated goal of rejuvenating degraded land. Eucalyptus plantations threatened to displace many villagers living unofficially in National Forest Reserve Land. The projected incomes led many local government representatives, particularly subdistrict chiefs and village headmen, to fell trees to make way for eucalyptus plantations. They had the idea that "the old forest cannot become money. We must cut it all down to plant economic forests" (Arawan 1993, 10). Environmentalists across the country argued against such projects, claiming that eucalyptus would severely deplete the soil (Lohmann 1991, 1993, 211). The governor of Uttaradit Province even researched the negative impacts of eucalyptus on the environment and agriculture and opposed such economic forests within his province.

Phrakhru Pitak opposed the plan in Nan, arguing that clearing natural forests to plant eucalyptus was not conservation but destruction. He wrote to the governor of Uttaradit requesting information about the ecological effects of eucalyptus to use in his fight. Without his permission, his letter to the governor was published in a national newspaper. The Nan provincial authorities complained to the provincial sangha hierarchy that such research and opposition to a government program was inappropriate behavior for a monk. Despite the challenge, Pitak convinced his ecclesiastical superiors of the dangers of the plan and, especially, the Buddhist basis of his motivations to end it. He maintained that his concern was not who benefited politically or financially from the plan, but long-term environmental damage and the consequent human suffering if it was implemented.

Through this case, Pitak began to develop his approach to the sangha administration, which was skeptical at best and often critical of socially engaged monks. Most members of the sangha administration held conservative views of the application of Buddhist principles in society, and especially criticized activities that challenged state-led projects. Pitak maintained a balance of respect for his superiors, while explaining his motives in Buddhist terms and eventually involving high-ranking monks in his programs. Finally, through his and other activists' efforts, the "Green Nan Program" was halted, but not before many areas were cleared (Arawan 1993, 10).

Pitak was increasingly adamant that logging (legal and illegal) and state-led development policies that encouraged commercialization and cash cropping were the primary causes of deforestation. His position created opposition. While he was able to convince the provincial hierarchy of the Buddhist basis for opposing the "Green Nan" program, many government and military officials and business people questioned his motives. In the early 1990s he received threatening letters. He told me he was once shot at while traveling in the forest. Although he did not know who shot at him, he suspected it was someone connected with logging. The high number of assassinations of social activists in Thailand since the open political period of 1973–76 set the stage for such violent responses, even to the work of engaged Buddhist monks. As recently as 2005, the environmental monk Phra Supoj Suvacano was killed in Chiang Mai Province, allegedly by tangerine growers who wanted the land he helped protect. Pitak, following the advice of close associates (Delcore 2000, 180), toned down his rhetoric. Into the 1990s, he learned from the experiences of other environmental monks who faced strong challenges because of their work. Phra Prajak Khuttajitto was arrested twice in 1991 and ultimately went into hiding and derobed before his trials more than ten years later. Achan Pongsak Techadhammo faced scandal when a photograph allegedly of him sitting with a woman was sent to newspapers across the nation. Pitak not only tempered his public criticism of social and political powers, but began to cultivate support from potential opponents at the early stages of each of his projects. He recognized that in a climate of criticism toward the sangha generally, socially active monks came under particularly close scrutiny.

In 1987 Dok Dang again experienced severe water shortages. The villagers requested the district government to send water in trucks for drinking and personal use. Through Phrakhru Pitak's teachings and their own experiences, people gradually began to make connections between deforestation and the lack of water. The monk worked with villagers and a local development NGO to set up the Dok Dang Conservation Association to protect the village's forests. This informal association aimed to conserve first one, then six separate forest areas surrounding the village that had not yet been drastically damaged. Pitak asked the villagers not to clear new fields, but to use more efficient methods of farming in order to protect the remaining trees. The village committee monitored use of the forest, forbidding people from cutting trees unless they received permission from the committee. The only accepted uses for such wood were for public buildings, such as the temple, and for houses.

The village households were divided into six groups (*muat*), the heads of which formed the association's committee. Each group was responsible for one of the protected areas of the forest. The committee's duties included investigating complaints of violations of their regulations, such as cutting trees, and assessing fines when they deemed necessary. The sanctions were both social, as the entire village would know of violations, and legal, as the committee used the threat of bringing in the police if violators refused to pay. The committee declared the protected land a "forest preserve," for which the entire village shared responsibility and benefits of use.[16]

The project was both strengthened and threatened by the declaration the same year of the area around Dok Dang as National Forest Reserve Land (NFRL). The central government had passed the National Forest Reserve Act in 1964 and periodically used it to claim land for protection. The Act's aim was to protect what was left of Thailand's rapidly diminishing forest cover, declaring reserved land as restricted for permitted use only. The program was not without controversy. The land claimed as NFRL was not all primary forest cover; much of it was occupied by people, some of whom had lived there for several generations, often without legal title. According to Santita Ganjanapan (1996, 261), "[The] legal definition of forest is land which is not owned by anyone under the 1941 Forestry Act, regardless of presence or absence of vegetation cover. Therefore, completely deforested land continues to have the status of forest." Some land declared as forest reserves had no natural forest cover, only monoculture plantations, such as eucalyptus, or no vegetation at all. The Royal Forest Department also gave permission in many sites to capitalists who wanted to log the forest or establish new economic forests of eucalyptus and other plantation trees.

At the heart of the debate surrounding NFRL was the question of whether people living in forests protected or threatened them (Santita 1996). The government's policy assumed that people should be removed from forested areas to prevent them from overusing or destroying natural resources. In contrast, most environmental NGOs and ecology monks—and forest dwellers themselves—argued that people living within a forest would best care for it. Forest dwellers, this position maintains, know how to live in harmony with the environment because their lives depend on its resources (on the human-and-forest debate, see Fahn 2003, 137–66; Pinkaew 2001). Since the NFRL policy was instituted, there have been repeated struggles across the nation as the government has ordered people to move out of National Forest Reserves. Sometimes people have been allowed to continue living "illegally" on the land after it has been declared to be within a Forest Reserve. They never know when they, too, may be ordered to move.

In Dok Dang, the NFRL declaration lent stronger sanctions to the informal regulations of the local Conservation Association. Yet, because legally people are not allowed to live in reserves, the villagers were afraid that the government would use the declaration as an excuse to take their land. They feared that they would be forced to move before they could benefit from any trees they planted, gardens they put in, or anything else done to improve the land (Arawan 1993, 9). Phrakhru Pitak similarly worried that, using the legal definition of NFRL, the Royal Forestry Department would grant permission to businessmen to plant commercial trees in the area if they determined that it was degraded. He used this argument to encourage the villagers to take care of the land and the forest.

Gradually, the areas that the villagers protected became more productive. By the early 1990s, they reported that bamboo shoots, mushrooms, and various vegetables grew in greater amounts than had been there in recent years. Whether due to their actions or not, water began to flow again, enough that in following years the people of Dok Dang did not have to request water again from the district government. Shortage of water for drinking and bathing remained an ongoing problem, however.

Other problems remained as well. Some people still secretly cut and sold trees. Many villagers hunted animals within the protected areas even though Phrakhru Pitak wanted to preserve the whole environment, not just the trees, following Buddhist concerns for all sentient beings. Ongoing tensions existed in the village between recognition of the benefits and urgency of protecting the forest and people's more immediate livelihood needs. Despite his best intentions, Pitak had not yet found a way to bridge these tensions. Searching for new approaches that might help resolve the competing pressures of short-term subsistence needs and forest conservation, he turned to the ideas of other activist monks.

Ritualized Projects

In 1990, continuing his visits to other activist monks, Pitak met with Phrakhru Manas Nathiphitak in neighboring Phayao Province. Manas began actively working on conservation issues in his home district in 1979, also in response to the negative impact of logging and resulting drought. Besides performing the first tree ordination as an environmental tool in 1988, Manas earlier adapted a Northern Thai rite, *suep chata,* or long-life ceremony, to make people aware of the importance of rivers and waterways for their lives. Phrakhru Pitak returned to Nan inspired to increase his conservation activities from mostly preaching and encouragement to more active engagement in environmentalism. He cites inspiration from monks such as Phrakhru Manas to adapt familiar rituals to new situations as the primary means of getting people's attention and spiritual investment in environmental projects.

Drawing on the models of tree ordinations from both Manas and Phra Prajak Khuttajitto, Pitak's first environmental ritual was the tree ordination and sanctification of the community forest in Dok Dang in 1990. The explicit use of a familiar ritual invested with new meaning and a spiritual concept of community strengthened villagers' commitment to the project. In addition to the tree ordination, villagers performed a ritual requesting permission and support for the consecrated forest from the village guardian spirit.[17] In this way, Pitak encouraged people to incorporate their own beliefs into the project. Unlike after his previous efforts, once he sponsored the tree ordination people began more seriously to conserve the forest. Although there had been a few violations, twenty years later Dok Dang still maintained its community forest.[18]

With the help of local NGOs, Phrakhru Pitak introduced alternatives to common agricultural practices that contributed to deforestation, such as planting cash crops and using chemical fertilizers and pesticides. In particular, following a growing trend among NGOs nationwide, he encouraged villagers to use integrated agricultural techniques—mixing different plants and raising animals to complement each other in ways similar to natural ecosystems—to reduce their need to clear new fields. Although few people in Dok Dang implemented these techniques because of initial costs and pressure from government agricultural bank and seed company representatives, their awareness of such alternatives helped to alleviate the tension they felt between conserving the forest and their need for making a livelihood from its resources. They again approached the forest as a source of renewable resources, such as bamboo, mushrooms, and grasses for making brooms. When I visited the village in 2006, the former headman claimed that most villagers used the protected forest in such a manner to supplement their incomes from cash cropping done outside the community forest. He himself shifted from cash cropping to making a living selling medicinal herbs collected from the forest or grown in his yard. He did, however, raise a concern about the future of the forest, saying that the four headmen to hold office since he stepped down in 2001 were not as committed to maintaining the forest's protected status or encouraging villagers to conserve it.

Since the initial tree ordination in Dok Dang, Phrakhru Pitak has sponsored numerous other projects, including tree ordinations in other villages to mark new community forests, "long-life" ceremonies (suep chata) to conserve and clean up the Nan River, the establishment of fish sanctuaries, and numerous educational seminars for monks and lay people, including farmers, teachers, and government officials. He established *Klum Hak Muang Nan* (the "Love Nan Province Association"), a group that acted as both an umbrella organization for other NGOs in the province doing environmental and sustainable development work and an organization in its own right, sponsoring and supporting environmental programs of Phrakhru Pitak and other ecology monks.

Phrakhru Pitak received recognition and support for his work from several national NGOs, such as Wildlife Fund Thailand, the Thai Inter-religious Commission for Development, and the Village Foundation. In 1993, the Village Foundation and Matichon newspaper awarded him the prestigious Model Citizen Award for his work in the northern region of the nation. That same year, he was promoted within the sangha hierarchy, receiving the ecclesiastical title and name of Phrakhru Pitak Nanthakhun (Plate 8). This promotion testified to his ability to balance his environmental work with the sangha's expectations of monks. Throughout the 1990s, Phrakhru Pitak spoke frequently at seminars for other activist monks and NGO conferences and workshops aimed at sharing information, methods, and experiences in a national debate on appropriate development. By 2006, he told me he was too busy with administrative work and too tired to travel to many seminars or meetings outside of Nan. His reputation, however, continued to inform the work of other environmental monks across the nation.

Throughout his career, Phrakhru Pitak cultivated his relations with his superiors in the sangha hierarchy carefully. The social and sometimes political actions of environmental monks tend to go beyond expected practice of most Thai monks, often placing them in conflict with the hierarchy, which traditionally upholds the ideal of the sangha as removed from society, even while it supports the government. Yet Pitak won over the provincial sangha leadership through his devotion to teaching the dhamma and working to relieve people's suffering. He purposefully involved high-ranking monks in all his projects, usually inviting the highest-ranking monk in the area to be the chairman of a given project and conduct any rituals connected with it.

Ever aware of potential damage to the reputation of the sangha as a whole through radical actions, Pitak carefully grounded his practice in respect for his superiors, a solid knowledge and conservative interpretation of the dhamma, and a commitment to preserving Nan's local cultures. This balance between social action and religious exegesis is crucial to implementing social change based on Buddhism.

The case of Dok Dang, and Phrakhru Pitak's conservation efforts there, was not an aberration in Thai history. The timing was right for monks such as Phrakhru Pitak to engage in activities that appeared contrary to the Thai ideal of the sangha as meditation masters removed from society. The conflation of several historical and sociopolitical trends in Thai society enabled the emergence of development monks in the 1970s followed by environmental monks in the mid-1980s, their growing—albeit often controversial—presence into the 1990s, and their acceptance by the early twenty-first century. The history of changing state/sangha relations, evolving and competing concepts of development as Thailand modernized in the late nineteenth and twentieth centuries, and the rise of global and national environmental movements all helped set the scene for the social engagement of a segment of the Thai sangha.

Phrakhru Pitak joined in the construction of a new form of knowledge and religious practice, one that has reverberated across Thailand, the Buddhist world, and beyond. The process is still evolving. Environmental monks have moved from being radical and controversial pioneers challenging the status quo within the sangha, the state, and society to setting the standard for social engagement for mainstream monks. They work primarily on the local or provincial level, with expectations of solving social problems. Yet with fame and acceptance come appropriation and neglect. Many of the environmental monks' methods, especially tree ordinations, have been appropriated and used for a wide range of activities, especially the celebration of the king's fiftieth anniversary of his reign in 1996–97. The attention and support that radical monks received as they challenged the state and big business have dwindled. They now compete for limited funds with a growing number of NGOs, and are subject to the changing interests of Thai society; while environmentalism was the burning social issue in the 1980s and 1990s, the predominant cause in the 2000s was HIV/AIDS. As monks find their way into this even more controversial social issue, the question must again be asked: To what degree are they independent thinkers and activists, versus following the pressures of social attention? Ultimately, as Phrakhru Pitak's story shows, the answer is more complex than this dichotomy. They act within social, political, and religious constraints, yet they act creatively, making their own choices while negotiating social pressures and expectations. In the end, they innovate, and translate their innovations into terms that impact the people and society around them.

The key innovation these monks initiated was the use of rituals to engage people's attentions and commitments, and introduce them to environmental and social justice concepts. Based on traditional rituals, these rites incorporated new teachings that emphasized people's interconnections with and responsibility for the natural environment. The rituals enabled the monks to respond to social pressures and promote social change. While ending suffering remained the primary goal of environmental monks, society quickly associated them with the most dramatic and public of their actions—the tree ordination.

3

The Rituals

It's important to use ideas, philosophy, and rituals from Buddhism, from the teachings of the Buddha, to deal with contemporary problems. We need to use ideas that villagers already accept and are familiar with, and gradually adapt them to deal with new problems. The changes cannot be too rapid or drastic, because then people will turn away from them. But these changes are happening too slowly to deal with social problems in Thailand today. . . . New interpretations are important because the social and natural conditions now are not the same as at the time of the Buddha.

—Phra Somkit Jaranathammo, January 24, 1993

TREE ORDINATIONS take a variety of forms and incorporate different audiences. Some are simple, involving one monk accompanied by a group of villagers wrapping old robes around the large trees in a given forest. The better-known form brings ten to twenty monks together in a formal ritual, chanting Pali scriptures and consecrating water, the tree to be ordained, and the surrounding forest. The form depends on the target audiences; the monk initiating the ritual aims to use the ceremony less to consecrate a particular tree (although that remains central to his purpose) than to impart lessons of Buddhism and environmentalism to the participants and to reach out to those less aware of the problems local people face. Tree ordinations, in short, are a form of *upaya* (Pali), or expedient means, used to wake people up, not to spiritual realization but to the causes of immediate suffering and ways of relieving it.

The Buddha taught people in ways or at the level at which they could best understand his teachings. For some, this meant deep philosophical treatises. For others, he and the monks who followed him used parables or metaphors to push people into greater understanding or realization of Buddhist teachings.[1] Environmental monks do the same thing, seeking ways of connecting issues of deforestation and environmental destruction with the suffering people face in their lives. They use tree ordinations and other adapted rituals such as long-life ceremonies for waterways to frame the suffering brought about by environmental destruction in familiar terms (especially for the villagers) or shock people (primarily the middle class and state actors) into rethinking the underlying causes of environmental problems and their scope. Rituals offer a means of, as Phra Somkit said, using "ideas that villagers already accept and are familiar with, and gradually adapt them to deal with new problems." Rituals form the central aspect of lay Buddhist practice in Thailand. They embody and symbolize Buddhist principles, and teach the morality and values the Buddha preached. Rituals translate abstract moral concepts into concrete actions in which villagers can engage.

Some of the monks' approaches challenge people by recategorizing nature, treating it in a manner similar with humans. Yet, long-life ceremonies and tree ordinations are not intended for rivers or forests, which are not sentient beings. Neither do environmental monks claim them as such. Instead, they use adapted rituals as elaborate metaphors invoking the sanctity of nature that teach both Buddhist values and ecological principles.

Environmental rituals serve as performances on both a local and a national stage. They are "embodied experiences" (D. Taylor 2002, 155) that encode, combine, and transmit spiritual and political meanings. Anthropologist Diana Taylor describes the ways in which testimonial and performed protest enabled survivors of the "Dirty War" in Argentina to keep the memories of those who had disappeared alive and active, shaming those responsible. "The embodied experience and transmission of traumatic memory—the interactions among people in the here and now—make a difference in the way that knowledge is transmitted and incorporated," she argues (2002, 155). She draws from the ideas of biologist Richard Dawkins, who coined the term *memes* as a cultural replicator (paralleling the biological concept of "genes"). Both genes and memes, according to Dawkins, provide for transmission, but can also change in the process. "Ideas and evidence change, at times beyond recognition. Cultural materials, Dawkins concludes, survive if they catch on. Memes need to be 'realized physically' (207) in the public arena" (D. Taylor 2002, 156). While less traumatic, Buddhist rituals used to promote environmental action serve to validate certain knowledges, especially those of rural Thai farmers, and interpretations that bring the religion into the here and now. They are a means of physically realizing and transmitting cultural ideas that prioritize local understandings and knowledge of the world over that of the dominant, urban society. Laying claim to moral superiority and embodying the close relationship between rural people and the natural environment, environmental monks go beyond preaching or individual projects to a deeper emotional and spiritual level. Rituals enable them to create and transmit new ideas, validate specific cultural forms, such as farmers' intimate knowledge of the environment, and contest the centrality of the economic and political forces that exploit rural people's resources. Tree ordinations in particular could be considered a "meme" that caught on.

Tree ordinations and other environmental rituals go beyond Taylor's concept of performance, though, because they are religious ceremonies. In his classic essay, "Religion as a Cultural System," Clifford Geertz describes the interplay between function and affect embedded in ritual performances. Religion—and rituals—are significant because of the tensions between the intensity of religious experience that arises during ritual performances and the ways in which participants remember and reflect on these experiences "in the midst of everyday life" (Geertz 1966, 120). Rituals do not merely affirm the social or cosmic orders, but create them.

> Religion is sociologically interesting not because, as vulgar positiv-
> ism would have it, it describes the social order (which, in so far as
> it does, it does not only very obliquely but very incompletely), but
> because, like environmental, political power, wealth, jural obliga-
> tion, personal affection, and a sense of beauty, it shapes it. (Geertz
> 1966, 119)

In his description of participating in rituals to consecrate Buddha images, Donald Swearer (2004, 90) similarly reflects the affective rather than cognitive experience involved. Both Geertz and Swearer emphasize the full engagement of participants as they immerse themselves into the ritual world and accept the often subtle messages encoded in them. While rituals have practical functions, their real power comes in the affective experiences they provoke in participants. Participants carry these experiences and meanings with them into their daily lives, even as their actions may not always reflect the details. Nevertheless, as Geertz (1966, 122) argues, they are changed by the ritual experience.

Using rituals as both embodied "memes" and affective experience serves three main purposes for the environmental monks: First, it strengthens the relevance of the religion in a changing society, highlighting the moral aspects of social problems such as environmental destruction. Second, it educates, or at least raises the awareness of, people concerning environmental issues and their resultant problems. Third, it builds new alliances among different actors, for example, introducing middle-class environmentalists to villagers, or engaging state agents in rural problems. Ultimately, monks hope to foster greater communication and understanding of the broader factors contributing to the suffering emerging from environmental destruction.

In this chapter, I examine how environmental monks frame rituals as a central means of getting people involved in, committed to, and educated about their projects. Their methods vary, from anthropomorphizing nature as a metaphor to engage villagers, to involving state actors and sangha authorities before they can oppose the monks' activities. Environmental monks reach out to academics and activists on a regional and national level, cooperating with them to design and implement projects, and tapping into broader discourses of environmentalism, social justice, and social change. Monks see rituals as a means of gaining attention for and minimizing opposition to their causes as local, regional, and national media cover the events.

Tree ordinations in particular require a balance between the spiritual meanings invoked through ritual (especially the emphasis on suffering) and the political negotiations needed to enact successful changes in how forests are categorized and used, and whether government actors cooperate with or oppose activist monks. Environmental monks use the rituals to make political statements. Through their challenge to state-led development and materialist economic growth, monks join national political debates. The rituals couch their criticisms in religious symbols and invoke a moral authority in support of their political concerns. Conducting rituals provides a means of making veiled political critiques, hopefully avoiding the controversies encountered by more outspoken monks such as Phra Prajak Khuttajitto, twice arrested in 1991 for his direct challenges to government and military authorities.

The first tree ordinations performed in the late 1980s and early 1990s shocked the Thai public. Over time, reactions evolved. Villagers participated from the beginning, seeing the rituals as incorporating their belief system (including spirit beliefs) and helping them deal with practical difficulties. NGO activists joined with monks early on in their effort to challenge the state on a range of issues. Other groups, from the sangha hierarchy to the Thai media and even government officials, gradually shifted their responses as tree ordinations grew in popularity and the rituals became routinized in the lexicon of Thai Buddhist practice. Today many people consider tree ordinations part of a monk's duties, expecting monks who live near forests, large or small, to protect them (Phra Kittisak Kittisophano, interview, 10/8/2006). State forces have even appropriated the ritual to reframe debates on responsibility for environmental problems. And in 2010, beauty contestants participated in a tree ordination ("Beauty Contestants Ordain Tree" 2010), further demonstrating how this ritual has evolved, becoming a mainstream cultural practice devoid of much of its original meaning and challenges to society. Before examining that process, I first look at the emergence of monks' use of rituals to address environmental concerns, and how they targeted different audiences.

Anthropomorphizing Nature

As development and environmental monks introduced new ideas aimed at relieving the suffering they saw as caused by rapid economic development and increasing consumerism, they sought innovative ways to get villagers not only to participate in their projects such as integrated agriculture, but also to understand and commit to the underlying principles. Monks engage in development and environmental work as aspects of promoting the teachings of the Buddha, but this approach is not immediately obvious to the laity with whom they work. Villagers' perception of Buddhism focuses on merit-making with the aim of realizing a better life, usually in a future rebirth. They rarely read the scriptures, and take a pragmatic approach to religious practice, which for villagers primarily entails rituals rather than meditation. They emphasize community participation, joining together to sponsor merit-making rituals, annual village protection rites, and planting and harvesting ceremonies, among others.[2]

To help villagers understand the meanings behind their work, the monks introduce rituals adapted to new issues, such as tree ordinations and long-life ceremonies for rivers. Rituals that environmental monks perform challenge people to rethink their relationships with each other, their livelihoods, and the environment. In the process, the monks aim to build and support community and increase people's self-sufficiency through interrupting their dependency on outside market forces. They push people to recognize and respect the mutual dependence between nature and humanity, as well as between individuals within a community.

While Buddhists respect all sentient beings, a bias exists in the religion toward humans. Only humans (and in Thailand only men at that) can ordain as bhikkhu, a prerequisite for achieving enlightenment.[3] As environmental monks turned their gaze on the natural world, recognizing the interdependent relationship between it and the people with whom they lived, they tapped familiar modes of enacting the religion to deal with new problems. Several monks adapted rituals usually reserved for humans as a means of making issues about nature more relevant and immediate for villagers. Through treating nature as human, they changed the rules that applied to both, particularly reframing the ways in which people tended to assume nature was there to serve them. The use of ordination ceremonies in particular shifted the hierarchical relations between humans and nature. Monks hold the highest social status in Thai society; by symbolically raising trees to this status, environmental monks aimed to revise the ways people think about their relationship and interdependence with nature. At the same time, they hoped to strengthen the environmental projects through incorporating a sacred, moral aspect.

The process through which monks began to anthropomorphize nature did not occur as intentionally as it appears in hindsight. Nor did it begin with tree ordinations. The idea of treating nature as human already existed, as villagers saw the natural world as inhabited with spirits with whom they interacted in a broad social hierarchy. Treating major components of the natural world such as waterways and forests with the same respect and interactions that villagers hold for spirits and monks was a logical approach for the villagers. Below I outline the evolution of this process as it occurred in northern Thailand, from performing long-life ceremonies for waterways to requesting spirits to protect forests to ordaining trees. From a strictly Buddhist perspective, these actions are radical reinterpretations, but from the villagers' orientation in a world in which humans, spirits, animals, and plants all interact, using one set of principles and practices to address problems that affected others makes sense.

Requesting Long Life

Phrakhru Manas Nathiphitak of Phayao Province, like other environmental monks who followed him, initially tried talking and preaching with villagers about the importance of protecting the forest and the water on which they depended. Despite his effort, their water problems only grew worse, as logging concessions in the area continued (see chapter 5). Pulling people together to discuss the problems and possible solutions created a sense of community and ownership over the projects that emerged. Manas did not credit any particular person with the idea of performing a *suep chata,* or long-life ceremony, for a local stream; it arose during discussions among the people affected by the drought. Manas coordinated this event in 1973, and his involvement brought in many people who otherwise may have questioned applying such a ritual to water rather than humans.

The organizers invited all the villages in the district lacking water to participate, first cleaning up the areas along the stream. "Everyone joined in, old and young," Manas said. "It became a way to make merit" (personal communication, 9/30/2006). Northern Thai villagers already observed special days to clean up community space as a form of merit making. The targets were public areas, such as temples, school grounds, and roadways through the villages. Asking people to clean along the stream bed focused their attention on how they used the water, and the condition of the communities through which it ran. Phrakhru Pitak later adopted the same technique along the Nan River, having volunteers document pollution in order to change people's behavior and use of the river. In Manas's home district of Mae Chai, however, not enough water remained to document pollution. The stream was truly "ill."

The suep chata ceremony is a Northern Thai ritual for people who are ill, old, or face difficult circumstances. Although not explicitly a Buddhist ritual, monks perform it for laity who request it. Villagers see monks as having considerable merit, which can be transferred to the ritual recipient through the rite.

Originally a Brahmanic rite, the ceremony uses objects symbolizing good life piled into a pyramid shape formed by long sticks (signifying long life). The participants incorporate offerings to the Buddha and various deities, including flowers, joss sticks, clay animal figures, betel nut, *miang* (fermented tea leaves), cigarettes, and gold, silver, and white flags. White cotton string connects the pyramid with the monk and the person for whom the ritual is performed, conducting the spiritual power of the ritual among the objects and the participants.[4] After accepting the pyramid offering, the officiating monk chants the story of a young man who extended his life through kindness to animals, followed by a popular Jataka tale of one of the Buddha's former lives and a dhamma lecture (Wells 1975, 209–13).

Several monks, including Phrakhru Pitak and Luang Pu Phuttapoj, told me that they personally do not believe in the ritual's power to change people's lives directly. They perform it for two reasons. First, it carries great meaning for the lay participants, who do believe in its ability to offset illness or misfortune. Second, the chanting and dhamma talk provide an opportunity to expose participants to the teachings of the Buddha. Combined, the Buddhist teachings and the beliefs of participants contribute to the ritual's effectiveness for creating an increased sense of well-being and a willingness to take care of oneself. This combination is another example of upaya, or skillful means, and foreshadows how monks use tree ordinations as well.

Phrakhru Manas adapted the long-life ritual for a stream that was running dry. The symbolism of the stream suffering illness and misfortune emphasized the importance of water to life generally and the livelihoods of the villagers specifically. Manas saw the ritual as an opportunity to bring villagers together to reflect on the problems they faced and to find ways to help each other. He wanted to use Buddhism together with local beliefs to help the villagers, something he saw as his responsibility as a monk (personal communication, 9/30/2006).

In a document written for Manas to give to English-speaking visitors, one of his disciples explained the ceremony as follows:

> The Long Life River Ceremony is adapted from the ceremony for people. When they get sick or have bad luck they do the ceremony to encourage them and it will bring good luck. "Long Life River" is also the ceremony for paying respect to gods who look after our rivers. The ceremony . . . also encourage[s] people to concern and love their environment [*sic*]. (Wilaiwan 1996, 4)

Shortly after the long-life ceremony for the stream in Mae Chai, government officials invited Phrakhru Manas to perform the rite for the lake and wetlands surrounding the provincial capital of Phayao. Since then he conducts the rituals for the Phayao wetlands and Mae Chai stream annually. People in other locations began to request the ritual as they too sought means of dealing with difficult environmental circumstances. No one questioned the appropriateness of a monk conducting such a ritual at the time, although Manas noted a few people thought he was "crazy."

As the businesses and people who stood to gain from the logging and other enterprises that villagers believed threatened the water sources became aware of the ceremony and its growing popularity in the province, the criticisms grew. When Phrakhru Manas expanded the scope of his work and his approach, more people, including his sangha superiors, began to question the monk's involvement in explicit social issues.

Ordaining Trees?

Despite the long-life ceremony for waterways and the increased concerns of
the people of Phayao about the causes of drought, the logging continued. In
1986, the Chiangrai Company again entered the forest of Mae Chai District
to mark trees for felling. By this time, the company had cleared eight of its
original ten concession areas first granted in 1973. Phrakhru Manas, the district officer, and village leaders of Mae Chai were concerned that no forest
would remain after the company completed the remaining two concessions.
They organized the villagers into a conservation group, *Klum Hak Pa Mae
Chai,* or the Mae Chai Forest Lovers Group. They coordinated a petition to
the company and the Royal Forest Department to cease logging in order to
protect the watershed areas. The company agreed for one year, but in 1987 it
resumed its work (Wilaiwan 1996).

People in Mae Chai, desperate to save their water source, took more dramatic action. They closed the forest and blocked the access roads to prevent
the logging trucks passing. Phrakhru Manas sought ways to support the villagers without escalating the conflict. When drought hit the district again in
1988, he came up with the idea of performing what was to become known
as a tree ordination.

Phrakhru Manas adapted the text of a Buddha image consecration ceremony (*buat phraphutta rup*), another traditional Northern Thai ceremony, to
sanctify the tree and the forest.[5] During the ritual, villagers placed tree saplings at the base of the Buddha statue, which were then sanctified along with
the image. After the ceremony, villagers planted them, and would not cut
them down because they considered them sacred. They called the saplings
"ordained trees" (*ton mai thi buat lao*), coining the name for the adapted rite.

Phra Somkit explained to me the distinction between bhikkhu ordinations and tree ordinations, noting they are not really similar (personal communication, 1/24/1993). Chanting during a tree ordination focuses on
teaching the dhamma and general moral lessons that can be applied to conserving the forest. For a bhikkhu ordination the chanting serves the purpose
of formally changing the status of the monk. The ceremony officially confers
a new name on the monk and changes his status from layman to bhikkhu.
Trees and forests may be consecrated during what are now called tree ordinations, but the classifier used in the Thai language to denote them remains the
same. Once ordained, a bhikkhu, on the other hand, shifts from the general
classifier for people (*khon*) to the sacred classifier used solely for sangha and
royalty (*ong*).

These differences, while clear to the monks performing the rituals, are not always noted by village participants. Mark Blum raises the concern about the implications of anyone believing the trees are actually ordained.

> [M]y concern is with what the idea of ordaining trees or "perform-ing long-life ceremonies" for rivers means both to us in the West and to Buddhism as a religion. At the very least these actions imply agency in the receiving body, which in a Buddhist context is defined as karmic accountability. . . . However symbolic tree-ordination may be in Thailand, the disconnect between what may be nothing more than political theater and the religious importance of the ordination of monks (for whom this means abiding by 227 precepts) for main-taining Buddhism itself is jolting and worth further scrutiny. (Blum 2009, 209)

Blum continues to examine what he believes are the roots of Buddhist inter-est in the environment, mainly American Transcendentalism. Finding no concrete evidence of "the spread of this rhetoric to Thailand" (Blum 2009, 210), I concentrate on how environmental monks use ritual as upaya, tap-ping into villagers' beliefs and practices to teach them in ways they under-stand, and performance, embodying and validating villagers' knowledge on a public stage.

The selection of chants used during tree ordinations demonstrates one way in which monks adapt these rites to particular situations and audiences. On one hand, the texts are the same as those used for many different rituals, ranging from the consecration of Buddha images, houses, and businesses to celebration of the king's birthday (Wells 1975, 277). These chants are *paritta* (Pali), or "protective chants" (*suat mon,* Thai), intended to ward off danger (Swearer 2004:300). Among the most commonly used are the Thirty-Eight Mangala Sutta, the Seven Tamnan (*Chet Tamnan*), and the Twelve Tamnan (*Sipsong Tamnan*). Given their association with various consecration ceremo-nies, it is not surprising monks choose them to consecrate a forest.

Phrakhru Pitak described his selection of verses from the Seven or Twelve Tamnan for tree ordinations depending on the lessons he wants to impart at a given ritual. He called the Thirty-Eight Mangala Sutta "lessons for life," which teach morality. For shorter rituals, Pitak chooses from among the thirty-eight verses to emphasize the specifics he feels are needed for a particular community (personal communication, 10/27/2010). Among the teachings of these thirty-eight sutta are instructions on associating with wise rather than bad people, listening well to wise and respected men, supporting one's parents and family, abstaining from sin, including strong drink, and upholding the Four Noble Truths (Payutto 1985, 320–24; Wells 1975, 253–54).

During the ritual, the Mangala Sutta is chanted while candle wax is dripped into water to create holy water, or *mantra,* while connected by a white string that runs from the monks' hands to the alms bowl with water to a Buddha image (Plate 9). Writing of a Buddha image consecration, Swearer (2004, 42) states that "the didactic function of the Pali chant takes second place to the ritual transference of the power stored in the image, through the agency of the chant and the medium of water, to the assembled congregation." At tree ordinations, water is similarly consecrated, and the participants receive the ritual power as the lead monk sprinkles the holy water on them. As discussed below, at one tree ordination ceremony, local leaders strengthened their oath to protect the newly consecrated forest by drinking the holy water, further demonstrating the power of the ritual.

Throughout the ritual, the chants, the consecration of water, the tree, and the surrounding forest, and the sermon given by the head monk all contribute to the affective experience for the participants. The specific chants are less important than the chanting itself, as described by Swearer:

> Divisions among the *sutta* and *paritta* used in the *suat mon* are of secondary importance to the sense of the chant as a whole, even though a particular sequence will be followed, with each section initiated by the officiating monk. This observation, while seemingly of minor significance, raises an important question about the nature of *suat mon,* especially for the Western student accustomed to think in terms of specific written texts with titles. To approach *paritta* chanting in this way bifurcates what is perceived as an integrated, sacred whole. Comprehending the *dhamma* in a ritual context rather than as written text integrates the apocryphal 84,000 facets of the Buddha's teaching into a seamless unity at the level of oral/aural experience. In rituals with powerful positive kammic potency (*phithī kam*), the historical and literary aspects of the texts chanted are unimportant. In this context the power of the ritual experience depends less upon correspondences to a written text than upon sound uttered and heard. The *suat mon* is so quintessentially an oral/aural and visual experience that to observe monks chanting from a book is qualitatively different from watching them with

closed eyes reciting continuously for an hour or more solely from memory. (Swearer 2004, 89)

Observing many tree ordinations, I witnessed this effect among the congregations. As the monks chanted, people closed their eyes, their hands held together, and their bodies occasionally rocking to the rhythm of the sound. Afterward, people scrambled to receive some of the sacred water sprinkled by the monks in an effort to take a small material piece of the ritual home, even as the water quickly evaporated.

While monks choose a variety of texts for tree ordination rituals, emphasizing the consecration of the tree and the forest and the opportunity to teach Buddhists responsibility and connections with nature, villagers view the rituals differently. For villagers, the ritual meaning is more literal, as they often consider the trees as ordained—not surprising given their belief in spirits inhabiting the natural world, including many trees. Their behavior toward trees wrapped in orange robes is similar to the respect they show monks: they *wai,* bowing with palms together, to such trees when they pass. Much of the popularity of tree ordinations and the criticisms they receive from the sangha and media are grounded in the villagers' version of the rite and the popular perception of the trees as formally ordained. Environmental monks play upon the tension between what they see as the scriptural meaning of the rituals, which teaches religious and environmental principles, and the popular meaning among villagers, which transforms a tree into a sacred object similar to a bhikkhu, to get people's attention and promote their message.

Phrakhru Manas was criticized by many people, including his own preceptor and the media, for ordaining trees. The regional head of the sangha demanded an explanation for why he ordained trees, noting this ceremony was reserved for ordaining bhikkhu. The ordination also made the news, with articles appearing in numerous local and even national newspapers. Questions were raised about ordaining trees rather than people. Manas told me that one article, which was published before the ceremony occurred, accused him of being perverted and part of a group that sought to undermine national development through opposition to logging concessions. This same article said he was "crazy," and called for him to derobe.

Phrakhru Manas remained unfazed. He suspected the head of the logging company had complained to the sangha authorities, and may have even been behind much of the media criticisms. He argued that even though the ceremony he conducted was not found in the scriptures anywhere, it served a valuable purpose. Not only did it bring attention to the problems of deforestation, especially those based on greed and ignorance, but the ritual brought people together to help each other. It fostered the development of the "mind and spirit" (*chitchai*) essential to Buddhist practice.

Despite open criticism of Manas's actions, performance of the ritual to preserve and protect forests spread. Monks from neighboring provinces, including Phrakhru Pitak, visited Manas to learn about his approach and see the impact of the rituals. Soon tree ordinations were conducted across the nation. In 2006, Phrakhru Manas responded to my question about the number of tree ordinations he performed since 1988. "Could be 1,000," he said, "or maybe 10,000. Who knows?" (personal communication, 9/30/2006).

Phrakhru Manas is a quiet, articulate, and unassuming man. He has told his story countless times over the past two decades, yet still relates it with passion. He laughs at his own motivations for becoming a novice—to avoid farming with his father—yet his commitment to helping people is genuine. In many ways, his story foreshadowed the work of all environmental monks, even with individual variations. His ideas about environmentalism emerged from a consciousness and a criticism of state-led development—the greed, ignorance and, occasionally, anger that accompanies an emphasis on material growth and financial gain. At the same time, he witnessed the loss of values and community that activist monks and many NGOs argue have existed in Thai villages for generations (see Seri 1986). Notwithstanding the idealization of village life, Manas sought to maintain a sense of community in the face of pressures on the villagers to engage in a materialist and individualistic economy.

Despite harsh criticisms, Phrakhru Manas stressed the urgency of getting people to value the forest holistically, and to break away from behavior that only appreciated the forest for financial gain. He considered treating nature in a similar fashion as humans a matter of skillful means; the Buddha taught that because people were at different stages on their spiritual journeys, one must teach to them appropriately. Adapting rituals for new purposes and meanings, Manas sought appropriate and effective ways of teaching villagers the value of nature.

The Spirit(s) of Conservation

Among the monks who borrowed Phrakhru Manas's concept of using rituals to promote environmental awareness and change was Phrakhru Pitak Nanthakhun of Nan Province. Pitak visited Phrakhru Manas, as well as several

other environmental monks, in early 1990. He had established a forest conservation committee in his home village, but the results and commitment to
it were halfhearted. He returned home from observing the work of Manas
and other monks and initiated a stronger conservation and sustainable agriculture program in his village, culminating in his first tree ordination.

In preparation for the tree ordination, Phrakhru Pitak worked closely
with the villagers, especially the headman, to redesign their forest conservation program and establish a community forest that everyone would help
protect. Following village practice, the villagers decided that they needed to
inform the village guardian spirit, one of the region's "lords of the land"
(Shalardchai 1989), of their actions. They set up a spirit shrine behind the
tree to be ordained (Plate 10), and requested permission from the guardian
spirit and other spirits in the forest to create the community forest and assistance in protecting it.

Most Thai Buddhists believe the universe is inhabited by spirits and gods.
The classic treatise on Thai cosmology, *The Three Worlds According to King
Ruang* (from the thirteenth century, translated by Reynolds and Reynolds
1982), describes the interplay between the heavens (the realms of *thewada* or
celestial beings), the earth (where the humans live), and the hells (the place
of *phi* or lower level beings living out the consequences of negative behavior).
All sentient beings, according to this Buddhist cosmology, can be reborn at
any level of these three worlds depending on the cumulative merit of their
actions in each life. Even the gods, who lead lives of pleasure and comfort,
will eventually pass away and be reborn. Only humans can achieve enlightenment, to be released from the cycle of rebirth and suffering.

While Thais view the three worlds as distinct, they are not isolated from
each other. Usually the thewada and phi of the upper and lower realms are
benign and do not harm humans. If provoked, however, the phi in particular
may harass, hurt, or even possess some humans. Thais believe some phi are
malevolent and go out of their way to avoid or appease all spirits. Some spirits
may simply appear to people as their paths cross. Guardian spirits, considered
both thewada and phi, illustrating the vague nature of these concepts, monitor and protect particular places. Some are considered "lords of the land,"
associated with the *mueang* or principalities of the past. People fear the spirits,
thewada and phi alike, because of their supernatural qualities and powers.

Buddhism does not deny that spirits exist. Instead, its teachings emphasize developing one's ability to control fear through recognizing the imper-
manence of all things, including one's self, by confronting the idea of spirits
and the fear they invoke. This is a learned skill, often developed through

years of practice. Kamala (1997, 79, 96–105) examines how forest monks isolated themselves in remote, usually forested areas in part to encounter phi and confront and still the emotions that arose.[6] In the case of the creation and consecration of the village's community forest, Pitak did not object to the villagers' incorporating their belief in the guardian spirit. He saw it as another means of instilling spirituality into the project, and garnering people's support and commitment to it. Afterward, he described the combined effectiveness of the two rituals, the spirit ceremony and the tree ordination, as follows:

> Holding a tree ordination, establishing a shrine for the guardian spirit and placing a Buddha image as the "chief" of the forest to forbid cutting trees are all really clever schemes. It's not true Buddhism to conduct such rituals. But in the villagers' beliefs, they respect the Buddha and fear some of his power. Thus we can see that there is nothing so sacred or that the villagers respect as much as a Buddha image. Therefore we brought a Buddha image and installed it under the tree that we believe is the chief of the forest and ordained the tree. In general, villagers also still believe in spirits. Therefore we set up a shrine for the guardian spirit together with the Buddha image. This led to the saying that "the good Buddha and the fierce spirits help each other take care of the forest." This means that the Buddha earns the villagers' respect. But they fear the spirits. If you have both, respect and fear, the villagers won't dare cut the trees. (Quoted in Arawan 1993, 11; author's translation)

Pitak articulated a clear statement of upaya here, especially in his use of the phrase "clever schemes." To achieve his primary goals of relieving farmers' suffering and protecting the forest, he manipulated the ways the villagers view the world. He acknowledged that "it's not true Buddhism to conduct such rituals," yet recognized the power of ritual as performance to reach the villagers and engage their commitment.

Most villagers would agree with the assessment that since the tree ordination there has been greater cooperation in protecting the community forest and less encroachment within it. "Ordaining the tree and asking the spirits to help have equal success. The spirits and the Buddha work together to protect the forest," one village elder commented to me in 1993.

While many of the villagers developed an understanding of the principles of ecological conservation through the education sessions held by

Phrakhru Pitak prior to the ceremony, the impact of both the Buddhist principles applied to forest conservation and the power of the spirit's charge to guard the forest cannot be denied. The local people's awe for the sacred aspects of the project, both Buddhist and animist, their respect for Phrakhru Pitak, and the newly introduced concepts of conservation all work together to heighten the villagers' cooperation and responsibility to preserving the remaining forest.

The element of fear may have had more of an impact than Pitak intended. Over the two years following the ordination ceremony, four deaths and several illnesses occurred that villagers attributed to retribution from the spirits for violation of the terms protecting the community forest. The people who died or became ill were all believed to be cutting wood or hunting within the protected areas, both of which the villagers agreed to stop when the forest was consecrated. A village spirit ritual specialist determined forest spirits (whether the guardian spirit himself or unnamed phi inhabiting the woods was never stated) who were offended by these people's actions caused their misfortunes.

Although some environmental monks, particularly Achan Phongsak Techadhammo, criticized him for using the fear of spirit beliefs to achieve the ends of environmental conservation, Phrakhru Pitak saw it differently. The villagers believed in and respected the spirits of the forest. Their relationship with these spirits, along with the various thewada and other phi that share their world, defined and reaffirmed their understanding of how the world works—in its natural, supernatural, and human aspects. The monk also recognized that Northern Thai belief systems are not static. They have evolved over time, adapting to incorporate various elements of Indian culture, including Buddhism, that have entered the region over several centuries. He recognized and used the sacred geography rather than trying to alter it to achieve his aims.

Just as Buddhism was used in the twentieth century by the government to encourage a shift in villagers' attitudes toward the forest in the service of "development" (see chapter 4), Phrakhru Pitak sees its potential for doing so again—only this time in the service of conservation and rural people's needs. Recognizing the continual evolution of people's beliefs and practices, Pitak integrates traditional beliefs with Buddhist practices to promote an ecological ethic. While the government and pro-development forces emphasize what they see as "pure" Buddhism (thereby invalidating non-Buddhist— i.e., spirit—beliefs), the monk seeks to incorporate all attitudes toward the natural world. Rather than "civilizing" the forest through imposing Buddhist concepts in order to conquer and use it, he hopes to instill values that recognize the importance of the forest as an integral component of the environment, which includes humans (Buddhist and non-Buddhist alike), animals, and spirits.[7] Through the Buddhist concept of interdependence, he teaches that humans need the forest for a well-balanced life.

Combined with concrete, practical methods of achieving this balance, such as integrated agriculture, spiritualizing conservation increases the potential of people's investment in projects. Environmental monks integrate the natural world into the human world, even treating aspects of nature in a similar manner as humans, in order to challenge villagers to rethink their relationships with nature. They accept the criticisms they receive as a result, seeing the process as one of skillful means, using concepts and practices with which people are familiar to introduce more complex philosophies and principles. In some cases, environmental monks anthropomorphize nature. In others, they engage the political context, using ritual to challenge social powers (including those of the state, the sangha authorities, and the middle class) and inculcate a sense of moral responsibility. This approach frequently plays out in the performance of tree ordinations.

The Politics of Tree Ordinations

No formula for performing tree ordinations exists. Each monk approaches the ritual in his own way, adapting it for the immediate circumstances. In Pitak's case, he chooses chants relevant to a particular place and time. One of the beauties of the ritual, and the Buddhist environmental movement as a whole, is its flexibility, allowing for creativity to meet specific needs. Even as the ritual, along with many other aspects of the larger movement, has been taken on by both NGOs and the government, especially since the project to ordain fifty million trees in honor of the king's fiftieth year of reign in 1996–97 (Delcore 2004b; Isager and Ivarsson 2002; Tannenbaum 2000), the malleability of the rite and environmental monks' creativity in using it offer the most potential for keeping the monks' work effective into the future.

In July 1991, I attended the second tree ordination sponsored by Phrakhru Pitak. That year he pulled together ten villages comprising a subdistrict in Nan that share common forest resources. Although the tree ordination was the culmination of months of preparation and was one aspect of a larger conservation program, the actual ceremony involved only a day and a half of activities. Pitak invited more than twenty monks from Nan and other northern provinces to assist in the ceremony. Recognizing the value of support from the sangha hierarchy and the local government for the project's success, he consulted with and involved members of the provincial sangha administration, especially the senior-most monk in the subdistrict, the district officer, and other local bureaucrats. Many local government officials and mid-level members of the sangha hierarchy participated in the ceremony. Given the independent nature and potentially controversial aspects of the activities of most socially engaged monks, Pitak's attention to convincing the sangha hierarchy and the government of the project's importance was significant for assuring its success.

The night before the ceremony, representatives of Wildlife Fund Thailand (WFT) showed slides about conservation, especially of forests, for the villagers. The organization's co-sponsorship of the project placed Phrakhru Pitak's work on a national stage and gave it further legitimacy. Not only is WFT one of the largest environmental NGOs in Thailand, it has royal patronage. The involvement of NGOs in the work of environmental monks is essential to much of their success, although at the same time it raises potential political issues as many NGOs are openly critical of government policy. As Delcore (2004b) argues, as NGO participation in tree ordinations increased, so did their influence on and interpretation of the ceremonies.

The Politics of Giving Forest Robes

The ordination ceremony began in the morning with a modification of a traditional ritual, *thot pha pa* (the giving of the forest robes). Development monks earlier adapted this ceremony as a means of both raising funds for village projects and securing villagers' involvement in them. For this environmental project, several nurseries and some wealthy patrons offered twelve thousand saplings, along with the usual basic personal necessities, to the monks. The saplings symbolized the forest in which robes were traditionally acquired, as well as the environmental focus of the ritual.

Villagers incorporated their own innovations in the manner in which they presented their offerings (primarily the personal necessities of soap, paper, toothbrushes, and, of course, robes) to the monks. They paraded their offerings in three groups, representing the three administrative units to which the ten participating villages belonged. While they carried model trees with simple offerings of money and necessities, they did not dance or drink, the typical accompaniment to a pha pa parade (Darlington 1990, 132–37).

Rather, each of the three groups performed skits that presented their ideas of conserving the forest.

All three skits emphasized the urgent need for the villagers to conserve the forest. Two were straightforward, pantomiming planting and caring for the saplings. They celebrated local crafts, with vehicles decorated in locally woven textiles. The most dramatic of the three included political commentary. The villagers acted out an incident of the forest being cut down, passing the blame from minority mountain people (in this case, the Hmong), to the Northern Thai villagers, until it finally settled on the government for not protecting the forest (Plate 11).

Through the skit, the villagers tapped into a debate that has raged across the nation since the environmental movement emerged in the 1980s. On one side stand those who blame people living in forested land, both ethnic minorities and rural Thai, for deforestation through their agricultural practices, particularly swidden agriculture. The Hmong, being one of the more recent groups to migrate to Thailand and living at the highest altitudes, often take the brunt of the criticism. This attitude is grounded in a reading of the Western concept of "pristine" nature, and tends to write out the existence of people living in the forest (Pinkaew 2001, 2002).

Anthropologist Pinkaew Laungaramsri elaborates on the Thai state's interpretation and use of this concept:

> [T]he adoption of North American wilderness thinking by the modernizing Thai state within the country's particular stage of capital accumulation has resulted in an ambivalence between "nature conservation" and "economic development." The Thai deployment of "wilderness" actually reverses the original. Unlike the romantically-conceived model of the North American national park, Thai wilderness thinking stands inside the heart of modernity and omits the key characteristic of the wilderness. Used as a tool to modernize the country and its people, Thai "nature conservation" abandons the wild freedom of areas once beyond the reach of the state and assigns new functions to the landscape now designated as "protected." Most crucially, this process has been integral to the capitalization of natural resources through the "development" paradigm. (Pinkaew 2002, n.p.)

Pinkaew quotes a Thai senator in relation to the debates over the proposed community forestry bill that would provide rights to people living in forested land. The senator's position illustrates the attitude of much of the government toward local people in forests. "Local people are like weevils," he said, "they eat up all the wood. If we pass this bill . . . it is like we open all the protected forests to all the communities" (Pinkaew 2002, n.p.).

Opponents to the state's position argue that indigenous people are best suited for protecting the forest, having developed an indigenous knowledge that allows them to live sustainably (Anan 2000; Yos 2003). Larry Lohmann, a strong proponent of allowing local people to maintain the forests in which they live, even labels the state's position as "racist" because it targets minority groups (1999, 2000). Both he and Pinkaew (2001, 2002) see this position as based on a social construction of nature that either ignores people living in "wilderness" areas, or equates them as part of the "other" that makes up a nature distinct from "civilization," that is, the dominant majority (Pearmsak 2002; Roth 2004).

Government policy was largely based on the view that people should be removed from protected areas, and these areas should then be used for national development. It adopted a top-down approach to forest management with the creation of the Royal Forestry Department (RFD) in 1886. Following the forestry model of the British in Burma, the RFD primarily treated the forest as a resource and oversaw long-term forest concessions by various logging companies. People living in the forest were considered as either part of the forest or obstacles to accessing the forest's resources. They were no longer allowed full management of their own environments. Pearmsak Makarabhirom (2002, n.p.), a program officer at the Regional Community Forestry Training Center for Asia and the Pacific at Kasetsart University in Bangkok, noted the consequences: "Local communities have long managed and used forests for their own livelihood. Since the central government took over forest management from the people, however, local communities have suffered and forest management has failed for lack of community participation."

Proponents of local involvement in forest management not only push for community participation, but also criticize government policies for failing to care for natural resources. Government policies have led to deforestation and environmental destruction as forests have been cleared for large-scale monoculture cash crops, such as feed corn, cabbage, temperate fruit trees, eucalyptus, cassava, pineapple, and other crops. People suddenly find themselves living "illegally" in their homes after the government proclaims areas as national parks or National Forest Reserve Land, thereby making them protected areas (Pearmsak 2002). Ethnic minorities in particular suffer discrimination and economic hardship as a result (Lohmann 1999, 2000; Pinkaew 2001).

Even environmental monks fall into the "people and the forest" debate. Most of them, including Phrakhru Pitak, support the right of people already living in the forest to remain as its best guardians. A few, most notably Achan Phongsak Techadhammo of Chiang Mai Province, take the position that people, usually highland minority peoples such as the Hmong, should be removed from the forest (especially watersheds).

That Northern Thai villagers participating in the tree ordination in Nan Province took a position in this debate, as opposed to leaving it to the academics, environmentalists, and government agents, was significant. They picked up on the economic underpinning of the arguments, recognizing that often people are removed from the forest to make way for economic development—first logging concessions, then commercial agricultural production. The skit concisely illustrated the tensions between seeking a livelihood in the forest and commercial plantations that often require cutting the forest to make room for cash crops. The villagers examined the arguments that targeted first the Hmong, then the Northern Thai, and ultimately blamed government agents for allowing companies to cut the forest and promoting cash cropping among the villagers. Through their public performance, they embodied and articulated a controversial position, and did so with impunity due to its ritual context.

The political debate concerning forest conservation and the economic interests involved in its destruction underlies all conservation activities.[8] It was unusual, however, for these issues to be brought so openly to the surface, especially during a Buddhist ritual. Besides illustrating the villagers' understanding of the complex political issues surrounding deforestation, the skit showed their trust in the setting. Pitak used the thot pha pa and tree ordination rites to reach out to the villagers and frame his position in deforestation debates (tactfully incorporating all the parties involved, villagers, NGOs, and government officials alike). Similarly, the skit performers took the opportunity to criticize the government openly, shielded by the sanctity of the Buddhist context.

Once Phrakhru Pitak ritually accepted the forest robes and other traditional offerings, he and the highest-ranking monk present accepted the saplings, thus sanctifying them and conferring merit on the donors and the participants. Participants then planted a few of the saplings around the temple grounds and at the site of the tree ordination. Most were given to the villagers to reforest areas that had been denuded, similar to the pattern established by pha pa ceremonies conducted to raise development project funds. These new trees were chosen carefully; they were species, such as fruit trees, that were productive without having to be cut down. Having been sanctified and given by the monks further protected them as the villagers would see cutting them as a form of religious demerit (*bap*).

To Destroy the Forest Is to Destroy Life

After the thot pha pa ritual, the participants climbed into trucks, vans, and buses to make the five-kilometer trip into the mountains to the tree chosen to be ordained. The tree stood taller than any others, making it the "king" of the forest. Northern Thais often identify such a tree within a forest, and revere it as representative of the forest as a whole. During his sermon, Phrakhru Pitak commented that more than twenty years ago, when he walked along this route through the deep forest to school, this tree was not unusual for its height or size. Now it clearly stood out as the tallest remaining tree (Plate 12). From its location, one could see for miles across a landscape dotted with cornfields, visible because of the deforested hillsides.

Over two hundred people accompanied the more than twenty monks to the site, which had earlier been prepared by volunteer development workers. A four-foot-tall Buddha image had been placed on a concrete stand at the base of the giant tree. The thick vegetation around the site had been trimmed, and a tent for the monks put up.

In this ceremony, as in all tree ordinations, the monks did not claim to be fully ordaining the tree. The ceremony was used symbolically to remind people that nature should be treated as equal with humans, deserving of respect and vital for human as well as all life. The monks used the opportunity of the ordination to build spiritual commitment to preserving the forest and to teach in an active and creative way the value of conservation. The main emphasis of Phrakhru Pitak's sermon during the ritual was on the relationship between the Buddha and nature, and the interdependence between the conditions of the forest and the villagers' lives.

Toward the end of the ritual, two monks quickly wrapped orange robes around the tree's trunk, marking its consecration (Plate 3). A crowd of photographers from local and Bangkok newspapers and participating NGOs, one anthropologist, and two film crews documented the act. The robes stood as a reminder that to harm or cut the tree—or any of the forest—was an act of demerit. While it was not unusual to find bodhi trees (the kind of tree under which the Buddha achieved enlightenment) wrapped with sacred cloth, in those cases the tree was already seen as holy; the cloth served more to honor the tree than to sanctify it. The innovation here was that the tree ordained was not previously treated as sacred but was made so through the ritual. The orange robes symbolized its new status.

As in most Buddhist rituals, the ceremony included the sanctification of water in a monk's alms bowl. A small Buddha image was placed in the bowl and candle wax dripped into the water while the monks chanted. A white string connected the bowl with the large Buddha image by the tree, passing through all the monks' hands. Traditionally, this holy water (*nam mon*) is sprinkled on ritual participants, conferring a blessing and merit on them. This water is seen as ritually powerful, and people always make sure to receive some drops of it (Olson 1991).

On this occasion, Phrakhru Pitak used the consecrated water in an original manner. Each of the ten village headmen drank some of the water in front of the large Buddha image to seal their oath to protect the forest (Plate 13). This use of a sacred symbol to strengthen such a pledge reinforced the notion of environmentalism as a moral action. It made the protection or destruction of the forest karmic action: protecting it would confer good merit (*bun*), destroying it bringing bad (*bap*), the balance of which would ultimately affect one's rebirth or even quality of living in this life. Beyond that, it drew on the belief of the villagers in the magical powers of the holy water; while specific sanctions were not mentioned for failing to uphold the headmen's pledge, the implications were that breaking it would involve going against the power secured by the use of the water.

The most overtly political aspect of the ceremony was the plaque nailed to the tree prior to the ordination (Plate 14). No formal mention of the sign was made during the ritual, nor was much discussion or fanfare made concerning its content or placement. The sign read, in Thai, "*tham lai pa khue tham lai chat*," which can be translated as, "To destroy the forest is to destroy life." The word *chat* (life) appears clear-cut, but it carries several meanings, all of which relate to the issue of conservation on various levels.[9] Chat can mean life, birth (as in rebirth), or nation. The sentence could thus be read, "To destroy the forest is to destroy life, one's rebirth, or the nation."

The first meaning is the most straightforward from the point of view of environmentalists whose concerns do not necessarily involve either religious or nationalist connotations. It also implies the Buddhist idea that one should respect and care for all life as everything is interconnected.

The second meaning, to destroy one's rebirth, invokes the concept of karma. It raises the idea that destroying the forest is an act of demerit and consequently has a negative influence on how one is reborn.

The third interpretation, that of destroying the nation (meaning both territory and people; F. Reynolds 1977, 274; 1994, 442), is the most complex. It evokes nationalist feelings, linking the condition of the forest with that of the state. It draws upon the moral connection between nation (*chat*), religion (*satsana*), and monarchy (*mahakesat*), the trinity of concepts that makes up Thailand's identity (F. Reynolds 1977, 1994). Even this meaning is double-edged. While it invokes the villagers' loyalty to the nation and the king in protecting the forest (a concept latter used for the king's fiftieth year of reign celebrations), it also calls upon the nation itself to uphold its moral responsibility to preserve the forest. Given the political undertones of the conservation issue, and the stance of Pitak and the NGOs involved, it is unlikely that this implicit meaning was present by mere coincidence.

The use of the word *chat* on the sign signifies the complexity and importance of tree ordinations. Monks are reinterpreting concepts of religion to promote environmentalism at the same time the latter is linked through moral ties with local and national political and economic issues. Throughout the ordination and the larger project of which it is part, Phrakhru Pitak extended his traditional role as spiritual and moral leader of lay villagers to embrace an activism that necessitated political involvement. The same kind of expansion is recreated in every project run by environmental monks, from tree ordinations and the establishment of sacred community forests to tree planting ceremonies and long-life ceremonies at sites threatened by environmental destruction.

NGO Involvement

Phrakhru Pitak did not orchestrate the 1991 tree ordination by himself. Not only did local people, especially the ten village headmen and the subdistrict officer, and local NGOs participate in the planning, but national NGOs and academics from Chiang Mai University (CMU) joined in as well. This case showed how rituals serve as a microcosm of the complex relationships between various NGOs, academics, and environmental monks as they plan and implement community-based conservation projects. It also illustrated the fine line between supporting local needs and imposing outside agendas, something Delcore (2004b) argues occurred with NGO involvement in the tree ordinations conducted nationwide in 1996–97 in honor of the king's fiftieth year of reign.

Three levels of NGO involvement emerged during the 1991 ritual, each with a different sense of what the broader project entailed, commitments to long-term support, and connections with the central government's preference for centralized control of forest and natural resource management. Indigenous NGOs, which grew up within Nan Province, formed the first level.[10] These NGOs were directly aware of the issues facing the people of Nan, and the goals and motivations of Phrakhru Pitak. The second level consisted of regional NGOs from across northern Thailand. Several of these NGOs joined a network of NGOs and academics from CMU that sought to support developmental and environmental projects across the region. Critical of state-led development, the network emphasized both grassroots projects and intellectual concepts underlying development goals, putting them at a slight remove from the immediacy of the project in Nan. Finally, national environmental NGOs contributed to the project both financially and with educational information. These NGOs were the farthest from direct engagement with Pitak's project, despite their presence during the ritual. Their support emerged from broader agendas that challenged state environmental and forest policies. They sought local projects that could represent their goals.

Indigenous NGOs were made up predominantly of people from the province. While many of these NGO workers obtained a higher education, they remained committed to helping the people of Nan. Having grown up there, they were aware of the issues the people faced, especially the impacts of economic development and the state's encouragement of cash cropping. Indigenous NGOs tended to be small-scale, focusing on specific issues, such as health care, sustainable development and agriculture, or preserving native plant species. Initially working independently, many of Nan's indigenous NGOs joined the umbrella organization, *Klum Hak Mueang Nan* ("Love Nan Province Association," referred to hereafter as HMN), established in 1993 by Phrakhru Pitak and several close associates. They sought to bring together individuals and organizations that cared about the social and environmental situation in the province. The organization included indigenous NGOs, village organizations, monks, and a few state officials (Delcore 2000). Even before the formation of HMN, indigenous NGOs supported Pitak's efforts. This was a reciprocal relationship, as their association with a well-known and respected monk gave them legitimacy and integrity in the eyes of both the people and officials.

As with his first tree ordination the year before, Pitak requested indigenous NGOs help him educate the villagers in advance of the 1991 event. For several weeks leading up to the ritual, Pitak, accompanied by one or more NGO workers from different organizations, visited each of the ten villages.

He showed slides that integrated moral lessons, such as the importance of selflessness and generosity, with concern about the nation's environment, especially its water and forests. Pitak made a strong connection between people's behavior and deforestation and its consequences, particularly the severe flooding in southern Thailand in 1988. That flooding, blamed by both environmentalists and government officials on logging and deforestation, led to the passing of a national logging ban in January 1989 (Pinkaew and Rajesh 1992). Pitak incorporated photographs of bloated bodies floating through flooded southern villages into his slide show after talking about the destruction caused by logging.

The NGO workers who accompanied him helped set up the show and spoke about the value of community cooperation in dealing with issues of deforestation. The NGOs represented ranged from a small, local seed-saving organization to a provincial-level foundation with ties to Scandinavia that promoted highland people's handicrafts and integrated agriculture. Depending on who went with Pitak, the topics discussed ranged from preserving local identity and cultural practices and values to the ecological basis of integrated agriculture. Villagers usually listened carefully. Not only did the NGO workers come with a respected monk, but they represented external expertise grounded in the workers' education. The fact that they were from Nan Province further empowered these workers. To many villagers, they stood for the potential of local people.

The second level of NGO involvement included regional, Northern Thai NGOs, especially the Northern Development Foundation, a coalition of NGOs and academics from CMU. Some of the indigenous NGOs from Nan participated in the discussions and cooperative projects supported by this network. When the network lent its support to Phrakhru Pitak's 1991 project, the participants received a history of the project and Pitak's motivations from a NGO worker from Nan, himself a close associate of the monk. Before committing their support, network members discussed how it fit their newly formulated concept of community forestry.[11]

The network used what anthropologist Anan Ganjanapan, one of the main academic participants, calls the "community rights approach" to research and development projects. Anan describes the approach as follows:

> With critical views of political and capitalist economic systems, the protagonist of this approach tends to suggest that popular participation in sustainable development will be possible by recognizing villagers' rights in their own communal organizations and in managing

their own resources. Because such collective rights are fundamental to human beings, participation enables people to reproduce both ideology of power and people's way of thinking in their articulations with the changing environment and society at large. (Anan 2000, 4–5)

The NGO workers conducted participatory action research, which engaged villagers in collecting data and identifying areas of need, then met regularly with each other and the academics. They discussed strategies for getting villagers to establish their own network of natural resource (especially watershed) management. Related to this network was another research project that involved in-depth anthropological studies on villagers' perspectives and practices related to resource use and management within the larger contexts of changing society and environment. The academics and NGO workers together encouraged villagers to learn from each other across villages and support each other in managing their resources (Anan 2000, 16–17).

An NGO worker from Nan brought Phrakhru Pitak's plan to conduct the tree ordination and establish the ten-village protected community forest to the network meeting at CMU less than a month before the ritual date. One of the villages involved already participated in the network's joint research project with a researcher from CMU. The network participants agreed to support the community forest project in Nan, and encouraged its members to attend the ritual.[12]

Because the project was grounded in participatory action research and targeted these areas with specific projects, the network had a good sense of local people's struggles, concerns, and wants. Nevertheless, they had less of a feel for these aspects than the NGO workers based in Nan. Through network meetings and discussions, the participants—NGO workers and academics—set up their own agenda and intellectual groundings for their work. Even with participatory action research, the network as a whole had a difficult time understanding every community's situation and needs.

The network did work as an invaluable mediator between local communities and NGOs in other places, regional and national NGOs, and even the state. Through discussions, the participants learned about and had input into developing stances on a range of political issues that affected their development and environmental work, such as the community forestry debate. At the same time, however, when the NGO members lent their support, financial or through participation, to specific projects such as the tree ordination in Nan, they brought with them definitions of concepts that had been developed outside the local area. Many of the network members were based in or near Chiang Mai city, came from the growing middle class, and held higher education degrees. The differences between their backgrounds and perspectives and those of the local people in Nan created underlying tensions.

One tension came from the different ways the various actors involved defined the forest. The network developed its own concept of community forestry. The process involved discussion, debate, and revision, resulting in a complex theoretical paragraph describing the concept. For the villagers, community forestry essentially means having access to a shared resource, and determining together how to use that resource. In Pitak's home village, a committee walked the forest to mark the boundaries of the community forest, which was consecrated by the tree ordination ritual and protected by the guardian spirit lord. While the network had no input into this process, my sense from the meeting that laid out the definition of community forest was that participants did not include spiritual considerations explicitly. The academics and NGO workers accepted the value of tree ordinations and even the guardian spirit ritual in Pitak's village, but saw them as useful tools rather than carrying genuine spiritual meaning.

Beyond the regional NGOs and the northern NGO/academic coalition, national NGOs took an interest in Phrakhru Pitak's project. Wildlife Fund Thailand provided both financial and logistical support for the ritual. Two representatives of WFT, one Thai and one an American volunteer, came to Nan the day before the ordination. A fair-like atmosphere prevailed that day as villagers, NGO workers, government officials, and monks joined in to celebrate the event. Typical of Northern Thai pha pa ceremonies, the activities that day included musical performances and lots of food.

The celebrations concluded that evening with a lengthy slide show sponsored by WFT. The two WFT representatives narrated slides emphasizing the urgency of nature conservation, highlighting the value of the forest for a wide range of life, including human, and teaching basic forest ecology. The American volunteer, Dave, held people's attention largely due to the novelty of a foreigner publicly speaking in Thai. His presence implied an involvement and concern for the area's environmental problems from an international community.

An international community did care about what happened with this project, although it was not the environmental community the villagers assumed from Dave's presence. Beginning in 1985, WFT oversaw the Thai implementation of an international project, The Buddhist Perception of Nature, "a project created to improve awareness, attitudes, and actions concerning the natural environment" (Nash 1987, 31). The Buddhist Perception of Nature Project was the brain child of Nancy Nash, a consultant with World Wildlife Fund in 1979 when she proposed that world religions should be incorporated into conservation efforts (Scott 1987, 4). She credited the Dalai Lama for her inspiration (Nash 1987, 31), which probably explained the project's emphasis on Buddhism.[13]

The Buddhist Perception of Nature Project sought ways to educate Buddhists across Asia about nature conservation, grounding its approach in an interpretation of Buddhism as inherently ecological. Professor Chatsumarn Kabilsingh of Thammasat University wrote a book sponsored by the project that drew from Buddhist teachings "to formulate an ethical approach to nature and environmental protection and to promote nature conservation through the teachings of the Buddha" (Chatsumarn 1998, xv). A simplified version of the book was published in 1987 in Thai and English under the title, *A Cry from the Forest.* The project distributed the book to temples and teachers' colleges across the country to support their efforts at promoting nature conservation to the larger populace (Chatsumarn 1998, 3–4). Including an English translation, even though it was primarily used in Thailand, lent the book an aura of authority and the sense that the ideas were "modern" and "Western." The book and the project conveyed a generic Buddhist interpretation of nature. Certainly no villagers from Nan provided input into the ideas presented.

WFT took the efforts of spreading the message of conservation through Buddhist monks one step farther. For about a decade, they had a Buddhist-based project that financially supported environmental monks and sponsored educational seminars. These seminars, sometimes co-sponsored with the Thai Interreligious Commission for Development (TICD, another national NGO), brought experienced environmental monks together to share their stories, problems and solutions.[14] Monks with an interest in conservation who did not know how to initiate projects attended some of the seminars, gaining practical knowledge, ideas for interpreting and using Buddhist scriptures to support their work, and, probably most importantly, connections with other monks engaged in similar work.

I attended a three-day seminar organized by WFT and TICD in July 1991 entitled "The Role of the Sangha in Natural Resource Conservation." The organizers extended three hundred invitations, mostly through regional and local environmental NGOs, to monks involved or interested in environmental conservation. Based on experience and responses to the invitations, they planned for approximately sixty monks to attend the seminar. During registration on the first day, more than two hundred monks showed up. The unexpected number highlighted both the growing interest among the sangha for environmental conservation, and the effectiveness of the outreach work by organizations such as WFT and TICD.

WFT and the Buddhist Perception of Nature Project provided a key level of support and legitimacy for projects such as Phrakhru Pitak's. WFT's royal patronage further strengthened environmental monks' projects, and helped minimize criticism that environmental and developmental work was not appropriate for members of the sangha. Yet the royal connections were less directly employed than they were during the 1996–97 tree ordinations in honor of the king.

The actual engagement of WFT remained somewhat superficial. Besides providing funds and occasional logistical help for specific events, usually high profile ones such as Pitak's tree ordination, WFT seemed to have little on-the-ground knowledge of or commitment to the monks' broader projects. Instead, the organization offered its own interpretation of Buddhism and encouraged monks to follow its conservation agenda, which emphasized wildlife conservation. While WFT actively sought out monks as primary researchers for the project, Chatsumarn admitted that few monks had the time or inclination to join (seminar presentation, 6/2/1993). Most of the research on Buddhist ethics and their connection with conservation was carried out by academics such as Chatsumarn herself, an urban-based university professor.[15] The philosophical and political commitments were strong, but there was little experiential understanding of the problems in villages or villagers' own interpretations of nature. The focus remained on encouraging and supporting activist monks, and providing a specific interpretation of Buddhist scriptures linked to conservation activities based on a particular definition of nature as distinct from people.

Few environmental monks used a concept of environmentalism or an interpretation of Buddhism that fell directly in line with that pushed by WFT. The organization drew from a Western notion of environmentalism that emphasized the conservation of nature as pristine and needing protection from human encroachment, one similar to the position of the state criticized by Pinkaew (2001, 2002). Instead, most environmental monks, including Phrakhru Pitak, focused on a concept of environmentalism grounded in their own interpretations of indigenous Buddhism that emphasized relieving suffering, centered on humans and their interdependency with the natural world. While a subtle difference, through their use of ritual to embody this concept and convey its affective meaning to villagers, these monks articulated a distinct approach of their own rather than one informed primarily by the West.

I contacted WFT via e-mail in the late 1990s to ask about the Buddhist Perception of Nature program. The response stated the program had ended because its funding had been cut. The dependence on outside funding and the seemingly arbitrary timing for ending it confirmed my sense of the superficial commitment of WFT to the individual monks engaged in environmental work. A series of scandals that hit the Thai sangha, including several well-known environmental monks, in the early to mid-1990s probably contributed to WFT and its funders' quiet decision to end the Buddhist program.

Despite WFT's stepping back from Buddhist environmentalism, many NGOs at all levels continued to get involved, particularly through sponsoring tree ordinations. In the early 1990s, this support helped the movement get through many challenges. Environmental monks faced criticism for inappropriate behavior for ordaining trees and engaging in political issues, death threats from powerful people who stood to gain from the exploitation of natural resources and village economics, real and fabricated scandals aimed at undermining public confidence and respect for activist monks, and environmental monk seminars scrutinized by armed military and police. NGO and academic involvement bolstered the monks' efforts to defend their actions as both appropriate for monks and good for the nation and its people. They brought the monks positive publicity and coordinated seminars that enabled individual monks to learn from each other and gain moral support for their work.

In the process, through these NGOs environmental monks' messages reached beyond the village level to the predominantly middle-class Thais who donate to and join national NGOs, and to whom these NGOs target their own messages. Through supporting environmental monks, the NGOs are publicly announcing that they agree with the monks' message of people's responsibility to protect the forests. In particular, the middle class is challenged to think about consumption—how their own lifestyles affect both the natural environment and the rural people. The rituals highlight the idealized image of rural life as one of simple living. Although villagers participate actively in consumerism, their level of consumption falls well below that of the middle class living in cities. As the latter shifted their opinions of tree ordinations from one of surprise or shock to backing and even appropriation, they acknowledged the subtle message of consumption and responsibility. The monks pushed them to consider the value of the natural environment for the nation as a whole, and contributed to the growing popularity of environmentalism across Thailand. Perhaps the strongest message for the middle class was the reinvigoration of Buddhism in their lives—pulling them away from materialist values to reaffirm basic Buddhist values instead.

Expanding the Audience

Early in the movement, tree ordinations shocked the Thai public. People struggled with the concept of treating trees as humans, misunderstanding the motivations of the monks performing them. Initially, monks such as Phrakhru Manas and Phrakhru Pitak aimed the messages of these rituals at the villagers, working with their spiritual understandings to get them to rethink their relationships with, their impact on, and responsibility toward the natural world. Given the centrality of rituals and spirit beliefs to rural religion, this approach made sense. As news of these rituals went beyond local areas, which it did even with Phrakhru Manas's first tree ordination, the misunderstandings and criticisms erupted immediately. While the collaboration of NGOs helped mediate these criticisms among the mainstream, middle-class public, the monks soon became aware of two other audiences for their messages. In another example of skillful means, some monks adapted the context of environmental rituals to pull in sangha authorities and state officials, both groups that held the potential of undermining environmental monks' work.

The years 1991 and 1992 were a tumultuous period for environmental monks. While monks such as Phrakhru Pitak expanded their work through highly publicized events like the tree ordination and consecration of a ten-village community forest in Nan Province, other better-known monks faced attacks on their reputations. Pitak recognized the difficulties activist monks faced due in part to opposition from their ecclesiastical superiors and government officials. As he moved forward with his environmental work, he made efforts to incorporate public officials and sangha administrators in his projects.

Phrakhru Pitak did this by inviting sangha, government, and military officials to participate in public rituals. An effective example was the suep chata, or long-life ritual, that he conducted for the Nan River in 1993. Through the long-life ritual for the river, Pitak expanded his focus from predominantly forests to include water. The Nan River, which runs from the highlands of the province south and west to feed into the Chao Praya River in the heart of Thailand, is part of the vital river system that supports the nation's agriculture. Without the water in the rivers, Pitak argued, the Thai people could not live.

A key argument in Pitak's work surrounding the Nan River was that if the people of Nan could clean up and care for the river upstream, then people downstream would follow suit. The ripple effect would spread to people caring for waterways across the nation, recognizing life's dependence on water. The Nan River, along with the other tributaries of the Chao Praya, formed the life blood of the nation and needed to be respected.

To symbolize respect for the river, Pitak and the newly formed HMN decided to hold the long-life ceremony as part of what they called the Love the Nan River Project. The ritual would highlight the ill health of the river and focus people's attention on how they treated it. They again followed a model set by Phrakhru Manas, adapted to fit a larger context. They also drew from the example of a nearby village that had performed such a ritual for its irrigation system the year before, providing a more local model. That ritual not only emphasized the problems the villagers faced due to drought, but helped to unify different village factions that competed over the use of water. Participating together in the rite strengthened village ties and healed rifts as people set up a system for sharing the water in conjunction with the ritual. The village monk, who did not consider himself an environmental or activist monk, agreed to perform the ceremony annually to ensure a good water supply and hoping to minimize future tensions among villagers.

Phrakhru Pitak's decision to invite high-level officials to participate in the long-life ritual for the river echoed the village ceremony in terms of bringing different social factions together. Pitak located the rite on land belonging to the military just outside Nan city. The military formed the main opposition to the work of Phra Prajak Khuttajitto, the monk twice arrested in 1991 for challenging a government and military land reallocation program. Pitak was determined to avoid similar conflicts. As the host of the long-life ceremony, the military could not later criticize the project to protect and conserve the Nan River. Similarly, Pitak invited the governor of Nan Province to open the ceremony, with several high-ranking provincial officials attending as ritual sponsors. Not only did these officials gain religious merit for their sponsorship and participation, but their presence condoned the project's long-term goals of conserving the river and other waterways in the province.

In 1993, Phrakhru Pitak received an ecclesiastical promotion around the same time he was awarded the Model Citizen Award jointly by the

Village Foundation, a national NGO that promoted village life and alternative development, and the Matichon newspaper. Pitak's decision to celebrate these two personal events together with the long-life ceremony for the river automatically pulled in members of the sangha hierarchy. Monks from across northern Thailand attended to honor Pitak's promotion and award.

Ecological and Cultural Fair

The event itself entailed more than just the ritual. HMN organized a two-day fair celebrating the river, educating people about its ecology and current condition, and honoring the monk. Over three months leading up to the fair and ritual, volunteers from HMN walked along the northern part of the river, documenting its pollution. They noted where pesticides and fertilizers ran off mandarin orange plantations, villagers washed their cars, motorcycles, and laundry, letting soapsuds float downstream, and piles of trash collected after being carelessly dumped into the river. They photographed problem areas, and recorded water animals and plant life. They placed handwritten signs reminding people of the value of water, and asking them not to wash their laundry near the river.

To highlight the ecological concerns underlying the event, the organizers borrowed an approach from an upstream village, establishing a fish sanctuary at the ritual site. The year before, Don Kaew Village created a fish sanctuary where the village temple stood along the river's banks.

The success of the fish sanctuary at Don Kaew spread quickly. Not only did Phrakhru Pitak use its model in conjunction with most of the long-life ceremonies he performed for waterways, but villages across Thailand adopted it. Don Kaew's headman claimed he heard of a village in northeastern Thailand that established such a fish sanctuary, giving him the idea. Nevertheless, he received a national environmental award in 1999 for beginning a trend that affected the fish population nationwide.

The day of the ritual a festive air hung over Nan city. Tents stood on the river bank, housing rows of bulletin boards covered with informational posters and photographs documenting the state of the river and its ecology (Plate 15). Children's drawings reminded viewers of the people whose lives depended on the river. Wildlife photos competed with images of sudsy trash clogging the water. Charts documented pollution levels and causes. Volunteers from NGOs from Chiang Mai and Bangkok helped put the informational displays together. A string with colorful flags swung from poles demarcating the portion of the river designated as the fish sanctuary.

For two days, people celebrated the river and learned about its life and problems. Cultural diversity was celebrated with music, dance, and food from all the provincial districts. People from across the province paraded from Wat Aranyawat, Phrakhru Pitak's temple, to the fairground, dressed in clothes from their districts and dancing to local songs. They carried a large sign announcing the long-life ceremony for the river (Plate 16). Participants came from across Thailand, including members of several national NGOs. About one hundred guests of the Village Foundation, the organization granting Pitak the environmental award, came, made up of NGO agents, upper- and middle-class sponsors, and villagers from northeastern Thailand. Many journalists attended, documenting every aspect of the event.

Under the tent, Phrakhru Pitak and several important monks from Nan and other northern provinces sat on a platform. Provincial authorities occupied the front seats facing the platform, dressed in government uniforms. In comfortable chairs (compared with the metal folding chairs for the rest of the audience), the governor and his wife waited for him to open the ceremony. To the side, yet in a place of honor, approximately two hundred monks from across northern Thailand witnessed the rite.

Under the main tent stood a colorful, eight-foot-tall pyramid framed by sticks and poles and covered in objects signifying long life (ranging from white paper flags to betel nuts, rice, and other food) (Plate 17). Once the ceremony began, Phrakhru Pitak captured people's attention as he celebrated his promotion and award, and conducted the ritual itself. The monks chanted texts of morality tales and Pitak gave a sermon about the importance of water and the river. The pyramid was blessed, linked by white string to the monks and a Buddha image. The monks chanted and sprinkled consecrated water across the crowd. At the conclusion of the ritual, a long line of monks filed past Pitak offering blessings and small gifts of congratulations.

The ceremony took only an hour to complete, after political speeches by the governor and local military leaders. As the monks left the platform and congregated in small groups to chat, members of the audience, primarily middle-class women and the wives of the dignitaries present, spontaneously began to dismantle the pyramid. It stood under the tent about one hundred yards from the river's edge, too far, they stated, for the spirits of the river to acknowledge and accept. Within a few minutes, they recreated the pyramid on a concrete dock that extended into the river at water level. As cameras snapped, officials released several boxes of small fish into the river. Not only did they repopulate the river with the fish, but they gained Buddhist merit for releasing wildlife, a practice found across the Buddhist world.

Acceptance of Buddhist Environmentalism

The long-life ceremony for the Nan River marked a turning point in the environmental monks' movement in several ways. First, the ritual expanded the ecological focus of the movement, even though forests remain the primary emphasis even today. Water always held a central place in the environmental movement, largely because of concern about the construction of several large hydroelectric dams across the country. In fact, the successful protests against the Nam Choen Dam in 1988 by a coalition of factions— environmentalists, students, civil servants, monks—marked the beginning of an effective environmental movement in Thailand (Rigg 1995, 13). The long-life ceremony took a different tack. Rather than protesting developmental plans for rivers, the project followed a proactive approach, working to educate and integrate people, protect and conserve water, and highlight the value of rivers running freely.

Second, and perhaps most significant, was the involvement of many key government, military, and sangha officials. Most of the activities of environmental monks done up to that time emerged from the grassroots, targeting specific local issues and involving local people. The monks faced criticism from the authorities, governmental and sangha, questioning whether such work was appropriate for monks. Some environmental monks, such as Phra Prajak, took a confrontational approach, openly challenging the government's development policies.

The Love the Nan River Project incorporated a wide range of people. The idea to perform the long-life ritual emerged from discussions among Phrakhru Pitak and various NGO workers from Nan. The participation of government, military, and sangha officials implicitly indicated acceptance of the underlying goals of the project and the fact that it was led by a monk. Over the course of the next few years, mainstream society gradually accepted environmental monks. Controversies continued to arise, but the Love the Nan River Project marked a shift in social thinking about environmental monks.

People attended the long-life ceremony from across the nation. With the exception of a group of villagers from the northeast brought by the Village

Foundation, most of the guests were urban, middle-class people. Most who came from outside the province belonged to national or regional NGOs; others saw it as an opportunity to join a groundbreaking event with a monk who was rapidly gaining national attention.

One NGO worker from Nan who worked closely with Phrakhru Pitak criticized the ritual and the fair, even while he spent considerable time organizing them. Unlike the earlier tree ordinations, the Love the Nan River Program emerged from discussion outside any particular village. It was coordinated from the city, through HMN. In his efforts to include various officials and build better relations and cooperation with them, Pitak seemed to pay less attention to the villagers. The ritual itself was sited along the river on military land away from any particular village, further removing rural people from direct investment in the program. Similar to a tree ordination described by Delcore (2004b) that recreated social hierarchies, this long-life ceremony prioritized people in positions of power, sidelining the villagers. As the NGO worker noted, though, the program needed the same kind of commitment from villagers as the tree ordinations and consecrated community forests, not just the cooperation of authorities. The challenge for environmental monks lies in framing their message in ways that are accessible to many sectors of Thai society while maintaining their positions and respect as monks.

Ritual Bridges

According to Phra Prajak Khuttajitto, activist monks serve as a bridge—between the poor and the rich, rural people and the state, and villagers and modernity. Environmental monks need to reach multiple audiences to increase the possibility of success of their projects. They articulate their primary audience as villagers. For the monks living in the villages where they work, this emphasis is obvious. Yet one of the main causes they cite for environmental degradation is the growing consumerism across the nation. All Thais watch television and listen to the radio. They see the ads promoting "modern" lifestyles, full of fancy cars, expensive clothes, and shiny appliances. The urban middle class sets the standard of what it means to be a modern Thai, and the villagers aspire to this image along with the rest of the nation. Environmental monks recognize the necessity of changing this image, and seek ways, such as the suep chata ritual and fair and increasingly public tree ordinations, to bring in audiences less immediately affected by the changes in the environment wrought by this lifestyle.

This use of ritual—to invoke villagers' community, loyalty, and sensibility to the urgency of environmental protection; to minimize potential criticism from the sangha and military; to challenge and push the state; and to engage the urban middle class in social and environmental issues beyond their direct experience—is a good example of the "radical conservatism" of socially active monks across the nation.[16] They enact and embody recognized symbols within Thai culture and religion, drawing on a "conservative" interpretation of them devoid of the elaboration that they feel much of contemporary Thai Buddhism has added to its practice. They invest these symbols with new meanings relevant for the immediate and long-term problems facing the villagers and the nation. The resulting interpretations and practices have the potential to motivate both rural and city people to change their lifestyles to prevent further destruction. Initiating and rejuvenating projects through ritual bring a sacred, moral, and affective perspective to environmental and development work. This approach goes beyond promoting integrated agriculture or sustainable livelihoods, which are done by many environmental and alternative development NGOs (many quite successfully). The monks draw on their moral authority through the use of ritual to share their concerns about the impacts of state-led development on the lives of their followers and the natural environment on which they depend, and the responsibilities people have to care for the forest.

Using ritual to highlight social problems and challenge social power provides environmental monks with an effective tool to meet their goals. Rituals form part of the bridge that monks use to help villagers negotiate a changing social, economic world and minimize their suffering in the process. Given their status in Thai society, monks can use ritual to reach across social divides, framing their message in ways accessible to different audiences.

Part of their challenge lies in genuinely bridging these divides rather than recreating them. Finding the balance between social criticism and acquiescing to social hierarchies (thereby reinforcing power inequalities) is not easy. Monks do not all agree on where this balance lies. Some, such as Phrakhru Pitak, believe including and working within power structures are necessary for creating substantial change, even though the changes are subtle and take longer to impact the local level. Others, like Phra Prajak, emphasize social justice aspects of their projects more, avoiding cooperation with authorities, despite potential negative repercussions.

Rituals provide a means of negotiating both the political and economic aspects of environmentalism. While rituals are only one tool used by environmental monks, they are a tool available only to the monks, thereby setting them apart from other social change agents such as environmentalists and government officials. Rituals also form another bridge for the monks themselves—between a conservative practice of Buddhism and a radical interpretation that promotes social justice, change, and nature conservation.

In the chapter that follows, I examine the precedents that enabled the emergence of activist monks, particularly environmental monks, and the social history within which they acted. Two divergent precedents within Thai Buddhism provided paradigms for environmental monks. First, forest monks (*phra pa*), devoted to meditation and forest wandering in search of enlightenment, had a significant impact on state/sangha relations at the turn of the twentieth century and contributed to a Buddhist concept of nature as meditation and dhamma teacher. Second, independent "development monks" (*phra nak phatthana*) sought alternatives to government-sponsored economic development beginning in the 1970s. Both of these groups challenged and redefined the sangha's place in Thai society, opening the space for the emergence and at least partial acceptance of environmental monks. I turn now to an examination of these historical processes and the social constraints within which individual monks made their choices to engage in environmentalism.

4

The Precedents

Economic and spiritual development must work together to solve problems.
—Phra Phuttapoj Waraporn (Chan Kusalo)[1]

IN JULY 1987, excited members of a Northern Thai village gathered in the
hot sun along the main road into town. Beneath constantly blaring loud-
speakers, a woman collected donations while a group of older men banged
drums and gongs. The high-toned sound of a Thai flute drifted through the
restless crowd. Women chatted despite the noise, and teenagers put the final
touches on a model tree hung with paper money, notebooks, soap, a set of
orange robes, and other offerings for the village monk. As the crowd grew,
the tree was placed in the back of a pickup truck and the people formed a
long line behind it. Final announcements were made over the loudspeaker
marking the beginning of the parade. Led by the makeshift band and the
pickup, the crowd danced its way through the village to the main gate of the
temple compound. There, older women, dressed in the white robes of the
devout, threw confetti over the paraders as the music, laughter, and cheer-
ing filled the grounds and the people entered the temple to present their
offerings.

This festive occasion, a *thot pha pa* ("giving of the forest robes") ceremony (commonly known as a pha pa ritual), was not typical although it
followed the standard structure of the popular merit-making ritual (Wells
1975, 111–12).[2] The tree was paraded, donations and robes presented to
the monk, refuge taken in the Buddha, the dhamma, and the sangha, the
five basic precepts of Buddhism reaffirmed by the participants, and religious

93

merit made. But the purpose of the ceremony and the motivations of the participants were not simply to make merit or give money to the temple. People conducted the ritual to raise funds for a new development program in the village—the Dhamma Agricultural Project for Self-Reliance. Initiated by the Foundation for Education and Development of Rural Areas (FEDRA), a nongovernmental organization founded by a senior monk, Phra Phuttapoj, better known as Luang Pu, or "Revered Grandfather," the project proposed to integrate small-scale approaches to economic change with Northern Thai religious and cultural practices. It drew on the moral authority of Buddhism, especially as embodied by Phuttapoj (Plate 18). Following the monk's philosophy, the program stressed both economic and spiritual development (Thepkavi n.d.).

Luang Pu Phuttapoj was one of the first independent "development monks" (*phra nak phatthana*) in Thailand, monks who initiated rural development projects aimed at alleviating the suffering they believed the government's capitalist-oriented development policies produced.[3] The cases of development monks such as Luang Pu Phuttapoj illustrate how elements of the Thai sangha responded to the state as it pushed its version of development, and how they established their own definitions of development. They show how individual monks, often in cooperation and dialogue with each other and with other social activists, experimented with the cultural meanings and religious definitions underlying development.

The precedents of development monks redefining the terms and goals of "development" in the 1970s and 1980s set the stage for environmental monks such as Phrakhru Pitak Nanthakhun not only to challenge state-led development, but also its effects on both the environment and the people whose lives depend on it. They laid the foundation for environmental monks to create and promote alternative forms of knowledge of development and the relationship of Buddhism to them. Environmental monks built on the cultural experiments of development monks who had gone before them. The key is a cultural history, as defined by Fox, that traces

> how human actors originate ideas about their society out of cultural meanings already constituted, and then how they experiment with these ideas. Such experiments may contest the present and may conceive a revolutionized future, or they may fail to do so and confirm the present. That is, once made into public answers, a set of cultural meanings compels but also enables future cultural experimentation. It stipulates the form that new utopian experiments, attacking

present conditions—or that ideologies, defending them—will take.
(Fox 1991, 108)

The interactions of development monks with the state, rural people, and NGOs involved a series of negotiations and cultural experiments upon which environmental monks built.

Three main aspects of the work of development monks established the precedent of monks engaging in social issues independently of government oversight that enabled the emergence of environmental monks a decade later. First, development monks see it as their responsibility as monks to take on community development projects in order to relieve the suffering they blame on state-led policies. The spiritual values on which development monks ground their projects set their movement apart from government programs. These monks see the primary goal of their work as promoting Buddhism, aiming to counter the root evils of greed, ignorance, and anger fostered through materialism.

Second, they engage in concrete, grassroots projects. Development monks work closely with villagers to deal with specific needs or problems in the villages. In many cases, their manual labor on specific projects, such as digging wells or planting trees, rather than their positions as monks gained the initial respect and cooperation of the villagers. The Buddhist aspects of the projects often were introduced afterward.[4] The integration of both aspects can be summed up in the goal of most development monks to promote spiritual and material growth simultaneously, with the latter defined through the former.

Third, development monks use familiar rituals to integrate their spiritual and economic goals. They recognize the power of ritual for conveying religious values and conferring them on mundane projects. Rituals engender the commitment of participants to the projects, as they publicly display their acceptance of the underlying values and goals the rituals embody (Rappaport 1979). Development monks adapt rituals in minor ways, such as using the pha pa ritual to raise funds for projects as well as providing the monks with basic necessities. Their use of rituals for social action established a precedent for environmental monks to adapt rituals as the symbolic basis of their movement. Throughout all their work development monks continuously reaffirm their commitment to promoting and maintaining the religion for the good of the people.

The use of rituals as a means of changing people's attitudes and behavior, and engaging them fully in social change projects, did not arise in isolation from the mind of a single person. In Thailand, the pressures of state-led development that emphasized production, gross national product (GNP), and gross domestic product (GDP) over quality of life created inequalities and suffering, despite the surface-level successes of the economic boom in the mid- to late twentieth century. The situation demanded creative responses that could reach beneath the surface. The rise of development monks was one such response, which emerged from deep-seated values and reframed them in ways that people could grasp and use to deal with contemporary problems. In the process, development monks laid the groundwork for monks to use Buddhist teachings and rituals to continue to respond as the consequences of rapid economic development spread to affect both the human and natural environment.

Buddhist Roots of Modernization in Thailand

The challenge of a critical anthropology remains understanding how development and politics are woven together in particular localities, differently deployed, and given form and substance through cultural practices. . . . Far from arriving fully formed, an artifact dispatched by the distant West, the disputed formations of development, in all their malleable guises, are forged through the crucible of cultural politics, reworked through livelihood struggles. (Moore 1999, 675)

Donald Moore points out the importance of examining development in its historical and geographic contexts. For development in Thailand based on Buddhist principles, that means going back to the beginnings of the religion itself, to consider the economic and political circumstances of its origins. More relevant here is the history of Siam (renamed Thailand in 1939) in the colonial world of Southeast Asia, and how the Siamese used Buddhism to approach, understand, and adapt concepts of modernity and development.

Buddhism began in what is now India more than 2,500 years ago during a time of dramatic social and environmental change. Population size and density grew simultaneously with the expansion of agriculture. Increased trade and agricultural surplus supported the rise of urban centers from which monarchs centralized political power. The republics that had dominated political systems in the area faded under the superior strength of larger monarchies and their armies. Trevor Ling (1973) argues that it was within this urbanization—and the resulting sense of "anomie" it created among people who could not adjust fast enough—that the Buddha (and other spiritual mendicants) sought alternatives and a means to deal with suffering.

The degree of environmental and social upheaval at the time did not equal what the world later went through due to colonization, the growth of global trade and capitalism, industrialization, globalization, and the resulting environmental changes since the nineteenth century. Modernization and the creation of nation-states initiated a discourse of political-economic development that dominated the process of change in many countries. In Siam, the process led to a dynamic—even dialectic—relationship between the Thai sangha and the evolving state.

Following Keyes (1989a), I see the dramatic changes that Siam underwent in the nineteenth century, especially the Buddhist reform movement instigated by Prince Mongkut in the 1830s, as key to understanding the kingdom's modernization process. Keyes describes the "radical rethinking of the Buddhist theory of action which took place in the nineteenth century" (Keyes 1989a, 122) that set the stage for reassessing the basis of political power, forming a modern Thai state, establishing a mass education system, and promoting a capitalist concept of development that remains dominant today. These processes eventually enabled the rise of several activist forms of Buddhism, including environmental monks, in the late twentieth century that both supported and challenged the government's development agenda and its relationship with Buddhism.

The process had its roots in the late eighteenth century with the fall of the Siamese kingdom, Ayutthaya, to the Burmese and shortly thereafter the establishment of the Chakri dynasty—still in place today—in Bangkok.[5] Within the next few decades, several distinct but interrelated currents of change intersected. First, the Chakri king, Rama I (r. 1782–1809), began what David Wyatt refers to as a radical rethinking of the legacies of Ayutthaya and Buddhist discipline in order to structure the direction of the kingdom. "At work here, of course, was an active, creative intelligence . . . not merely content to transmit the past but wanting to shape the past and in so doing to shape the future" (Wyatt 1984, 147). At the same time, the kingdom came into increased contact with the West. Missionaries, traders, and representatives of colonial governments exposed the Siamese elite to new ways of thinking about the world—both religious and scientific. The resulting period of questioning and exploration under Mongkut sparked a religious reformation that affected not only the structure and practice of Siamese Buddhism, but influenced power relations and the structure of the emerging Thai state, and moved Siam into the modern era.

The basis of Siamese society leading into this era of rethinking the world was Buddhist cosmology. According to Craig Reynolds (1976, 204), "Buddhist cosmography stood at the core of Siamese Buddhist belief for centuries, serving as an all-embracing statement of the world as seen through Siamese Buddhist eyes, as well as a primary instrument for educating subjects of the Siamese kings in Buddhist values." Epitomizing the connections between Siamese society and Buddhist cosmography was the *Traiphum Phra Ruang* (*The Three Worlds According to King Ruang*; translated by Reynolds and Reynolds 1982), a royal Buddhist treatise apparently dating to the thirteenth century that represented the religious universe of the Siamese people.[6] The *Traiphum* ranked all beings in a cosmological hierarchy of ritually acquired merit and *karma* (Sanskrit; *kam*, Thai) accumulated from moral actions in previous lives. All Siamese subjects were located within this socioreligious hierarchy with the monarch at its pinnacle because of both his positive merit (*bun*) and virtue (*barami*). The *Traiphum* explained natural phenomena, categorizing all sentient beings according to their merit accumulation and providing order to the moral and physical universe. The text explained "planetary motion and the recurrence of the seasons, and . . . such subjects as geography, biology, and meteorology" (C. Reynolds 1976, 209).[7]

At the same time, multiple traditions of Buddhism existed throughout Siam and its tributaries. The various principalities that made up the region had distinct cultures, languages, histories, and religious customs; even individual temples often followed the specific disciplinary rules and rituals of their abbots' lineages (Kamala 1997, 3–5, 23–40). Regional leaders were legitimized and supported through their subjects' beliefs in their merit and virtue. People across the kingdom made merit through offerings to the sangha and other ritual practices, holding their place within the cosmological hierarchy.

This cosmological order of the world was challenged as the Siamese elite was introduced to new systems of thought, especially Western science and geography (Thongchai 1994). Prince Mongkut, the crown prince under the reign of Rama III (r. 1824–1851), led a movement to rethink the basis of the Siamese worldview, religiously and scientifically. Ordained as a monk for twenty-seven years before ascending to the monarchy in 1851, Mongkut was well versed in various forms of Theravada Buddhism, including Mon, Burmese, and Sinhalese. He engaged in dialogues with Christian missionaries, leading him to examine Buddhism as a universal religion comparable with other world religions (Keyes 1989a, 124). Skeptical of religious practice centered on ritualized merit-making and myths based in Buddhist cosmology, and their lack of scriptural basis, Mongkut instituted religious reform in the 1830s and 1840s (Keyes 1989a, 125). Critical of the laxness of the Siamese sangha, he established the Thammayut sect, emphasizing Pali studies and a stricter interpretation of the *Vinaya,* the discipline of the sangha. Similar to the modernization of other aspects of Thai society that Mongkut later initiated as king—introducing modern scientific concepts, economic practices, and education—his reform of the religion aimed to eliminate practices he felt were too ritualistic, metaphysical, or overly influenced by local or regional culture.[8] Mongkut was fascinated by Western science, yet maintained a distinctly Siamese and Buddhist orientation toward the world. Jackson described the significance of his interests:

> Mongkut attempted to develop an interpretation of Buddhism consistent with Western science and learning and this attempt marked the beginning of a fundamental epistemological shift in doctrinal Thai Buddhism. The theoretical shift, which continues to have significant religious implications today, involved the rejection of the layered or hierarchical notion of truth which underlay traditional Buddhist teachings and its replacement with the notion of a single, universal, and all-encompassing truth. (Jackson 1989, 44)

As king, Mongkut linked the sangha hierarchy—now headed by the Thammayut sect—with the absolute monarchy based in Bangkok, using it to legitimize the central government and weaken the influence of regional forms of religion and the power of regional political leaders. Ultimately, this shift in power enabled the central Bangkok government to use the sangha to pull peripheral regions under its control in the early twentieth century (Kamala 1997; J. Taylor 1993a). The Thammayut sangha received royal patronage and, despite its smaller numbers, became politically dominant in the religious hierarchy.

Two key events occurred during Mongkut's reign that contributed to the rethinking of Buddhism and power relations within the kingdom. First, Siam formally opened its borders for trade with Europe through the Bowring Treaty with Great Britain in 1855. Not only did this treaty mark a change in Siam's internal economic system, centering trade and power in Bangkok and beginning to emphasize a monetary measurement of economic progress, it integrated the kingdom into the colonial economic system of Southeast Asia and "ultimately led to a radical restructuring of the Thai state" (Jackson 1989, 25).

Second, just before the end of Mongkut's rule, his minister of foreign affairs and a high-ranking nobleman, Chaophraya Thiphakorawong, published *Kitchanukit* ("A Book Explaining Various Things") in 1867. In the book, Thiphakorawong defended Buddhism to the West, but acknowledged that it did not adequately explain the natural world (C. Reynolds 1976, 216). The book strengthened Mongkut's rationalization of the religion, distinguishing the religious from the physical world, and allowed for a more active interpretation of religious practice.

Yet Mongkut's process of "rationalizing" Buddhism was as much an effort to preserve Siamese identity in the face of strong Western influences as it was an acknowledgment of new ways of thinking about the world (Johnson 1997, 248). Even while reforming the Buddhist sangha, Mongkut reintroduced various royal Brahmanic rituals into the court. Mongkut, followed by his son Chulalongkorn (Rama V, r. 1868–1910), restructured ancient rites to bolster the Siamese in the face of new knowledge coming from the West. Mongkut did not merely acquiesce to Western views of the world, but integrated them with reinterpretations of Siamese religious practice to form a uniquely Siamese response to modernization. This pattern of creative reinterpretation of religious rites reemerges frequently through the history of the interactions between Buddhism and social change in Thailand, a process we witness again in the late twentieth and early twenty-first centuries with the development and environmental monks.

King Chulalongkorn formalized the connections between the Buddhist reformation, the liberalization of Siam's economy and greater international involvement, and the bureaucratization of the kingdom as he centralized the state. The legitimizing role the sangha played toward the state was strengthened as Bangkok expanded its control to peripheral regions. Chulalongkorn restricted the autonomy of the outlying principalities, established Bangkok Thai as the kingdom's official language (versus regional dialects), expanded and standardized Siamese education, and used the Thammayut sect (versus various other sects, especially the numerically dominant Mahanikai) to define Siamese religion and identity. Kamala points out the importance of religious unity to the process of state building:

> In creating a modern Thai state the Bangkok authorities needed not only a common language but a common religion. The Siamese rulers' preoccupation with order, harmony, national unity, and modernization led them to believe that monks as well as laypeople—regardless of their ethnic identities—should have a common religious outlook.

They assumed that a rationalized form of Buddhism would provide the most unity and harmony. (Kamala 1997, 8)

Chulalongkorn appointed the monk, Prince Wachirayan, another of Mongkut's sons, as head of the Thammayut Order, from which position he could institute many of the reforms initiated by Mongkut (Keyes 1989a, 126), including educational reform across the kingdom (Tambiah 1976, 219–25; J. Taylor 1993a, 62–65). This process centralized the sangha hierarchy and bound it more closely with the government. Wachirayan's motivation emphasized strengthening the sangha more than centralizing Bangkok's control. As Tambiah (1976, 224) notes, "Wachirayan believed that the health of Buddhism required a nationally administered sangha and that the ecclesiastical machinery had to lean on the arm of the polity in order to be effective."

Under first Mongkut, then Chulalongkorn and Wachirayan, the Buddhist reformation "fundamentally altered" the religious culture of the kingdom (Keyes 1989a, 127) and the expectations of the sangha. Wachirayan in particular emphasized new conceptions of the world, influenced by the integration of science and reformed Buddhism, through changes in both clerical and secular education. Keyes describes the process as revolutionary, setting the stage for the social activism of the sangha in the late twentieth century:

> While aspects of cosmological Buddhism can still be found in contemporary Thailand, the fact remains that the religious culture of the country was fundamentally altered by the Buddhist reformation, especially as the premises of the new world-view were made basic to both clerical and secular education. Even those in rural areas who continue to participate in traditional rituals have learned through attendance at schools, listening to the sermons of modernist monks, and dealing with the representatives of the organizations—both governmental and private—seeking to mobilize them for "development" to see themselves as having some freedom from the constraints inherited from previous karma to redefine their place in the world through their own actions. (Keyes 1989a, 127)

During the modernization period, Siam established the threefold concept of religion, monarchy, and nation, formalizing the connection between religion and state even further (F. Reynolds 1977, 1994). Three Sangha Acts enacted in 1902, 1941, and 1962 brought the sangha legally under the government's control (Ishii 1986, 51, 68–70,102, 115; Jackson 1989, 64–82; Tambiah 1976, 230–62, 1978, 118–23). Each of these acts created a state-imposed organizational structure for the sangha that paralleled the contemporary forms of government: in 1902, Siam was still a monarchy and the hierarchical, centralized sangha was headed by a Supreme Patriarch; in 1941, a decentralized sangha structure was established that paralleled the democratic, constitutional monarchy in place at the time; and in 1962, a top-down structure was reintroduced to match the autocratic government of Field Marshall Sarit Thanarat. Underlying the acts, especially that of 1962, was an effort to garner support not only for the current government, but to legitimize its development policies as well. The 1962 act in particular aimed to use the sangha to foster Sarit's development agenda (Ishii 1986, 115).

Economic Intensification

After coming to power through two coups d'état in 1957 and 1958, Sarit aggressively pushed Thailand into an intensive development policy. Based on a Western, capitalist model, Sarit promoted agricultural intensification and expansion toward an export-oriented and industrial economy. He introduced the five-year National Economic and Social Development Plans that laid out the goals for each period. He encouraged a shift toward cash cropping, bringing more forest land under cultivation, thus "civilizing" the wild forest (Stott 1991) and making it useful for humans. He also drew on traditional cultural values to promote his development agenda. Yoneo Ishii notes,

> Sarit thought that national integration must be strengthened to realise national development. To attain this goal he planned to start with fostering the people's sentiment for national integration through the enhancement of traditional values as represented by the monarchy and Buddhism. (Ishii 1968, 869)

Using the concept of a single, absolute truth and a centralized sangha organization, Sarit incorporated Buddhism into his development campaign through community development and missionary programs involving monks (Tambiah 1976, 434–71; Somboon 1977, 40–41). These programs included Thammathut, which sent monks to missionize in politically sensitive and economically poor border provinces; Thammacharik, through which monks worked with the Department of Public Welfare among minority mountain peoples to convert them from animism and develop them (generally through building infrastructure, bringing them into the national economic system, and assimilating them into Thai culture); and community development programs sponsored by the two national Buddhist universities. Their aim was to strengthen the sense of national identity of peripheral peoples through Buddhism. These programs were—and are still today—supported and overseen by the government rather than the sangha (see Somboon 1977, 1982). Keyes (1989a, 133–34) points out that these programs began an intense politicization of the sangha and an acceptance of the use of Buddhism to provide "the moral rationale for political objectives." Not only did these programs train the monks who participated in them in concepts and methods of community development, national unity, and social action, but the rural people with whom they worked were also exposed to these ideas, along with the notion of monks engaging in such nontraditional activities. One of the unintentional outcomes of Sarit's and his successor Thanom Kittikachorn's inclusion of the monks in their development programs was to plant ideas and techniques of sociopolitical engagement within the wider sangha. This process facilitated the rise of factions within the sangha who adapted these methods to challenge the government's development agenda and what they perceived as its negative effects on the Thai people's quality of life.

Quality of Life and the Problems of Development

> Western consumerism is the dominant ethic in the world today. You cannot walk down the streets of Bangkok, for example, without being bombarded by billboards touting the benefits of various soft drinks. Streets here are jammed with expensive, foreign cars that provide the owners with prestige and the city with pollution. Young people define their identities through perfumes, jeans, and jewelry. The primary measure of someone's life is the amount of money in his or her checkbook. These are all liturgies in the religion of consumerism. (Sulak 2000b, 178)

Sulak Sivaraksa, an outspoken, Buddhist social critic, summed up the criticism of state-led development. Since Sarit's push to advance the nation economically, subsequent governments have continued policies of industrial growth, agricultural export, and development of big business. Social, economic, and environmental problems have grown as well. Thailand's

economic growth continued into the 1980s, largely bolstered by the presence of the U.S. military and American concern to prevent the spread of
communism. In the 1980s, Japan took the lead as the economic miracle of
Asia, encouraging European economic powers to take Asia seriously. Thailand soon followed suit. Foreign investment poured into the country and
domestic investment grew. Internally, manufacturing overtook agriculture
as Thailand's primary source of export goods. Cities, especially Bangkok,
bulged with rural migrants looking to take part in the boom (Pasuk and
Baker 1998, 2–5). Thailand burst onto the global economic stage in the
mid-1980s as one of the "flying tigers." From 1985 until the economic crisis
of 1997, "Thailand was the world's fastest-growing economy," according to
economist Pasuk Phongpaichit and historian Chris Baker (1998, 1).

The economic crash in 1997 was not the first indication that there were
problems with Thailand's rapid growth. For more than four decades, the
gaps between rich and poor, urban elite and rural peasant expanded. Materialism and consumerism became the markers of success, even when people
could not afford the refrigerators, trucks, or televisions they desired. Debt
rose, and people saved less. Dr. Chalongphob Sussangkarn, president of the
Thai Development Research Institute, noted in 1996 that "household sav-
ings declined from 21.1 per cent of GNP in 1986, to 9.8 per cent in 1992,
and to 7 per cent in 1995. Consumption expenditure in 1995 rose 15 per
cent from the year earlier" (Laird 2000, 265). Stress-related illnesses were on
the increase, environmental destruction was rampant, and pollution levels
soared. Large-scale development projects such as dams destroyed forest, agricultural land, water quality, and people's ways of life.

In its Seventh Plan (1992–96) the government acknowledged the problems when the National Economic and Social Development Board (NESDB)
pointed to the deterioration of social cohesion, uncontrolled rural-to-urban
migration, the breakdown of family structure, the rise of new diseases such
as HIV/AIDS, cancer, and mental illness, and declining morality and social
values (Laird 2000:265). These concerns were reiterated just before the crash
in the summary of the Eighth Plan (1997–2001):

> [F]iercer competition for income and wealth in Thailand has brought
> with it greater materialism. This in turn has had a negative impact
> on people's behaviour, bringing about a lack of discipline, declining
> ethical and moral standards, and the rise of practices which centre
> around self-interest and the exploitation of others. These unfavoura-
> ble trends are threatening the traditional Thai values and ways of life,

and they have contributed to the collapse of families, communities, and local cultures. In addition, the social stresses that accompany economic prosperity have started to alter the patterns of sickness and mortality, bringing the diseases of modern life, such as cancer, heart disease, and high-blood pressure. (Laird 2000, 13–15)

A small number of intellectuals, scholars, and Buddhist monks identified the growing problems for people's quality of life as early as the 1960s. These thinkers turned to Buddhism for potential solutions to Thailand's growing social problems. A few innovative monks had begun the process of rein- terpreting Buddhism's place in society much earlier: Buddhadasa Bhikkhu founded his meditation center, Suan Mokh, outside of the sangha hierar- chy and government control in 1932, and his philosophy continues to guide socially engaged Buddhists in Thailand today. Phra Kruba Sriwichai mobi- lized Northern Thais in 1935 to work together to build a road up the sacred mountain of Doi Suthep in Chiang Mai so that pilgrims could reach it more easily. They were exceptional for their time, yet provided precedents on which Buddhist activists built in the 1960s. In that decade, Sulak Sivaraksa founded the influential journal, *Social Science Review,* in which he published numer- ous articles criticizing the direction of government development and calling for greater consideration of Buddhist principles in planning and implemen- tation. Dr. Prawase Wasi led a group of medical personnel who provided monks with health care information and offered support and knowledge for other kinds of rural development grounded in Buddhism. Economist Dr. Puey Ungphakorn argued that development plans must consider the qual- ity of life and social justice, foreseeing the problems within growth-oriented schemes (Demaine 1986, 99; Delcore 2000, 72). Most significantly, Phra P. A. Payutto (known at the time as Phra Rajavaramuni) began speaking and writing on the relationship between Buddhism and social change. The work and ideas of these thinkers led to the formation of a small number of non- governmental organizations focused on rural development issues.

A handful of monks initiated rural development projects during the 1960s as well. They worked independently, motivated by the problems they witnessed in the villages with which they were familiar. In Chiang Mai, Luang Pu Phuttapoj opened a school for rural boys called Metta Suksa Foun- dation. The school opened its doors in 1959 at Wat Chedi Luang, in the heart of Chiang Mai city, teaching practical skills, elementary education, and Buddhist morals. All the boys attending received scholarships; most would not have been educated beyond the government's mandatory fourth grade otherwise. Phuttapoj's expectation was that they would bring their new knowledge and morality back to the villages when they graduated, and help to improve the lives of their families and neighbors.

In 1962, Phrakhru Sakorn Sangvorakit was placed by sangha authorities in a village temple in Samutsongkram Province that did not have a monk. The economic difficulties the villagers faced were immediately apparent to him, but the villagers did not readily trust him as a social leader. He came from outside, and they had seen other monks come and go without impacting their lives. Phrakhru Sakorn decided to act first, and work on the moral issues he saw later. He began digging a well and building small canals to deal with the village's drinking water problem. He started constructing a new school building, working side by side with a few villagers. Gradually, more villagers realized his commitment to their well-being and slowly joined. He studied alternatives to supplement their meager income from rice production, and learned how to grow coconut trees to produce sugar. A couple of brave farmers took a chance on following his example. As they succeeded in generating a better livelihood, over time other villagers requested his help for growing coconuts and marketing their sugar (Seri 1988, 44–53). The young abbot described his teaching-through-example approach:

> Before I make a suggestion to the villagers, I have to know it very well; I had to learn everything by myself. I finished only elementary school and finished Dhamma course.
>
> I knew nothing about agriculture. But when I became their leader, I had to learn. My principle is: if I want the villagers to do something, I have to show them and not just tell them. I studied coconut trees starting from the soil, the race, the way to grow, the product from coconut to marketing. I read articles and books about agriculture. I contacted traders. I made experiments. I learnt from the experts and started to do what they told me and found out better ways. I learnt to build houses by observing and doing. (Seri 1988, 45)

Both of these monks, as well as others who ventured into development work on their own early in the movement, encountered problems with their approaches. Phuttapoj eventually realized that only a small number of the graduates of the Metta Suksa Foundation actually returned to their home villages. Phrakhru Sakorn watched the villagers' incomes improve through the sale of coconut sugar, and then their material desires and expectations follow suit. Both monks adapted their approaches in the 1970s as a Buddhist development movement took shape and grew.

Both monks might have participated in government-sponsored programs if they had been aware of them. Even with the degree of criticism independent development monks generally hold of state-led development schemes, the division between the monks involved in government programs and those who work independently is not clear cut. Many, such as Phrakhru Pitak Nanthakhun, do both, drawing knowledge and lessons from programs such as Thammathut and Thammacharik, or taking community development courses at the Buddhist universities, which they then apply to their own projects. Nevertheless, the development monk movement arose because of discontent and concern over the negative impacts of state-led development policies that became apparent in the 1960s.

Democratic Mobilization

Dissatisfaction with the direction of the nation's economic development, and the politics behind it, was strong across the country by the early 1970s. Rural populations were frustrated with the drive to intensify agricultural production, their growing dependence on middlemen to market cash crops, and the increasing number of large agribusinesses taking their land. They initially felt neglected as the government focused on industrial and urban growth, then overwhelmed with bureaucratic policies when Bangkok turned its attention to the rural areas. The emergent urban middle class was also dissatisfied. While education levels rose, no corresponding growth in government sector jobs occurred. More and more young, affluent graduates joined the private sector, where they were subject to economic fluctuations. Insurgency and labor movements grew in the provinces, and student and worker protests began in Bangkok (Wyatt 1984, 295–97).

Frustration with economic inequalities and uncertainties, and political corruption culminated in student-led protests that overthrew the military government on October 14, 1973. This protest began a turbulent, three-year experiment with civilian-run democracy, popular mobilization, and social change. Students poured into the countryside to help poor farmers. NGOs proliferated in this process, working with rural people to find alternative forms of development to the capitalist, production- and export-oriented policies of the government. Farmers themselves formed a political party, the Farmers Federation of Thailand, to promote issues of rural social and economic justice that gained popularity nationwide, and drew strong criticism and violent opposition from the right (Bowie 1991, 11–13). This period of social awareness, freedom of speech, social change, and political experimentation came to a violent end on October 6, 1976 when right-wing paramilitary forces attacked students at Thammasat University in Bangkok, followed by a military coup a few hours later (Bowie 1991, 4–5, 1997, 24–33).

During this time of heightened social awareness—of class inequalities, poverty, political corruption, land alienation—almost all segments of Thai society mobilized in one form or another. Even factions of the Thai sangha, which on the surface maintained an aloofness from society and politics, engaged in political and social movements. At the extremes were a group of young monks, predominantly from the two Buddhist Universities in Bangkok, who felt isolated in their temples and began to study Marxism and express solidarity with the poor.[9] Opposed to them, a right-wing faction of the sangha emerged that criticized the leftist monks, activist students, farmers, and workers alike, labeling them subversives and communists. The leader of this faction, a controversial and outspoken monk named Kittiwut-tho Bhikkhu, took the opposition a step farther in June 1976 when he made a speech entitled "Killing Communists is Not Demeritorious," a position he ardently defended as both Buddhist and good for the nation (Somboon 1982, 132–57; Seri 1988, 8). Both factions were most visible between 1973 and 1976. The leftist group dispersed after the events of October 6, 1976, and many fled to the jungle with thousands of student activists to join the Communist Party (Seri 1988, 7–8).

While these two groups were the most obvious and outspoken during the mid-1970s, they were the extremes. The development monk movement quietly grew during this time to include many more rural monks. The exact number is difficult to determine, as there is no official category in the sangha for "development monk."[10] Rather, the term is used by monks and their followers to identify their work. Individual monks initiated village-based projects aimed at alleviating the suffering they saw as caused by the materialistic direction of state-led development. Unlike the leftist or rightist monks, development monks sought a middle path toward both spiritual and economic development, and tried to avoid political implications.

Some development monks, such as Achan Banyat Anuttaro of Nakhorn Rajasima Province, were approached by student activists hoping to help rural farmers and to learn from the monks. Achan Banyat was initially labeled a "communist monk" by villagers and local police due to his work with the students. "They came to this conclusion," he stated, "because at that time groups of students came to help me, digging the pond and working in the temple and the village. This was before 1976, the most confusing period of democracy in our country" (Seri 1988, 70). Achan Banyat gradually won over both villagers and police, convincing them of his and the students' genuine motives to help the people.

As with the growing number of NGOs and students working in the countryside, development monks sought alternatives to the forms of development pushed by the government. Somboon Suksamran, a sociologist who studied "political" monks, captured the movement well:

> The "development monks" . . . are extraordinary in that their involvement is independent of the control and directives of the government and the *Sangha* authorities. It is a response to the rapid socio-political changes of the 1970s. Their concepts, strategies and approaches to development take into account the importance of improving the quality of life, strengthening self-reliance and self-respect, and preserving the individual community's culture. They also seek to assure the survival of the *Sangha* as a whole.
>
> The "development monks" are not only responding to the development needs of villages not yet reached by the government's efforts but are also initiating an alternative mode of development. The monks themselves are important agents of change. (Somboon 1988, 26–27)

Unlike the monks trained through the Buddhist universities or working on government programs, these monks initiated projects on their own or after contact with other activist monks or occasionally NGOs. They maintained that participating in government-sponsored programs could limit their control over the planning and implementation of development projects and their ability to respond to villagers' perceived needs.[11] More importantly, the ultimate goals of the government and the independent development monks differed: the government generally included the sangha in development projects because of the village leadership of the monks and the legitimacy they brought to the activities; the independent development monks saw their social action work as a crucial element of their being monks and Buddhists. They worked to solve the social problems and human suffering that result from industrialization and monetary-based economic development as a means of teaching Buddhist principles and practice.

Somboon (1977) criticized the government's blatant use of the sangha to promote its policies of national integration and the containment of communism through community development programs. The top-down nature of government development and its use of local abbots to promote a political agenda without consideration of religious principles or villager-identified needs could be damaging to both the government's agenda and the reputation of the sangha. He argued that

> if these monks are forced into exerting too much pressure on the villagers to get them to participate in community development activities which the latter do not perceive to be useful or traditionally meritorious, then these monks will become associated in the eyes of the villagers with the government and with politics. Such an association will undermine the position and influence of the abbots, as well as perhaps the position of religion in Thai rural society. (Somboon 1977, 119)

In contrast, Somboon described the development monks: "One of the most innovative movements in the last few years has involved monks who voluntarily organized themselves for development tasks in villages throughout the country. Their commitment to development is a commitment to liberate the rural population from oppression, exploitation, poverty and ignorance" (Somboon 1988, 26). Particularly striking is their independence from control by either the government or the sangha administration, combined with their creative application of Buddhist teachings in a manner accessible and meaningful to the villagers with whom they work.

Development in The Name of The Buddha

Farmers lined their water buffalos up along the temple wall, each animal decorated with colorful flower leis and ribbons. They waited anxiously for Luang Pu Phuttapoj and a committee of judges to assess each buffalo and select the best one. The "beautiful buffalo" contest took place at a seminar at Wat Pa Dharabhirom, Phuttapoj's temple and home to FEDRA, the NGO the monk founded in 1974 (Plate 19). As part of FEDRA's agricultural development program, seminars brought farmers from different villages together to discuss their projects and new approaches to farming that encouraged self-sufficiency and alternatives to capitalist-oriented agriculture.

At this particular seminar, farmers who had received water buffalos from FEDRA brought the animals back for the contest. The animals were part of the "buffalo banks" set up by FEDRA in various villages: Farmers received buffalos that had been donated to Phuttapoj by wealthy patrons so that they would not have to go into debt at plowing time by renting someone else's buffalo. Buffalos are central to rice farming across Southeast Asia, used to plow the paddy fields. In the latter half of the twentieth century, they had begun to be replaced by "iron buffalos," gas-powered plows. FEDRA encouraged farmers to use buffalos instead, arguing that they do not pollute or need replacement parts, and can be eaten when they fail. Farmers who received buffalos from FEDRA agreed to treat the animals well, not to harm, sell, or kill them. They returned the first offspring to FEDRA to be given to another farmer, but could keep others. Farmers saw caring for the buffalos as a form of making religious merit and showing respect for Phuttapoj. As with all of FEDRA's programs, the buffalo banks served a dual purpose: they helped alleviate poverty through enabling farmers to live self-sufficiently and without debt; they also taught the core Buddhist values on which Phuttapoj based his development work.

Phuttapoj established his first buffalo bank in the mid-1970s, shortly after founding FEDRA. At the same time, he initiated rice banks, to which farmers donate a portion of their harvest in exchange for the right to borrow rice when they run out before the next harvest. Without village rice banks, farmers would have to buy rice at inflated prices, often contributing to further debt. To avoid debt for other needs, FEDRA helped set up revolving funds and credit unions from which villagers could borrow with low interest rates. The villagers learned to manage the funds themselves as well, with the goal of breaking their dependence on outside organizations. In FEDRA's early years, Phuttapoj hired a group of women to create Mettanari, a women's development organization. He realized that he assisted only boys through the Metta Suksa Foundation, yet women contribute significantly to the quality of village life. Mettanari taught rural women skills such as weaving, sewing, and embroidery to supplement their agricultural incomes.

In these projects and others, Phuttapoj's work is typical of that of other development monks. The monks drawn to this work each found their own way into it, feeling responsibility as monks and community leaders to respond to the suffering they witnessed among villagers.[12] This suffering, they believe, is based in the promotion of the spiritual evils of greed, ignorance, and anger that underlie capitalist development schemes. The moral fiber of rural society is torn, and people are less concerned with their spiritual well-being than with acquiring money and material goods. Phuttapoj's philosophy of integrating spiritual and economic development epitomizes the approach taken by all development monks.

Phuttapoj believed that people could not (or would not) concentrate on Buddhist practice, especially meditation, if they were concerned about how they would get their next meal or medicine for a sick child. The starting point was meeting basic needs and helping people be able to help themselves. Then he incorporated Buddhist lessons.

Luang Pho Nan (Phrakhru Phiphitprachanat) of Surin Province reversed this approach. When he first went to live at Wat Samakkhi, he encountered a village rife with debt. People responded through gambling and drinking. He felt he owed the villagers his life:

> It came to my mind that I should not be indifferent to the problems of the villagers. I had lodging and food. I had no burden, no family, no wife, no children. I only had to practice Dhamma and perform religious ceremonies. I owed the villagers everything. They had their family burden, but still provided me with food and shelter. What could I do for them? (Seri 1988, 55)

Luang Pho Nan's first attempt to help the village was to build a road to connect them to the provincial town, about eight kilometers away. From 1965 to 1975, he and his novices, along with a few villagers, worked on the road. At the same time, he helped villagers connect with nearby irrigation canals to deal with the lack of water in the village. His efforts, while successful in their immediate purposes, did not positively affect the villagers' lives. Their debt grew and they continued to drink and gamble (Seri 1988, 55–56). The root of the problem was not poverty. Poverty, he felt, was yet another symptom of the personal state in which the villagers found themselves. They needed moral guidance so that the material changes could do good. He described his approach as follows:

> To help the people means, first, to make the people understand the good and the right according to their view: then gradually take them to the goal we set. Otherwise we will find out that our good will is more an obstacle to development than a promotion. We have to start from where they are. We should not rush to the conclusion from what we see with our eyes. The people drink, smoke, gamble. It is true. But what is the real cause? We have to find out together with them. (Seri 1988, 56)

Luang Pho Nan switched his focus to teaching villagers to meditate, beginning with a group of forty monks and villagers for an intensive, seven-day program in 1975. By the time I visited Wat Samakkhi in 1991, the program had become an annual event every April. People who initially scoffed at his teachings were now proud to host the retreat for hundreds of villagers, having given up their vices of gambling and drinking. Luang Pho Nan only introduced new development projects in 1978, several years after villagers began to meditate regularly with him. At that point he believed the spiritual foundation for development had been laid, enabling the villagers to participate fully and appreciate their accomplishments.

He went on to introduce a variety of projects with which the villagers cooperated in order to help themselves. They set up a cooperative to buy fertilizer in Bangkok at prices significantly lower than in the nearby provincial town. The Thai Interreligious Commission for Development (TICD)[13] helped the village establish a rice bank. Cooperatives were built for basic goods and medicine, all overseen and run by the villagers themselves. At the heart, Luang Pho Nan saw the basis of success in the village was the meditation practice. "We need the spiritual dimension in all development activities. Without spiritual life we cannot start carrying out a real development" (Seri 1988, 57).

Regardless whether development monks began with material activities, as Luang Pu Phuttapoj and Phrakhru Sakorn had, or teaching religious practice, as Luang Pho Nan did, they would all agree with Luang Pho Nan's statement about spiritual development. I heard repeatedly from every activist monk with whom I spoke that spirituality and economics must go together if the people and the nation are to progress in terms of quality of life rather than digress through a worship of materialism. Their early attempts at rural development were experiments, lacking clear precedents or teachers. Phrakhru Sakorn adjusted his approach to working with villagers on growing coconut trees. To build community spirit, he introduced self-help cooperatives based on a village credit union. Following the trend among development NGOs, he introduced integrated agriculture. Farmers grow a mix of crops, together with fish in the paddy fields, free-range chickens, and sometimes other livestock. They grow first to feed their families, reducing their dependence on food markets. If there is a surplus, they sell it so they can buy necessities they cannot produce themselves (Seri 1988, 51–52).

Luang Pu Phuttapoj recognized the limited impact on rural life the Metta Suksa school ultimately had, despite his original intentions. He expanded his work when he founded FEDRA in 1974. Metta Suksa brought boys into the town, but real change needed to occur in the villages directly to make any significant improvements in the lives of rural peoples.

Since the 1970s, the emphasis of these monks remains focused on spiritual development and quality of life, which they define in Buddhist terms, as the primary components of their work. A phrase coined by King Jigme Singye Wangchuck of Bhutan accurately describes the goals of Buddhist-based development in Thailand: in Bhutan, they measure development through "Gross National Happiness" rather than Gross National Product (GNP). The Thai state, on the other hand, and most of Thai society continues to measure success based on GNP.

Spiritual and Economic Development

According to Luang Pu Phuttapoj,[14] the major cause of suffering faced by the rural Thai is poverty. "The farmers are the backbone of the nation," Phuttapoj said, yet they are hungry (Thepkavi n.d., 1). The land of Thailand is fertile, with plenty of water, yet many people have a very low standard of living. They do not have enough food to eat when they are hungry, nor clothes to wear when they are cold. The priority of development should therefore be to fight poverty, to improve the quality of life of the rural people.

Before discussing how this is to be done, Phuttapoj stressed the need to examine the roots of rural poverty. These lie, he believed, in two main areas. First is the lack of educational opportunities for the peasants, which leads to limited knowledge, especially concerning the market system, a fatalistic attitude, and a lack of good leaders. Those who do receive an education tend to leave the village for steady work in the cities, sending only money back to their relatives, not the benefits of their knowledge or experience. The second root of the problem, according to Phuttapoj, is the laziness of the villagers. He described the villagers as unwilling to work hard if it can be avoided, an attitude brought on by the fatalism caused by the lack of education. They accept the bad weather that may destroy their crops, rather than seeking ways to change its effects. They rely more on magic and merit-making through *dana* (generosity) to solve their difficulties than hard work to overcome them (an attitude Phuttapoj shared with Buddhadasa Bhikkhu and P. A. Payutto).

This latter attitude reflects what Phuttapoj saw as the peasants' main approach to religion. The peasants focus on the tangible aspects of religion— the ceremonies and rituals, and the act of giving to the temple to make merit. They go to the monks to ask for blessings to solve their problems and bring happiness, to help them choose a correct lottery number, or to gain wealth. If they are not asking for intervention in this life, they aim to improve their situation for their next life. The emphasis on merit-making at funerals and transferring merit to the dead are two examples of this preoccupation, combined with the concern for accumulating merit before they die. They are, in Phuttapoj's eyes, merely acting on the external forms of Buddhism. The farmers do not internalize the teachings of the Buddha. They behave as good Buddhists when they enter the temple for a pha pa ceremony or on the annual Buddhist holidays, listening to the monk's sermon and taking the five precepts. But once outside, they do not uphold the dhamma in their everyday lives. They drink excessively, and spend what little money they have on material luxuries, such as alcohol, cigarettes, and televisions.

Phuttapoj taught that Buddhism's benefits appear in three realms: this life; one's next life; and in achieving enlightenment.[15] The third is beyond the expectations of most Buddhist lay people. They do not realistically believe that they can obtain liberation in this lifetime, nor is it possible for everyone to commit themselves to this end. Those responsible for earning an income and feeding a family cannot devote themselves to developing the concentration necessary to obtain enlightenment. Instead, most lay people focus on improving their karma to improve this life or ensure a better life in their next rebirth. If people are hungry, most of them place their hope in their next life, not in changing the circumstances in which they currently find themselves.[16] Most Thai monks emphasize the next life, teaching the importance of following the precepts and making merit in order to offset the ills and suffering of this life—itself the result of karma accumulated in previous lives—and be reborn into a better life.

The villagers' emphasis on accumulating merit and their hopes to gain materially from monks' blessings are understandable given their current standard of living. When they are lacking the basic necessities of food, clothes, shelter, and medicine, it is difficult to concentrate on abstract religious principles. Phuttapoj recognized this, and called for an increased awareness among the sangha, especially village monks, toward helping villagers to overcome these obstacles. He realized that religious activities alone will not solve their problems of hunger and insufficient clothes or shelter.

Economic development is not enough, either. It can create desire (*tanhā*, Pali) for material goods, exposing the peasants to lifestyles and values that emphasize material wealth as an indicator of success. Gaining material goods becomes the motivation behind people's behavior, causing them to turn away from traditional values, and often leading them into debt. Money does not bring contentedness or unity among people, Phuttapoj was quick to point out. Many rich people are unhappy; their wealth brings them only a desire to have more.

Luang Pu Phuttapoj emphasized that the technical knowledge of economic development experts must be combined with the moral guidance of monks or others who practice dhamma; for Phuttapoj, spirituality (chitchai) was equated with morality. Only in this way can poverty be handled without causing increased hardships or creating new problems.

Four main principles formed the basis of Phuttapoj's spiritual and economic development ideology: hard work (*khayan*), thriftiness (*prayat*), self-sacrifice (*siasala*), and cooperation (*samakkhi*) (Thepkavi n.d., 5–6, 8; FEDRA 1985, 3). Each of these relates to the later teachings of environmental monks. The first two work toward developing one's occupation, providing qualities that improve one's work and the benefits of its outcome. Hard work helps people to overcome the laziness that emerges out of poverty and hardship. Phuttapoj taught that diligence should come before enjoyment or relaxation; the latter are found in the satisfaction of work well done.

Directly related to diligence is thriftiness, a principle that protects against extravagance and wasteful living. People should save what they earn for the things they really need, rather than buying things that bring luxury or status. In particular, Phuttapoj worried about the tendency of villagers to buy televisions, alcohol, and cigarettes when their children need new clothes or better food. Internalized, this principle works to make the best use of the results of one's hard work, increasing the feelings of contentment.

Self-sacrifice and cooperation go beyond occupation to influence one's relations with others. Self-sacrifice relates to the Buddhist concept of *anatta,* or "no-self," while both principles invoke *metta*, or "loving-kindness." For those who cannot afford to devote all their time and efforts to the quest for enlightenment, trying to be compassionate toward others and escaping selfish aims help relieve suffering. Giving up one's self-interests while cooperating with others enables developmental activities to move in a direction that will benefit society as a whole, not just the individuals involved. These principles remain qualities that individuals should strive to uphold, guiding their interaction with and behavior toward other people.

Phuttapoj argued that these four principles represent the essence of the Buddha's teachings in a way that is relevant to the contemporary world. Crucial for his teachings was not understanding how the principles relate to the canon, but internalizing and practicing them as part of the dhamma. The intentions behind such practice are crucial to the success of one's actions, and how they benefit both the individual actor and society. Phuttapoj emphasized that changing society begins with developing individual practice of dhamma. His concept of spiritual development (*kanphatthana chitchai*) involved instilling a morality based on the dhamma within each person that governs actions in a way relevant to the well-being of the larger society. This principle can guide the direction of economic development and social change in a way that is then appropriate for Thailand.

This view of inner spirituality preceding broader social development within Buddhist social activism is clearly stated by Sulak Sivaraksa when he says that "the inner strength must be cultivated first; then compassion and loving-kindness to others become possible" (1986, 74). The experience of the Sarvodaya Shramadana Movement in Sri Lanka also exhibits the philosophy of development beginning with the individual (see Macy 1985, 1988; Bobilin 1988).[17] This interreligious development movement is founded on Buddhist principles, beginning with the use of the Four Sublime Abodes to develop each individual (Macy 1985, 38–40; 1988, 176–78). The four steps toward development based on the Sublime Abodes as described by Sulak are as follows:

1) *Mettā*: Loving kindness towards oneself and others. We all desire happiness. We should try to be happy. Through the precepts and meditation, a happiness state could be created. The mind will feel amity and harmony with oneself as with others. It renders assistance and benefits without ill-will, without the malice of anger and of competition. Once one is tranquil and happy, this tranquility and happiness could spread to others as well.

2) *Karunā*: Compassion can only be cultivated when one recognizes the suffering of others and wants to bring that suffering to an end. A rich man who does not care for the miserable conditions of the poor lacks this quality. It is difficult for him to develop himself, to be a better man. Those who shut themselves in ivory towers in the midst of an unjust world cannot be called compassionate. . . .

3) *Muditā*: Sympathetic Joy is a condition of the mind which rejoices when others are happy or successful in any number of ways. One feels this without envy, especially when a competitor is getting ahead.

4) *Upekkhā*: Equanimity means the mind is cultivated until it becomes evenly balanced. It becomes neutral. Whether one faces

success or failure, whether one is confronted with prosperity or adversity, for oneself or for others, one is not moved by it. Whatever one cannot do to help others, one is not disturbed about it (having tried one's best). (Sulak 1986, 75–76)

The Four Abodes provide the means for personal awakening, from which state the individual can then move on to awaken—or develop—the community and society.

Having developed oneself toward happiness and tranquility rather than toward worldly success and material progress, then a Buddhist is in a position to develop his community, starting with his family and his village. (Sulak 1986, 76)

Critical to this undertaking is providing people with the tools to help themselves, beginning with a moral grounding in the teachings of the Buddha that will enable them to recognize oppression and exploitation, and help them avoid poverty and overcome ignorance.

As part of this process, Luang Pu Phuttapoj attempted to make people aware of the importance of developing themselves first. For example, he met with a group of fourteen villagers and six development workers on their return from an observation trip to Isan, the northeastern region of Thailand, in May 1987. He questioned each person about what they had seen and learned, and how they would use this experience in their activities when they returned to the villages. While the purpose of the trip was to see how the problems of deforestation and poverty were being dealt with in Isan in comparison with the north, Phuttapoj personalized the experience for each participant. Why had they gone? How did it affect them personally? These were the types of questions he emphasized, although not ignoring the broader issues of how the methods observed might be applied to their own development programs. What he aimed to demonstrate was the importance of each person first understanding and enacting the principles learned on the trip in daily life, then moving on to share them with relatives and neighbors.

He based his teaching that day on the saying, "*khrong ton, khrong ngan, khrong khon.*" Literally translated, the phrase means "to control (or take care of) one's self, to control one's work, to control people."[18] Phuttapoj used the phrase to show the order necessary to enact dhamma in one's life. First, one must learn to control one's self—one's emotions, desires, and behavior. Rational thinking should govern action, not emotions or selfishness. Doing so forms the basis for being in control over one's work, rather than being controlled by it. The principles of hard work and thriftiness, and maintaining the balance between laziness and greed must all be considered. "Khrong ngan" (to control one's work) incorporates the concept of *sandot,* for when one is content with what one has and the work one does, then one is truly in control of one's labors. Finally, it is not until one has achieved control over one's self and work that relations between people can be affected. Control through compassion (karuna) and example rather than through political power demonstrates the value of the dhamma in guiding social relations. All three levels of control are necessary to achieve success in economic and spiritual development.

The interconnection between individual and social development is central in Luang Pu Phuttapoj's philosophy. While personal spiritual development and the cultivation of the dhamma are necessary starting points for social action, true practice of the dhamma involves the responsibility toward others and society. Although Phuttapoj expressed the individualistic orientation of mainstream Thai Theravada Buddhism, he was a strong part of the movement extending the religion outward.[19] These themes contributed to the latter interpretations of the dhamma in support of environmentalism.

This philosophy, combining the more traditional concern for the religious well-being of each individual with the call for social action, is straightforward for someone who has devoted seventy-five years to studying and practicing the dhamma. Phuttapoj's ideas are for the most part too abstract and intangible for the average villager to grasp. For this reason Phuttapoj highlighted the importance of traditional ceremonies. The ceremonies symbolize and make tangible the abstract moral concepts behind the religion. They remind the participants of the fact that they are Buddhists, and provide an opportunity to concentrate and think about the principles of the dhamma. The problems occur when the focus of the rituals emphasizes only the next life or enlightenment, ignoring their relevance for the present. Phuttapoj therefore always used the opportunity of ceremonies to preach his view of the moral responsibility of Buddhists toward society.

Luang Pu Phuttapoj's ideas cannot be made tangible through the ceremonies alone. In true Buddhist fashion, he took the Middle Way, using the ceremonies as reminders of the values and teachings of the Buddha, while at the same time enacting a new interpretation of these teachings. The latter came through his development projects, where his abstract concepts were put into concrete action. An analysis of economic change and the process of religious reinterpretation needs to be made at the level of social practice.[20]

In this way, Phuttapoj laid the foundation for environmental monks to act on their interpretations of the dhamma as they work for both community development and environmental conservation.

Economic Boom

After the crackdown on student activists in October 1976, and the return to power of military, right-wing rulers, the state worked even harder to legitimate itself and reaffirm its power. The leaders emphasized their connections with big business, touting the economic advantages they would bring to the nation. Initially, the country's economic future seemed dim, and it moved toward recession. In 1985, following and fueled by dramatic economic growth in Japan, Thailand entered a decade of rapid growth and social change. Foreign investment surged, but local investment was even stronger. The shift toward industry and export production exploded. According to Pasuk and Baker, "In a very short period the whole shape of the Thai economy altered. In 1980, three-fifths of exports originated from agriculture. By 1995, over four-fifths came from manufacturing. Over a decade the urban population doubled and the average per capita income doubled" (Pasuk and Baker 1998, 4).

The growth was not without consequences. John Laird summed up the problems well:

> Thailand as a whole had experienced an increase in material affluence while at the same time undergoing a decline in major aspects of the quality of life: increasing stress in society, a dangerously widening gap between rich and poor, continuing environmental decline, and a debasement of culture through rapid commercialisation that changed the values and expectations of Thais. (Laird 2000, 209)

While most Thais, especially the growing middle class, were pleased with the boom, others were concerned with its negative effects. Right after the 1976 crackdown, most social activists went underground for a few years. Anyone criticizing the government's approach was labeled a communist; in fact, many students joined the Communist Party of Thailand's insurgency in the jungle because of the lack of alternatives for opposition. A few NGOs, including FEDRA, quietly continued to work in the rural areas. By 1980, the military relaxed its counterinsurgency campaign, and amnesty was granted to many who had fled to the jungle. The insurgency began to wind down.

At the same time, Thai NGOs reemerged, bolstered by support from international agencies that had established themselves in the country to help with the refugees from Indochina. An increasing number of organizations and activists, including development monks, started networking and supporting each other's activities. More small-scale, indigenous organizations arose to deal with local, grassroots issues (Delcore 2000, 73–74).

These NGOs and development monks responded to the economic struggles. High on the list of development NGO activities was the movement for alternative agriculture. By the 1980s, the environmental problems of intensive, export-oriented agriculture were apparent, as was the expanding debt of rural peoples who participated in this approach. Alternative agriculture took many forms, but emphasized self-reliance, growing to eat first, and lessening a dependence on chemical fertilizers, pesticides, and herbicides. It involved integrating many different species that complement each other, such as nitrogen-producing beans with nitrogen-hungry crops. Pigs, chickens, and fish ate insects while producing natural fertilizer. They were fed the leftovers from fruit and vegetable crops—rinds, sheaths, etc.

In conjunction with alternative, or integrated, agriculture, NGOs promoted credit unions and revolving funds, local handicraft production and marketing, and other means of supporting rural life. Critics accused some NGOs of glorifying the past and denying villagers the benefits of "modern" life. While true of some organizations, most emphasized moderation, pointing out the inequalities of access to modern goods in Thailand's current economic condition.

With the economic boom, and its corresponding economic inequalities and social problems, people increasingly turned to Buddhist leaders for guidance. Temples and monks benefited financially from the economic upswing, and the sangha administration continued its support of the government, taking the official position that Buddhism and politics do not mix, considering any criticism of the state as a form of political action. Despite this, a small percentage of the sangha followed the models of monks like Luang Pu Phuttapoj, Luang Pho Nan, and Phrakhru Sakorn and moved into rural development and social justice work. Given the parallel concerns of many development NGOs and these monks, they soon cooperated on several levels.

Unlike most development monks, Luang Pu Phuttapoj had established his own NGO, although he cooperated with others, especially those focused on the issues facing northern Thailand. In the early 1990s, Phrakhru Pitak Nanthakhun set up Klum Hak Mueang Nan (Love Nan Province Association) to coordinate environmental and developmental efforts among NGOs and civil society groups. Other monks sought support from the growing number of NGOs across Thailand, gaining financial backing and knowledge from NGO staffs. Seminars and training sessions run by NGOs such as the Thai Interreligious Commission for Development and the Coordinating Group for Religion and Society contributed to the increase in the number of monks engaged in rural development work.

Monks soon networked among themselves as well. Informally, development monks across Isan began to meet regularly to share experiences and support, and to coordinate some of their development efforts. Luang Pho Nan and a handful of other monks who moved into development work early on formed the core of this group. FEDRA sponsored seminars for Northern Thai monks and established a Monk Outreach Program as part of its agricultural projects. In 1989, after a group of northern development monks visited colleagues and participated in a meeting of the development monks' group in Isan, they formed the Lanna Development Monks Group (*klum song phatthana chumchon lanna*), supported by Luang Pu Phuttapoj.[21] Although the Lanna monks' group did not last, another Northern Thai development monks' association emerged. Based at Wat Suan Dok, home of the Chiang Mai branch of Mahachulalongkorn University (one of Thailand's two Buddhist universities), the group continues to work today. As with the group in Isan, these northern groups coordinated the activities of development monks, provided training and sometimes financial support, and mediated with other organizations, both nongovernment and state. Also in 1989, Sulak Sivaraksa founded the International Network of Engaged Buddhists (INEB) that brought Buddhist activists, ordained and lay, together from across Buddhist Asia (and, to a lesser extent, the West) to promote social justice, human rights, appropriate development, and environmentalism grounded in the application of Buddhist principles in all the countries of its members.

With the expansion of organizations and people, including monks, across Thailand engaging in alternative forms of development from the 1970s through the 1990s, it is clear that the economic boom resulted in the growth of more than GNP or GDP. The question remains as to why some monks engaged in worldly activities such as development, breaking with the ideal image of monks as aloof from society, and how they were accepted by the people with whom they work.

Why Development?

The ideal image of a monk in Thai society is of someone removed from secular life, concentrating on Buddhist practice and projecting sanctity and tranquility. While genuine withdrawal rarely exists, and most monks interact with society in some form, activist monks are often criticized for stepping beyond the "proper" behavior of a monk through their engagement in mundane affairs.

In a study of seventy-seven self-proclaimed development monks conducted in the mid-1980s, Somboon Suksamran (1988, 34–35) listed several reasons that monks engaged in independent development work. All the monks interviewed, Somboon said, were aware of the criticisms and defended their activities on the grounds of their responsibility as monks, a position I found often repeated by the activist monks I met from the late 1980s until the present.

Two kinds of motivations stood as foremost in both my and Somboon's studies. First, these monks felt it was the sangha's responsibly to serve society, to give something back to the laity who took care of them. Luang Pho Nan phrased it well in the quote cited earlier: "I owed the villagers everything," he said (Seri 1988, 55). I found development monks to be acutely aware of their debt to their lay supporters and their positions as social leaders. Rather than thinking that the sangha should remain aloof from society, they believed they should engage in it in order to build the spiritual development of all people, to work to relieve suffering and give back to their lay supporters. Many monks talked with me about their concerns over the suffering people faced due to the consequences of rapid economic development that did not consider spiritual ramifications. Phrakhru Pitak Nanthakhun frequently mentioned dealing with people's suffering in talks he gave at seminars for development and environmental monks.

Second, development monks considered the future of Buddhism in Thai society. The rise of consumerism undermined the basic teachings of Buddhism, particularly those preaching detachment from desire (tanhā) and no-self (anatta). People now looked toward material accumulation for a sense of success and pride, which countered key Buddhist principles.

Since the push toward modernization began in Mongkut's time, the position of the sangha in society has evolved. While monks high in the hierarchy retained influence in society, the position of monks at the lower levels, especially in the villages, decreased. The modernization of education, for example, moved schools and teaching out of the temples. Health care shifted to medical centers and clinics. People in many areas turned less to the monks for advice and guidance, and more toward government officials. Monks needed to respond to maintain the relevance of the religion in society. As Somboon stated, "Thai society is rapidly changing and the *Sangha* must involve itself in order to maintain its status in society. In other words, the monkhood has to change or it will become obsolete" (1988, 35). In many ways, this process began with the Buddhist reforms initiated by Mongkut in the early nineteenth century; through rationalizing and reforming the sangha and minimizing their ritual involvement, he emphasized Buddhist philosophical concerns over social ones. With a centralized sangha hierarchy, many monks did not live in their home villages. They no longer embodied local religious and cultural understandings, but responded to directives from Bangkok. Mongkut started a process that ultimately limited monks' engagement in the lives of average lay people.

More practical concerns came into play as well. Some monks felt that if government officials fulfilled their duties more thoroughly, monks would not need to deal with social issues (Somboon 1988, 34). In some places, the villages were remote and difficult to get to, making it easier for a local monk to work with villagers than for district or provincial authorities. In other places, monks accused government authorities of being part of the problem. Phra Prajak Khuttajitto, for example, became famous in 1991 for accusing military and forestry officials of illegal logging in Dong Yai forest reserve and for poor planning of a relocation scheme for northeastern Thailand designed to reforest degraded lands. Instead, he claimed, villagers were moved off productive land that was then turned over to large companies (often with government connections) for monoculture plantations such as eucalyptus (J. Taylor 1993b, 1996; F. Reynolds 1994).

Somboon (1988, 35) also found monks raising concerns about the spread and impact of communism in remote areas. Without development projects, poverty could drive people to affiliate with the Communist Party of Thailand. His research primarily took place in the late 1970s and early 1980s when the insurgency was strong. When I began my research in 1986, the fear of communism had declined and was rarely mentioned by activist monks as a rationale for their work.

Charisma, *Barami*, and Changing Religion

Regardless of their personal motivations, development monks could not do their work without the acceptance and cooperation of the laity. This support comes from multiple constituencies—villagers, urban devotees, NGOs, and occasionally government officials. As seen in the case of Phrakhru Sakorn's coconut sugar project, often a monk must work hard and begin to make a difference materially in village life before the people will accept him. Yet that is true of any development agent, and does not place the activist monks in any special category. Being a monk in itself does not equate with success. The development monks who are most effective radiate charisma, and are perceived by their followers as having achieved *barami,* or spiritual perfection.[22] Villagers generally did not specify these perfections, but used the term *barami* to describe monks such as Luang Pu Phuttapoj.

Key to the effectiveness of development monks is the respect they receive from villagers. Watching farmers' reactions to Phuttapoj as he strode among them and their buffalos the day of the beautiful buffalo contest, his charisma and influence were readily apparent. Villagers fixed their gazes on him, waiting excitedly for a nod or acknowledgement. The pride of the winning farmer rippled through all the participants. Ultimately, it did not seem to matter to them whether their animal won; they saw themselves as champions as recipients of Phuttapoj's buffalos and, thus, his favor. Although the projects can fall victim to the same kinds of obstacles that occur with all community development—village politics, lack of funding, pressures of consumerism, etc.—the involvement of highly respected monks such as Phuttapoj helps to reinforce core values and maintain the status of the sangha on the village level.

Ordained at the age of fifteen, Luang Pu Phuttapoj passed away at the age of ninety-one in 2008, and had become a high-ranking, well-known monk. He was referred to as *Luang Pu* (literally, "Revered Grandfather"), a term reserved for senior monks for whom their followers have strong reverence. He was an imposing person; his demeanor exuded wisdom, confidence, and discipline. Although stern in requiring those around him to put forth the best they have, a word of praise or encouragement from him was always sincere and engendered loyalty. He was a charismatic person, in Weber's sense of the term (1946, 245–52), a natural leader with a spiritual gift. In Phuttapoj's case, the supernatural gift is accredited to his karma, to the merit (*bun*) he had accrued, which enabled him to acquire the knowledge, wisdom, and understanding of religion (and, in many ways, of life) he offered others. His charisma was at the root of his reputation for being particularly meritorious. People gave to him with the belief that the donations would result in greater merit for the donor than giving to most other monks.[23] His followers perceived him as embodying barami.

The history of Phuttapoj's buffalo banks offers insight into his spiritual reputation, and how it plays into his development work. The details vary depending on the teller, but the basic story of the origin of FEDRA's buffalo bank program remains the same.[24] A rich man, some say from Bangkok, others from Chiang Mai, was extremely ill. After visiting numerous hospitals and doctors, all confirming that his illness was incurable, in his desperation the man consulted a fortune-teller, a *mo du*. His only hope, according to the mo du, was to save the life of an important animal such as a water buffalo or cow and donate it to a Buddhist monk. The man immediately purchased a buffalo from a slaughterhouse and presented it to Luang Pu Phuttapoj. Here the details vary, ranging from immediately to gradually over six months, but all agree that the man recovered.

As word of this recovery spread, other wealthy lay people began to donate buffalos to Phuttapoj to make merit intended to forestall misfortune and ensure a long life. Phuttapoj was willing to accept the animals because their lives were saved, and the benefactors received merit from the act. Initially, they were kept at Wat Pa Dharabhirom, roaming the grounds of the monastery compound. As many as twenty buffalos were kept at the temple at one time. They began to require considerable time and care from the novices and monks, and to disrupt the peaceful environment of the wat, which should have been conducive to meditation and study. Phuttapoj had the idea that since the buffalos had been granted a longer life by the action of humans, they could provide a useful service to someone else in need, such as poor farmers. Through this process, the merit of the donors could accomplish even greater good.

Even though he told me he did not believe in the effectiveness of rituals, saying that true spiritual progress came from within through meditation practice, Phuttapoj often brought the recipient farmer and the donor together for a ritual transference and blessing at Wat Pa Dharabhirom. The ritual carried meaning for the lay participants, and further emphasized the religious foundations of the program and the responsibilities of the farmer to care for the animal. This ritual became the basis of one of the main programs of FEDRA, the buffalo banks. During the ritual, Phuttapoj used the opportunity to encourage donors to give directly to poor farmers, arguing that they would receive as much or more merit from the act as giving to a monk. His pragmatic use of the ritual to preach an atypical interpretation of the dhamma that promoted rural development foreshadowed later adaptation of ritual by environmental monks.

Phuttapoj's story is a good example of how an individual monk moved into independent development work. His decisions were in response to economic changes that were impacting the rural people around him. As is typical of most activist monks—both development and environmental monks—his charismatic personality contributed significantly to the potential of his work and the acceptance of it by rural farmers and urban supporters alike.

Themes from Phuttapoj's story are repeated over and over in the lives and work of other development monks. Their individual histories differ, but each one stands out for his devotion to the religion and the people for whom he is responsible. Seri Phongphit sums up the following characteristics of leading development monks:

1. They are recognized as having attained the essence of Dhamma.
2. Determination and consistency.
3. Moral integrity and sacrifice.
4. Openness and readiness to learn.
5. Love of nature.
6. Leadership.
7. Barami. (Seri 1988, 151–53)

In his descriptions of these characteristics, Seri emphasizes the spiritual and religious basis of each one. These monks practice the religion, and hold themselves to a high standard of religious behavior. Given the intensity of the social gaze focused on them due to their social engagement, activist monks must uphold a high moral image and practice. To undertake their work, activist monks' behavior and reputation have to be impeccable. This is particularly true as many of these monks aim to reinterpret aspects of religious practice in order to make their work more effective. Two aspects of development work in the name of the Buddha illustrate how these monks use their charisma and leadership to reframe the religion to encourage behavior conducive to their aims of spiritual and economic development: restructuring merit-making and the use of familiar rituals to promote new goals. Both of these efforts provide the foundation for environmental monks to continue to expand the use of religion for social change.

Merit-Making Rethought

Merit-making is the focus of Buddhism in Thai villages. When asked what Buddhism is, the majority of the villagers answer that it is *tham bun*, "to make merit." Most laymen, and even admittedly many monks, do not strive to obtain the ultimate salvation of enlightenment (*nibbana*, Pali; *nirvana*,

Sanskrit). In interviews I conducted in a village in Chiang Mai, not one person mentioned the idea of nibbana in connection with any aspect of religion. They recognized that obtaining this goal was beyond their abilities, and admitted that they would rather be reborn in a better life than to achieve the perfect salvation of nibbana.[25] The majority did not even think often of future rebirth, but considered that if they were healthy and happy in this life, it was due to merit they made both in previous lives and in this one.

The laity believes that merit can be acquired in three ways: by giving or charity (*dana,* Pali), morality, and meditation.[26] Merit can be made by doing good of any kind. Religious activities such as giving alms to the monks, supporting the temple, praying, listening to sermons, following the precepts, and practicing meditation all result in merit (Chai 1985, 37). Other types of meritorious activities include being generous to others, taking care of the poor, helping to improve the village or nation in development work, and caring for one's parents. The villagers do not tend to think of these latter activities, however, when they talk about making merit. They often consider the activities that result in the most merit as those involving *dana* (particularly giving alms or gifts to the monks), chanting, listening to sermons about the dhamma, and transferring merit to the dead. These are activities within the means of the average villager, although they differ somewhat from what the scriptures list as important meritorious acts.[27] Ordination as a monk is considered extremely meritorious, but obviously out of reach for women, who perform most merit-making activities.

For wealthier devotees, especially urban people, paying for a new temple building or repairing an older one rank high on the list of meritorious activities. Dana activities, especially rituals such as the pha pa ceremony used to raise funds and goods for monks' livelihoods, evolved parallel with the shift in economic priorities in Thai society, raising concerns among development monks that Thais care more about material than spiritual goals. People now prefer to give large-scale items, especially buildings, on which their names as patrons will be written. The ceremony itself often involves an elaborate celebration surrounding the actual donation. When wealthy patrons travel to give to a particular temple, they often pay for the trip from the funds raised. They expect to be fed and entertained, again drawing funds from the host temple and incurring resentment from the local villagers, something I witnessed several times in Chiang Mai. According to Seri (1988, 38), "This leads to a substantial loss of resources."

Development monks refocus merit-making on donations that benefit those less well-off, incorporating the concept of charity for the poor to the act. They do not simply want to return to older priorities that emphasize giving to or becoming monks. They aim to get people to recognize the value of giving to the poor. Part of his work, Luang Pu Phuttapoj believed, was to make the wealthy people aware of the plight of the poor and recognize their responsibility to help them. Giving to the poor is, in his terms, equally if not more meritorious as giving to a monk or building a new structure at a temple.[28]

The Thai Interreligious Commission on Development (TICD) held a seminar with monks in 1982 to discuss the use of rice banks in community development (Bobilin 1988, 93–98). One of the main conclusions from TICD's seminar was the importance of cultural values in development, including the need to restructure common means of merit-making as part of a new approach to instigating local development. TICD's *Newsletter* reported the experience of a village monk, Phra Athikarn Sanon Thavaro, the abbot of Kasanuan Temple, Nakorn Rajasima Province, in his efforts to help the villagers overcome the problems of poverty. As both the problems he faced and the philosophy and methods he used to deal with them are similar to those of other development monks, it is worth quoting him at length here.

I held that genuine trust from the people must come first. I had been working at that place for six years, starting by preaching the five precepts[29] in order to prevent villagers from falling into degraded paths. There were some who could follow, but many failed. Hence I thought that there should be other means or vehicles to lead the people towards the right direction. For the people would always proclaim, "We cannot eat Dhamma instead of rice; if we observe the precepts, we will be starving. Only the rich can observe the precepts."

[I] thought that I should adapt the traditional way of merit-making so that it would be more practical. People used to believe that merit-making was to do or to give things useful for the temple. That was the old belief. I tried to give a new understanding of it. I told the people that merit-making could be done to any other person, monks or not, and it could be done anywhere: there was no need that it must only be performed within the temple compound.

Then I thought that the villagers had been spending a lot of money on merit-making, especially on the special religious days which took place throughout the year. And as I could not stop them, I would rather change my role. So I became a cooperative staff member, collecting their money for them. According to the Lord Buddha's teaching, monks should not consume more things than necessary, and what was left should be returned to the people. So when we received more than we really needed, we would spend the rest buying rice and putting it in a storehouse for the people. Sometimes we decided to buy buffaloes to form a buffalo bank. The villagers agreed with this idea from the very beginning. And sometimes there were people from other places (usually middle-class people from towns) coming to offer robes for monks after the rainy season. Together with the robes, they also offered other things, as well as money. Usually, this money would be used for the maintenance of the temple. But I asked these people if I could use this money to help the poor. They agreed with me on my idea. They were glad that their offerings would be useful to the poor people. I felt that these sacrifices and solidarity would bring us nearer to the Dhamma. (Bobolin 1988, 93–95)

As with Phuttapoj, Phra Athikarn sought ways to shift concepts of merit-making from focusing on the sangha to helping the poor. The compromise most development monks arrive at is to accept alms donations, then use them in development projects. This process retains the original spiritual motivations of the donors, and lends a moral element to the projects as well.

Pha Pa Ceremony: Redefining Ritual and Power

Talking alone cannot change patterns of behavior, especially those reinforced by social power structures. Telling wealthy people that they can make as much merit through giving to poor farmers as to a renowned monk such as Phuttapoj did not convince them. As development monks sought to initiate new ways of thinking about development and merit-making, they realized the need for more effective means of bringing about change in people's attitudes, and thereby their relationships. In particular, as the monks sought funding for their activities, the class-based power structure that underlay their appeals to potential supporters, even through merit-making, became apparent. The hierarchical nature of Thai society was reinforced through both the forms of merit-making and the monks' own positions as above all laity. The monks needed a more experiential and powerful way of conveying their message. They tapped into the heart of popular religious practice to use ritual.

The pha pa ritual is one of the most popular Buddhist rituals in Thailand (Seri 1988, 38). People pool resources together to offer basic necessities for the monks—robes, soap, funds for the upkeep of the temple, spending money—so that the monks can concentrate on more spiritual issues. "Pha pa" literally means "forest cloth," the cloth ancient monks found in forests and charnel grounds and used to make their robes. The Vinaya, the disciplinary rules for the sangha, requires monks to find abandoned cloth that no longer belongs to anyone. Contemporary Theravada Buddhists recreate this act through hanging robes and other necessities and donations on model trees, emulating the forests in which ancient monks discovered their clothes. These trees are then paraded through the village to the temple with considerable pomp, dancing, and music, and formally presented to the monks.

The ritual pulls community members together in the care of the temple. Often people from outside the village participate, thereby symbolically tying the village into the larger society. The pha pa ritual is often sponsored by people from other villages or cities who make merit through large donations. The day of the ritual the patrons visit the recipient village, where a large party surrounds the act of donation. The outsiders are fed and feted, with music and perhaps movies or other entertainment, and alcohol, all pulling funds from the original donations.

Development monks began to shift the focus of pha pa ceremonies in the 1970s. They saw this ritual as having the potential to introduce new ideas about development, moving away from the emphasis on material goods toward quality of life through using it to raise funds for development projects. Specifying individual projects, such as building a well or a rice bank, or establishing a village credit union, sponsored by monks as the purpose of fund-raising through pha pa rituals got donors to think more broadly about the ways in which their gifts were used, while still keeping the traditional idea of the rite as supporting monks.

Development monks often work with NGOs and networks of activist monks to organize specific pha pa ceremonies and educate the participants. In 1981, the Coordinating Group for Religion in Society (CGRS), TICD, and several university student organizations in Bangkok joined with the monk Achan Khamkhien Suwanno to organize a rice pha pa ritual for the remote mountain village, Tha Mafaiwan, in Chaiyaphum Province (TICD 1981; Seri 1988, 38–40). In these and other cases, villagers and donors engaged in planning the ceremony and studying the needs for the funds. Fifty-three donors traveled from Bangkok to Tha Mafaiwan, enduring difficulties due to the remoteness of the village, to offer the funds raised to Achan Khamkhien. Rather than being entertained and fed, as is common, the donors used their own money to cover their expenses. They joined in village life, learning from the villagers about their situation. Instead of feeling isolated and inferior, the villagers felt empowered through the experience to take responsibility for the rice cooperative that was established through the ritual (Seri 1988, 39). In a proposal calling for donors, TICD described the process and its goals, and its basis in Buddhism, as follows:

> [I]nstead of giving requisites and donations to the temple for the purpose of erecting permanent structures, this time benevolent individuals will donate rice or money to the Tha Mafaiwan Temple so that the temple will have more capital to operate the cooperative and be able to lend rice to the villagers for consumption when rice is scarce. The rice will be returned to the cooperative later, thus greatly relieving the villagers' hardships. To make merits in this manner is truly in accordance with the principles of Buddhism because it not only makes the temple the breeding ground for good deeds where [sic] the villagers can depend on, both materially and spiritually, it also shows our benevolent attitude towards our fellow countrymen who are poorer and who suffer more hardships than we. Helping other people overcome their hardships in accordance with [our] capabilities, benevolent minds and desires to help our fellow countrymen is regarded as the key to the principles and teachings of Buddhism. (TICD 1981, 11)

The rice pha pa at Tha Mafaiwan epitomizes the ways in which development monks and the NGOs that support them reframe the use of rituals and tap into local cultural beliefs and values to deal with social issues, foreshadowing their use by environmental monks. This rite was unusual in the participation of urban folk who welcomed the opportunity to learn from local villagers. The charisma and reputation of Achan Khamkhien contributed to this process.

Far more common is the enactment of reinterpreted rituals and beliefs on a local level in which activist monks work with communities where they live. While rituals such as tree ordinations, pha pa ceremonies to raise funds for development projects, and long-life ceremonies for waterways have become popular across Thailand, the projects they support tend to be most effective on the grassroots level. When monks and lay people know and experience the difficulties of socioeconomic and environmental situations, they are best able to commit to the long-term efforts necessary to effect real social change.

5

The Grassroots

The forest is the watershed of Buddhism. Without the forest, the religion would run dry.
—Phra Paisal Visalo, September 29, 1992

Monks and the forest are like fish and water.
—Phra Prajak Khuttajitto, July 12, 1991

PHRAKHRU MANAS NATHIPHITAK (Plate 20) watched ants cross what was once a river.[1] Drought plagued his home in Phayao Province in northern Thailand. Villagers struggled to plant their crops and find sufficient water for their daily needs. Six years earlier, in 1973, the provincial government granted ten logging concessions in Mae Chai District, Manas's home and the site of watersheds for many of the region's streams. Although the logging was scheduled over a thirty-year period, the company immediately began cutting the forest's larger trees.

With trees gone from watersheds, the primary cause of the drought seemed obvious. Few trees remained to hold the rain in the soil, causing rapid runoff in the rainy season and drought in the dry season.[2] The people of the district came together to discuss the problem and seek solutions. Together with Phrakhru Manas, they decided to set up a conservation committee and to perform a common Northern Thai ritual, *suep chata,* a long-life ceremony. Usually conducted for people who are sick, old, or face misfortune, in this case the villagers asked Manas to perform the rite for the dried stream in hopes of reviving the flow of water.

The process, by Manas's account, was organic, emerging from discussions among the people affected by the drought in Mae Chai. No one approached

133

the problem explicitly seeking a Buddhist solution, or even a spiritual one. As the respected abbot of Wat Photharam, an important temple in the district, Manas assumed a leadership role, and listened to the concerns and wants of his neighbors and relatives. Relieving their suffering remained his primary motive, as he witnessed the challenges they faced due to the drought—and the logging behind it.

Lay villagers generally do not grasp the complexities of the philosophical notion of suffering. They recognize the immediate pain or problem, and seek a concrete response. The challenge for activist monks such as Phrakhru Manas is to uphold what most see as their primary responsibility of relieving the suffering of their followers while teaching the deeper meanings of the concept.

Phrakhru Manas sought ways of helping the villagers who turned to him. His interpretations of the causes of their suffering, the links between forms of development and environmental problems, and his creative approach typified the work of environmental monks, although the term had not been coined at that time. He used people's beliefs and familiar rituals to raise awareness about the causes of suffering. He targeted not only the link between deforestation and drought, but the deeper greed that drove the desire for logs and the potential wealth they symbolized. He promoted the idea that people's actions could change the situation they faced. Although he did not articulate a direct parallel, he based his work in the concept of karma—that people reap the consequences of their actions and the intentions behind them. He used ritual to build community and unity among the people affected by the drought.

Like development monks, Phrakhru Manas sought ways to help villagers cope with changes in Thai society, particularly the impact of the changing economy. In this way, the category of environmental monks emerged from development monks, both critically examining and seeking to minimize the effects of rapid economic development on rural life. The first environmental monks articulated the value of the forest and water for people's lives, and human responsibility for the natural environment, even as they later became concerned with other environmental issues.

Phrakhru Manas was one of the first monks to engage explicitly in environmental work. His initial projects—performing long-life rituals for waterways, organizing villagers into conservation groups, and challenging the logging companies—focused on local concerns. He drew from local people's concepts and beliefs to structure his approach, particularly the use of the long-life ceremony.

The emergence and growth of development monks paralleled and accompanied the rise of NGOs engaged in alternative development. Since the 1970s NGOs have become a major social opposition movement within Thai society. Both secular NGOs and development monks emerged because of concern over the negative impacts of government development policies on Thai society, culture, and environment.

Similarly, the earliest environmental monks, like several NGOs, made connections between development and environmental degradation and the resulting social problems in specific locales. These monks sought to deal with suffering on an immediate basis while teaching Buddhist principles and religious practice. Their resourcefulness and visions enabled them to connect with villagers and present abstract ideas, such as suffering (dukkha) and its causes, in terms villagers understood and recognized. Their creativity was radical in its interpretation of the teachings and the impact it had on people's lives. They got people's attention.

As the environmental movement emerged across the nation in the 1980s, the work of environmental monks soon pulled them into national political and environmental debates. They took on controversial issues and challenged powerful people. While similar concerns underlay their actions, no single approach unified all environmental monks. A movement of environmental monks emerged as monks began to meet together, through both visiting each other's projects and attending seminars organized by NGOs. Through sharing their ideas, challenges, and methods of dealing with environmental issues, monks gradually began to identify as environmentalists and to construct a new paradigm of Buddhist environmentalism.

The work of environmental monks takes two general forms, with some overlap. First, monks undertake localized projects that deal with specific situations and problems. These projects often come out of individual monks' experiences. Monks such as Phrakhru Manas are moved to action as they witness the disappearance of the forest and water, and other negative effects of government policies and the commercialization of natural resources on rural people. Their activities overlap with those of development monks in that they are concerned with rural people's livelihoods as well as the condition of the natural environment. Their projects include integrated agriculture, establishing forest conservation committees and community forests, wildlife sanctuaries, tree planting, and ecological education of villagers.

The other form their activities take is protest. Environmental monks joined with other social groups—students, journalists, environmentalists, NGOs—in objecting to large-scale development projects that would negatively impact both people and nature. Participation in protests and taking positions that often brought them into direct opposition to government policies and the goals of big business brought the Buddhist environmental movement into the public's eye and raised questions about the monks' activities. The broader implications of monks' involvement in protests and challenge of both state and business interests will be examined in chapter 7.

Concern about the well-being of people and nature at the grassroots remains the core of the movement. Environmental actions and the rituals that structure them are what symbolize and identify environmental monks, and are where they have had the most impact. These are also the ideas and actions competing powers within society eventually appropriated because of their effectiveness.

Grassroots Environmentalism

Philip Hirsch (1996) demonstrates that several different environmentalisms coexist in Thailand, grounded in social and material perspectives. That of the middle class is most visible, given the social and economic power of that group. Yet Hirsch argues that, "for most Thais, concrete livelihood issues at a very local level are the most significant consequence of environmental degradation." Consequently, the reality is "that the majority of Thais whose livelihoods are most threatened by environmental and resources degradation are poorer people living in rural areas" (1996, 30). He concludes that "a latter-day moral economy of control over resources may be seen to underlie much of the 'peripheral environmentalism' which, though more hidden and perhaps counter-intuitive than middle-class environmentalism, forms the backbone of the environment movement in Thailand today" (1996, 34). Hirsch downplays the impact of environmental monks in the formation of this "grassroots environmentalism," citing them as one aspect of how environmentalism at the grassroots takes a "Thai" rather than Western perspective (1996, 33). I would agree with Delcore (2000) that monks such as Phrakhru Pitak Nanthakhun have influenced the development of a broader environmental movement through the 1990s. As Delcore (2000, 153) points out, "Phra Khru's 'individual problematic' (his individual concerns and their social and cultural appeals) have helped shape the character of Thai environmentalism and the place of Buddhism in society." The same holds true for other environmental monks who have captured the nation's imagination.

Although less visible than the protests and controversial positions some monks have taken on well-known debates, such as the resettlement plan in Isan, grassroots activities form the core of the work of environmental monks. At this level, monks collaborate with villagers and NGOs to combat increasing poverty, debt, and desolation of rural people as they are entangled in the state's rhetoric of progress. As with development monks, they are concerned about the place of Buddhism in society and fear the loss of moral values due to growing consumerism and a cash economy. They bring their concerns together through a range of projects, from wildlife sanctuaries and protecting water sources and forests, to promoting integrated agriculture.

Wildlife Sanctuaries

Buddhist monks have long been associated with protecting wildlife. The Jataka tales, the stories of the Buddha's lives, illustrate the principles of nonviolence, compassion, and care for all living beings that form the core of Buddhist teachings. Across the Buddhist world, monks put these teachings into practice through caring for wildlife.

The creation of wildlife sanctuaries at Thai temples occurred before environmentalism emerged as a political force. These monks emphasized saving nature for nature's sake, along the lines of the preservationist approach to environmentalism in the United States. Monks protected wildlife as an application of the basic Buddhist principles of compassion and nonviolence. They did not consider the broader implications of protecting wildlife in terms of the impacts on people's livelihoods or the politics of nature conservation. While monks successfully protected wildlife in numerous temples, this mode of conservation cannot be considered "Buddhist environmentalism" as I am using the term here because of the narrow focus of its intention. As with the diverse environmental movement across Thailand, however, wildlife sanctuaries at temples foreshadowed more political and economic engagement of monks in environmentalism that followed.

A good example of wildlife protection in this mode occurred at Wat Phai Lom, a temple outside of Bangkok. The monks there joined with leading Thai naturalist Dr. Boonsong Lekagul in the 1960s to help protect the Asian Openbill Stork (*Anastomus oscitans*). The number of Openbill Storks across Asia was in significant decline by the 1950s. Despite being protected by law in Thailand since 1960, the birds had all but disappeared due to poaching and habitat destruction. An area near Wat Phai Lom was the only remaining colony in the nation. In 1970, due to the work of the monks and Dr. Boonsong, the Thai government declared this area an official bird sanctuary, offering the birds refuge, especially during their annual migration. The number of birds increased dramatically, from four thousand in 1964 to thirty thousand in 1980 (Williams 1992/1993). Yet as their population rebounded and spread beyond the limits of the sanctuary, the birds again faced poaching and habitat destruction.

Dr. Boonsong's involvement in the Openbill Stork sanctuary highlights the connection between the emerging conservationist movement and the awareness of some monks of the impact their actions can have. At the time of the storks' initial decline in the 1950s, Boonsong had become the nation's leading naturalist. Born in 1907, he enjoyed hunting in his youth. Gradually he became aware of the value of wildlife and moved into conservation. In the 1950s and 1960s, he emphasized preservation—protecting wildlife (especially birds), and keeping people out of the sanctuary areas. Boonsong's efforts led to the creation of the first national park in Thailand in 1962 under the National Park Act of 1961, beginning the ongoing debate about whether people can live in parks, that is, whether people and wildlife can coexist. National park policy in Thailand has generally limited human access to parks, including relocating people who lived in the newly designated park areas.

Even though the monks at Wat Phai Lom were primarily motivated by compassion and not the kind of social, political concerns that predominate for environmental monks today, the case of the Openbill Storks at Wat Phai Lom contributed to a key event in the history of Buddhist environmentalism. Nancy Nash, a U.S.-born journalist and environmental education consultant living in Hong Kong, claims that a visit to Wat Phai Lom in the 1960s with Dr. Boonsong planted the seeds of an idea to connect conservation activities with the world's religions (Rolex Awards for Enterprise 1997). In 1985, she established the Buddhist Perception of Nature Project. This project, based in Hong Kong, provided educational and financial support for Buddhists across Asia to engage in environmental conservation. The project published a book in Thai, Tibetan, and English entitled *The Tree of Life* that interpreted Buddhist teachings to support conservation efforts and provided an ethical basis for conservation work (Davies 1987). With international attention, the project promoted the idea of an explicitly Buddhist environmentalism, joining a growing international movement of using religion to protect and preserve the natural environment.

Wildlife sanctuaries also show a less ecological side of Buddhism. As with any religion, Buddhist principles are open to interpretation. As Wat Phai Lom protected and nurtured the storks, for example, a neighboring temple did not. The monks there felt inconvenienced or bothered by the birds' droppings and noise. Unlike their neighbors, they discouraged the birds from settling in their temple compound by smoking them out, more concerned with the quiet atmosphere of the temple grounds than the well-being of the birds (Williams 1992/1993).

In some places, questions arise as to the real motivation for the "sanctuary." I visited one temple in northeastern Thailand in 1987 that operated what it called a wildlife sanctuary. The conditions in which the animals there were kept were appalling. Small cages filled the temple's "wildlife refuge" holding animals collected from the nearby forest, including an endangered sun bear. The animals had no room to maneuver, sat in their own excrement, and drank water filled with mosquito larvae. The temple abbot brought out a baby sun bear to show us and made the bear perform various circus stunts, like walking on its hind legs. He claimed that if the bear had been left in the forest, it would have been killed by poachers and its organs sold on the black market as an aphrodisiac. While poaching of bears is well known across Asia, including Thailand, the life of the sun bear at this temple could hardly be called one of refuge, nor, I suspect, would it be condoned by many environmentalists. The "zoo" here seemed to be more of a way for the temple to bring in funds from tourists than a genuine act of compassion. The case demonstrates the importance of intention in order to label a particular action as Buddhist environmentalism.

A form of wildlife sanctuary that is clearly centered in Buddhist environmentalism as a social movement is the fish sanctuary. Traditionally, fish are one of the species, along with birds, turtles, and a few other small animals, that Thai Buddhists buy and release to make merit through freeing them.[3] The problem is that often the animals and birds return to their captors, are recaptured, or die when released. (Land turtles, for example, are sometimes let loose in water, where they drown.) In the 1990s, a new approach to making merit through protecting fish emerged.

I'm not sure where the first fish sanctuary in Thailand occurred. In Nan Province, the headman of Don Kaew Village coordinated with the monks at the village temple to establish a fish sanctuary where the Nan River passed the temple compound in 1992. The headman claimed he heard a news story about a similar sanctuary in the northeast, which he adapted to his village. He designated an area in which no fishing was allowed. The local monks came to the riverbank regularly to feed the fish, drawing them into the safe area and enabling them to repopulate (Plate 21). Once the fish population outgrew the sanctuary, some fish would leave it and could be caught. The project helped partially alleviate problems villagers faced with a cash economy. Having shifted to growing primarily cash crops, they bought most of their food, often at high market prices. The sanctuary provided a steady supply of fish for the villagers, while simultaneously protecting the animals from overfishing, a problem along much of the river. In 1999, Don Kaew's headman won a national environmental award for the success of the fish sanctuary.

The model soon spread. Phrakhru Pitak Nanthakhun borrowed the idea when he initiated a project in 1993 to highlight the problems of the Nan River. The project documented pollution and misuse of the river, a major tributary of the Chao Praya River, which runs through the agricultural center of Thailand and on through Bangkok. Following Phrakhru Manas's use of the long-life ceremony for waterways, Phrakhru Pitak sponsored a suep chata ritual and an informational and cultural fair to bring attention to the condition of the river. In addition to the ceremony and the fair, Pitak established a fish sanctuary at the ritual site on land belonging to the military just outside Nan city. The ritual participants formally marked the opening of the sanctuary by releasing several hundred fish into the protected section of the river, thereby also making religious merit. Communities across the province began to set up their own sanctuaries, often requesting Phrakhru Pitak's or other monks' participation to give the projects moral legitimacy. In 1999, Phrakhru Pitak claimed more than three hundred fish sanctuaries had been established across the province, and more were being established every year.[4]

These fish sanctuaries fall squarely within Buddhist environmentalism in a way most other wildlife sanctuaries do not.[5] Unlike the stork sanctuary at Wat Phai Lom, fish sanctuaries serve the double purpose of protecting fish and providing a secure livelihood for villagers. The morality of protecting the fish is emphasized, as it is at Wat Phai Lom for the birds, but the process goes farther to incorporate a broader understanding of the socioeconomic forces that endanger both fish and humans through environmental damage. It seeks a way through which both people and wildlife can coexist.

Water

Whereas the bird and wildlife sanctuaries mentioned above illustrate a particular approach to enacting compassion and care for all living beings that focuses on the animals and birds themselves, water conservation and fish sanctuaries offer another tack taken by monks. A very small number of monks began consciously to engage in these activities beginning in the late 1970s. The difference from wildlife sanctuaries was that these monks linked water conservation with the same problems that led monks into development work: the livelihood difficulties villagers faced due to changing economic situations. They linked the condition of the natural environment with livelihood issues, emphasizing the interrelationship between nature and humans. These cases are the first explicit examples of Buddhist environmentalism.

Phrakhru Manas's efforts to protect the waterways of Phayao Province described above formed one of the earliest cases of a monk's undertaking explicitly environmental activities to deal with the suffering of the villagers with whom he lived and worked. As he said, "Rivers are the life blood of the Mai Chai people . . . [W]ithout them, how can they survive?" (Wilaiwan 1996, 4). Manas worked quietly with the villagers of his home district to address the water shortage they faced. Like the development monks, he questioned the negative impacts of state-endorsed projects, particularly the logging concessions granted in his area. He focused on the local area without challenging broader state policies. He went beyond the development monks in raising concerns about the condition of the natural world, the rivers and forests in his home in particular.

Around the same time Phrakhru Manas began to organize villagers to conserve the water, the majority of the nation was struggling to find its way after a tumultuous political period from 1973 to 1976. The student protests that brought down a military government in 1973 were sparked in part by a hunting scandal in which army officers and soldiers poached animals in a national park (Stott 1991, 144). The helicopter in which the military personnel were bringing the animal carcasses out of the park crashed, leading to the encroachment discovery. On one level, concern for the inviolability of the park and the protection of the animals motivated the students in Bangkok. On another, the abuse of power by the military in violating the national park probably angered the students more. Nevertheless, environmental and wildlife issues literally exploded onto the national stage with this event. Environmental concerns were eclipsed when the military gave up power, and the nation experimented with popular democracy for a three-year period that emphasized social issues of poverty, class inequalities, and corruption.

While development NGOs gained a foothold during this period, environmental issues took a back seat. Monks like Phrakhru Manas balanced concern for the poverty, debt, and suffering of villagers with an awareness of the underlying causes of their struggles—the ecological impacts of logging and deforestation. Yet it would be almost a decade before such questions took center stage in Thai politics. Most scholars cite the successful popular protests against the construction of the Nam Choen Dam in Kanchanaburi Province in 1988 as the defining moment for the "coming of age of the environmental movement in the country" (Rigg 1995, 13). While the work of Phrakhru Manas was significant in the origins of Buddhist environmentalism, as with the environmental movement as a whole, it did not grab the attention of the nation until environmental issues began to be taken seriously across the board in the mid- to late 1980s. More than wildlife or water, forests became the central focus of environmental debates and the symbol of the environmental movement.

Forests

Phrakhru Manas's concerns about the impact of logging typified the impetus of many environmental monks to move beyond both Buddhist meditation practice and routine village duties such as accepting merit donations and performing rituals. Given the centrality of the forest for the lives of rural people across much of Thailand, it is not surprising that environmental monks focused on forest issues. Thailand had one of the fastest rates of deforestation in Southeast Asia prior to the 1990s (England 1996, 60). The monks perceived several negative consequences that impacted the lives of villagers: soil erosion; loss of water, especially when deforestation occurs in watershed areas; and loss of wildlife and plants.

In the north, logging and the fight against the communist insurgency led the state to take control of much of the highland forests. The Royal Forestry Department (RFD) was established in 1896 to help the kingdom negotiate between the British logging companies coming in from Burma and the northern lords who maintained rights to the forests and offered overlapping teak logging concessions (Pinkaew 2001, 68). Bangkok stepped in after numerous conflicts and legal battles, recognizing the growing economic value of the northern forests. Into the twentieth century, Bangkok continued to expand its control and definition of the kingdom's forests. The concept of the forest (*pa*) evolved from a mystical, powerful, wild, and non-civilized space (Stott 1991; Pinkaew 2001, 67; Kamala 1997) into a controlled and contested economic resource. With the intensification of economic development and agricultural expansion beginning in the 1960s, and the conflict from the 1950s until the 1980s with communist insurgents who used dense forests as their base, the forests became even more contested.

The symbolic and practical meaning of forests for Buddhist monks complicated the issue, and became a tool in the struggle over control of land and people. Meditation monks retreated to remote forests, especially in Isan, to practice *thudong*. Thudong entails following thirteen ascetic practices, including wandering and sleeping in the open air. The practice of thudong contributes to ridding oneself of defilements and strengthening one's mental skills and control of the mind. The "wild" forests were seen by the thudong monks (often referred to in Thai as *phra pa,* or "forest monks") as ideal locations to practice meditation because of the combination of peacefulness, being removed from society, and danger, as the forests were filled with wild animals, charnel grounds, spirits, and other obstacles to practice that the monks had to overcome (Kamala 1997). In the early twentieth century, the emerging nation-state realized the power of forest monks for bringing the people, and the forests, in remote parts of the kingdom under Bangkok's control. Lay people revered forest monks for their Buddhist practice and mental abilities, often respecting them more than local village monks. In some areas, there were no established temples or village monks. Forest monks were the main connection between these remote villages and established Buddhism. In this way, they offered the state a means to reach people who considered themselves unrelated to the central kingdom (Kamala 1997).[6] The monks became unwitting players in the state's efforts to expand and to "civilize" the peripheral regions. Yet the forests, even as they became less spiritual and more "civilized," never lost their special place for the sangha.

It is not surprising, then, that the rapid loss of the forest, especially in Isan and the north due to logging, intensified agricultural production, and monoculture economic plantations, impacted the sensibilities of both village and forest monks. For some, protecting the forests within and immediately surrounding temple compounds, especially *wat pa,* "forest temples," and meditation centers, became paramount (J. Taylor 1991). Others moved beyond their temple boundaries into activism aimed at stopping or reversing deforestation and the economic forces driving it.

Focused on meditation practice removed from society, relatively few forest monks actively engaged in social issues such as protecting the forest.[7] Village monks, on the other hand, experienced more directly the problems villagers faced because of the dwindling forest. Village monks not only appreciated the forest for the same peacefulness and dhamma lessons as forest monks, they also witnessed firsthand the negative impacts of deforestation on village life. As more villagers were pulled into a materialist, cash economy, their core values changed. People went to the cities in search of a better living, whether because of growing debt due to cash cropping or to acquire enough money to purchase status goods, such as a concrete (rather than wooden) house or a car. The lessons of Buddhism for living a simple life within a supportive community were often neglected.

Many of the monks drawn into environmental activism equated the loss of the forest with the loss of these values. They were aware of the changing circumstances within which villagers lived, and the need for Buddhism and monks to adapt to help villagers cope. The solutions, they felt, would be found in strengthening these values and getting villagers to change their behaviors.

Initial actions emerged from the historical role of village monks as teachers. Monks such as Phrakhru Manas and Phrakhru Pitak began by preaching an environmental ethic grounded in Buddhist principles. When villagers came to them to make donations or to request ceremonies to help them with illness or misfortune, or when monks were invited to chant at funerals or housewarming ceremonies, they used the opportunity to incorporate commentary on the close relationship between villagers and the forest. They sought to instill an awareness of the consequences of consumerism and clearcutting the forest to make money, highlighting the three root evils in Buddhism, greed, delusion, and anger.

Both Manas and Pitak quickly realized the ineffectiveness of preaching alone. People politely listened, but their behaviors did not change. More explicit action was needed. Some monks, such as Luang Pho Khamkhien Suwanno in Chaiyaphum Province and other Isan monks, followed an expanded version of the forest monks' approach of concentrating on the forest immediately surrounding their temples. In Isan, by the late 1970s significant amounts of forest had been cut down to make way for economic crops. In Chaiyaphum, first it was cassava, which received a high price in the early 1970s. Villagers not only converted much of their rice paddy land to the crop, but expanded their fields into the mountains. Many even invited relatives from poorer areas to join them in the cassava boom. Eucalyptus plantations followed, as businessmen encouraged by government policies moved into already damaged land. With growing profits they soon began to cut down remaining natural forests in order to plant eucalyptus. In the early 1990s, the government, in conjunction with the military, instigated a new policy, the "Land Redistribution Project for the Poor in Degraded Forest Areas," known in Thai by its acronym, *Kho Cho Ko*.[8]

Officially, Kho Cho Ko aimed at resettling villagers from degraded areas to new land. The land they left behind would be regenerated through reforestation initiatives. In reality the land from which they were removed was often converted into economic forests, particularly eucalyptus plantations. In addition, the land to which villagers were resettled was often worse than that they left. In many cases, resettled villagers found themselves moved to land that was already occupied, creating conflicts among rural farmers.

Some village monks felt the need to respond to the negative impacts of Kho Cho Ko. Beginning with the forest within their temple compounds, they established strict regulations concerning the use of the forest. They allowed the forest to regenerate naturally, although in a few cases they planted new trees. As the improved condition of the natural forests became obvious, especially in comparison with eucalyptus plantations, the monks convinced villagers to protect ever-increasing amounts of forest in and around the villages. The journalist Sanitsuda Ekachai described the natural forest protected by Luang Pho Khamkhien, directly across a rural road from a eucalyptus plantation:

> At Baan Thaa Mafai Waan, a mountain outpost in the province of Chaiyaphum, heaven and hell are only a few steps apart.
>
> A red dirt road, about five metres wide, cuts between two stands of trees that signify two very different possible futures for the 400 families who live here.
>
> On one side of the road is a lush, cool forest. The dense greenery makes walking difficult. The air is thick with moisture, the soil damp and soft with decomposed leaves. Sunlight filters through the protective canopy, courting the quiet world of green that lies beneath.
>
> On the other side, the trees are ranged in neat rows. This is a eucalyptus plantation. The hard, cracked, soil is covered with brown leaves that refuse to decompose. There is little shade; instead of airiness, the place is hot and dry. The land is cut by deep crevices, caused by severe erosion, as if Mother Earth were wounded. (Sanitsuda 1994, 72)

Sanitsuda (1994, 124–29) also reported on the positive results achieved by Phra Achan Somneuk Natho in Nakhorn Pathom Province, following a similar approach. Somneuk experimented, planting different kinds of trees to see which would grow well in the regenerating forest. He taught villagers about medicinal herbs that could be grown in the forest. The young monk stressed the importance of not micromanaging the forest because that would make it a plantation, not a forest. "I took a look at the tree plantations the Forestry Department calls forest and I felt like laughing," he commented. "How can you call them forests? I felt there was something fishy in a policy which insists on clear-cutting trees first in order to grow trees" (Sanitsuda 1994, 128).

Footsteps in the Night

Luang Pho Khamkhien expanded his efforts through encouraging other monks. Besides his work at Tha Mafaiwan Village, he oversaw the forest temple of Wat Pa Sukato, a few kilometers away. There, the monks again preserved a natural forest. Farther up Phu Long Mountain, the highest mountain in a more remote area of northern Isan, villagers of Mahawan struggled with deforestation and the spread of cash crops, especially cassava. While many villagers cut the forest themselves in search of a living, a few began to realize they were destroying their main resource. They established a small group to conserve the remaining forest near their village on the mountainside. They approached Luang Pho Khamkhien for help, seeing the success of his work at Tha Mafaiwan.

The challenge lay in the area's history. The mountain was declared a National Forest Reserve in 1971, a requirement before the RFD could give out logging commissions. Logging companies worked the area for four years, opening the dense forest, which enabled lowland people to follow. In 1977, people established a village and began to plant cassava. Not only would the encroachment from a nearby village need to be halted, but many of the villagers themselves would need to be convinced to stop growing cassava, with its negative effects on the soil and, ultimately, people's livelihoods.

At Luang Pho Khamkhien's request, a small number of monks moved to the mountain in the late 1980s. They established an unofficial sangha residence, called Wat Pa Mahawan. Although labeled as "wat pa," or "forest temple," the residence was illegally located within the forest reserve land. The RFD came to the area in 1991, two years later, but paid little attention to either the forest or the monks, according to Phra Paisal Visalo, one of the monks Luang Pho Khamkhien asked to live at Wat Pa Mahawan. In 1992, I made the long trip from Bangkok to interview Phra Paisal, a leading scholar in the environmental monk movement.

The trip from the provincial capital of Chaiyaphum involved a long bus ride to Wat Tha Mafaiwan, where a friend and I spent the night. From there it was only thirteen kilometers to Wat Pa Mahawan, which took an hour by hired truck. The road was dirt (or mud, given the recent rains), rutted and narrow in places. We had climbed a steep hill the day before, and now traveled across a plateau surrounded by mountains. Little forest remained as all the land had been planted with either corn or cassava. "Communist grass," an invasive form of imperata grass that takes over denuded land (and which villagers equated with the insurgents), grew thickly along the road. Burned remains of a few trees occasionally stuck up through the crops in the fields.

Our driver commented that twenty years earlier the area was all forest. The road did not exist. Many wild animals, including tigers, roamed freely. The forest now was almost gone, remaining only around the three temples run by Luang Pho Khamkhien. The driver quickly blamed the logging companies for opening the region. Farmers followed only seeking a way out of poverty.

When I asked the driver about the efforts of monks in solving the problems of poverty and deforestation, he replied that most monks could only conserve the forest at their temples. "Luang Pho [Khamkhien] is not like the others," he continued, adding that the abbot is more interested in the villagers' problems than most. His respect for the abbot animated his face as he spoke. When we left the truck to walk the last kilometer up the mountain to the temple, we learned the driver was Christian. His respect for Luang Pho Khamkhien came from the abbot's work, not because of religious faith.

As we entered the forest surrounding Wat Pa Mahawan, the temperature dropped. My eyes struggled to adjust to the relative darkness, and moisture beaded on my skin. Relief from the oppressive heat that occupied the farm land flooded through me.

The temple's few buildings were spread out along the steep trail through the forest, mostly hidden from one another. Wat Pa Mahawan was more of a "forest temple" than any other I had visited. Phra Paisal emphasized meditation practice there, in addition to helping the villagers protect the forest. Paisal first met Luang Pho Khamkhien when he was an NGO worker for the Coordinating Group for Religion in Society in the 1970s and '80s, and helped him deal with the poverty in Tha Mafaiwan Village. He ordained under Luang Pho Khamkhien for three months in order to study and practice meditation as a break from the intensity of NGO work. Luang Pho Khamkhien taught him ways in which meditation helps one step back from oneself to value both other people and the natural environment. Phra Paisal decided to remain as a monk in order to continue his work helping others, eventually coming to live at Mahawan. There he welcomed NGO workers from across Thailand when they needed to refresh their spirits. Phra Paisal quickly became a key figure in the Buddhist environmental movement.

Writing a semi-regular newsletter for members of Sekhiyadhamma, a network of engaged monks, on the connections between Buddhism and ecology, and providing spiritual and intellectual support for activists, Phra Paisal provided critical information and made concrete connections between the philosophy and practice of Buddhism and their practical application for dealing with social issues such as environmentalism, poverty, and political justice. Phra Paisal is one of the few activist monks who balance the details of activism with the big picture of how social, political, and economic issues intertwine. One of his criticisms of Thai sangha is that few monks see beyond the immediacy of their local situations. As monks lost significant aspects of their social role to an increasingly secular society over the past 150 years, their priorities shifted. Rather than being concerned with the conditions and suffering of the laity, they tended to focus on gaining status through the sangha hierarchy. As monks are promoted, their involvement with the sangha bureaucracy also grows, leaving less time for dealing with the concerns and problems of the laity.

Phra Paisal repeated these thoughts to me fifteen years later, still showing his concerns about monks' focus on local issues and hierarchy. "Monks are mostly interested in local issues," he said. "They are more engaged at that level, not national issues. As monks get older, they are promoted in the hierarchy, and don't have time for activism" (interview, 10/6/2006).

The predominant counter to this trend is increasing involvement in ritual as a means of interacting with the laity and maintaining a role for monks in society. Neither of these approaches, Phra Paisal feels, are what the Buddha intended because they focus on society rather than spiritual practice first (personal communication, 9/29/1992). Through his newsletter and talks at seminars for both monks and laity, he challenges monks to rethink their Buddhist commitment and practice and urges them to engage in social justice grounded in Buddhist principles. Meanwhile, he and the other monks at Wat Pa Mahawan continue to work with the villagers to protect the forest.

When Phra Paisal came to Wat Pa Mahawan in the late 1980s, villagers from the far side of the mountain threatened the forest as they crept in at night to cut trees. Trees could be sold and the land claimed for farming once it was cleared. Despite the efforts of a few Mahawan villagers to protect the forest, they had little power to stop the encroachers. Once the monks moved into the forest, their constant presence began to change both the actions of the encroachers and the attitudes of the villagers in Mahawan. Living and meditating in the forest, the monks noticed when people came in to cut trees. At night they would smell fires beginning and would run through the forest to put the fires out. Phra Paisal commented that the encroachers would hear the monks' footsteps in the night and would flee before they were caught. Even though the monks had no legal authority in the forest, their presence invoked moral authority and scared the encroachers off.

The commitment of the monks to the forest and to the villagers influenced the villagers to help themselves. The willingness to make changes in their lifestyle to save the forest spread from a few people to most of the village. One of the people in Mahawan who himself used to cut trees became the president of the village's conservation association. Together with Phra Paisal and the other monks, the villagers established four areas in the forest: protected forest that no one could use; community forest in which people could raise animals, collect firewood, and in which spirits live; living areas, including the sangha residence; and areas for their livelihood ("*tham ma ha kin,*" or "finding food").

When I visited Mahawan in 1992, the government had recently informed villagers that they were to be relocated through Kho Cho Ko. Their future was uncertain. Later that same year, the program was cancelled due to opposition and protests across Thai society, including members of the sangha. According to Phra Paisal, the government planned a less intense program, but the details had not been announced. When I interviewed him again in 2006, he still lived in the illegal sangha residence at Wat Pa Mahawan, the forest still stood, and the villagers had not been moved.

While in Mahawan the impetus to protect the forest originally came from a few villagers who invited the monks to help them, in other places environmental monks organized people into village forest conservation associations. Phrakhru Manas and Phrakhru Pitak both moved from preaching an environmental ethic into establishing community conservation associations in their home villages. These efforts foreshadowed the community forestry movement that has been debated nationwide for the past two decades.

As Phra Paisal pointed out, monks were organizing to protect their forests and work with the people who lived in them before the "community forestry" movement arose in the early 1990s (personal communication, 9/29/1992).

Community Forests

As the environmental movement developed in Thailand, forests quickly became the centerpiece. Dams remained a focus for protests and public action, but forest issues affected far more people's daily lives. The government's long-term policy aimed to remove people from forest land, arguing that farmers' agricultural practices, in particular the slash-and-burn techniques of mountain people in the north, severely damaged forest ecology. Through several programs, such as Kho Cho Ko, people would be resettled, leaving the forest as "pristine" wilderness. Anthropologist Pinkaew Launga-ramsri (2001, 64) argues that the concept of "nature" as "an untouchable, self-regulating and dehumanized entity" arose as a byproduct of state intervention since the early twentieth century. She shows how the government blames villagers for forest destruction, while linking forest conservation—through the state's definition and approach—with nationalism:

> [T]he forest has been portrayed and perceived as fragile, vulnerable, and susceptible to extinction, while swidden fields and village settlements are depicted as analogous to forest bulldozers. This alarmist and apocalyptic rhetoric has successfully gained widespread public and media support. Forest conservation is no longer just the RFD's agenda. It is spoken of as a responsibility of every Thai citizen. People who violate the law of conservation are considered as the destroyer of the nation. This imposed conservation authority has resulted in tension between local people and forest officials in many protected areas, particularly in north Thailand. Popular resentment and resistance as an expression of local people's distinctive ideas of conservation and forest use has emerged throughout the northern region. (Pinkaew 2001, 66)

Amidst this tension, academics teamed with NGOs to undertake participatory research, engaging local people in studies of their concepts and use of forest resources, and to fight for the rights of people to live in and maintain forest land. The community forestry movement emerged through the intersection of local resistance, regional NGO coordination, and academic theories. In 1991, at a meeting I attended of professors from Chiang Mai University and northern NGOs concerned about forest conservation, a definition of "community forests" was established as a working prototype. It emphasized that local people's indigenous knowledge of their land and their practical use of forest resources led them to conserve their forests. Central to the definition was the idea that because local people had the most reasons and the knowledge to protect the forest, their rights to use local forest must be preserved. A similar project began based at Khon Kaen University in the northeast. Given the urgency of demonstrating connections between people and the forest where people do not have title to the land (especially in the face of possible relocation through programs such as Kho Cho Ko), a nationwide movement evolved calling for a Community Forestry Bill.

Several versions of the bill emerged, differing on such issues as whether hunting would be allowed in community forests, whether trees could be cut down to build houses, or whether community forests could be established in national parks or only national forest reserves (Fahn 2003, 160). Beyond the details of how community forests would function, larger issues loomed. The environmental journalist, James Fahn, describes the deeper debates underlying the Community Forestry Bill:

> The vision of farmers living sustainably in the forest basically assumes they will adopt (or return to) a more traditional, self-sufficient lifestyle. But even if that's achievable, some preservationists ask whether it's fair to force them to live under such strictures. Wouldn't they be better off resettled outside protected areas rather than serving as a living exhibit in an open-air museum? Environmental democracy groups respond that these are loaded questions—loaded with the assumption that everyone holds the same modern, urbanized vision of development that has produced the preservationist ethic itself. We tend to assume that other people want the same things we want, that they want the same form of development we have; but the two sides in this debate have very different notions about what form development, and conservation, should take. (Fahn 2003, 160)

Environmental monks joined both sides of these debates, although most stood on behalf of local people's rights to live in the forest. Many monks believed that preservationist conservation would not work. If poverty drove people to cut down trees, simply forbidding them from doing so would not change the underlying causes of deforestation. The monks needed to work with farmers to find alternative forms of development grounded in Buddhist principles that encouraged forest conservation. Many drew from the precedent of development monks and incorporated natural or integrated agriculture—a form of development that differed from the government's capitalist economic development plans—into their environmental activities.

Integrated Agriculture

Most environmental monks come from rural backgrounds. Because they often work in areas in which they grew up or currently live, they are aware of the immediacy of the environmental, social, and economic issues that villagers face. Conservation for them is not only a matter of protecting the natural wilderness, but also of helping villagers find viable ways of living in balance with the natural environment.

Phrakhru Manas Nathiphitak and Phrakhru Pitak Nanthakhun are two examples of village monks who witnessed the impact of logging and deforestation and moved into campaigns to protect and regenerate the forests. They saw that teaching about the problems of deforestation and people's interdependence with the forest did not affect the situation or promote change in people's behavior. Even organizing community conservation committees to set regulations and monitor forest use had mixed effectiveness. In some cases, most villagers participated, increasing the ability of the committee to limit destructive forest use. In other places, villagers had limited options to make a living, and often violated conservation regulations in order to feed their children.

Phrakhru Pitak recognized the complexities surrounding deforestation and its causes. Rather than blaming only the state and big business, he understood the ways economic motivations impacted all the players, from government officials to rural farmers. Comprehending the interrelated complexities could lead to more effective approaches to change people's behaviors to protect the forest. Blaming a range of players enabled him to work with them all without implicating himself as favoring one group against another.

Pitak listed seven causes of deforestation in Nan Province:

1. Corn production: One look at the denuded hill sides in Nan makes one aware of the negative impact of growing feed corn. Yet the Government Agricultural Bank (GAB) promoted corn

production as part of the state's agricultural intensification program that began in the 1960s. In Nan, dry rice can be grown on the mountainsides in limited amounts. As farmers moved into a cash economy, they turned to corn and other cash crops (primarily string beans) to supplement their rice production. Growing corn, however, often led to debt. Farmers bought seeds along with chemical fertilizers and pesticides on credit with either GAB or seed companies. When harvests were not sufficient to repay the debts, farmers cleared more forest to enlarge their corn fields. Corn quickly wears out the soil, contributing to erosion and, as with any intensive monocropping, using up soil nutrients. Corn production led to a vicious cycle of deforestation and debt.

2. Logging companies: Since most of the mountainous land in Nan Province had been declared National Forest Reserve Land in the 1970s, wood harvesting was banned. Add to that the government ban on commercial logging put in place in 1989 (Pinkaew and Rajesh 1992). Nevertheless, the Royal Forestry Department, according to Phrakhru Pitak, looked the other way when these companies gathered what they claimed was "old wood" laying on the forest floor. Such logging removed obstacles for small-scale loggers to follow.

3. Small-scale capitalists: Among those who followed the logging companies were capitalists and businessmen seeking opportunities to profit from the rich forests of the province. Often referred to in northern Thailand as "influential people" (*phu mi itthiphon*), these businessmen included a range of middle-class and elite people, even some police, according to Pitak. Sometimes they cut wood illegally themselves. Other times they hired villagers to cut it for them or bought logs whose origins they claimed not to know. An example of such an influential person was the headman of Pitak's village when he first returned to become the abbot. The headman authorized villagers to cut wood to build the new temple, but the wood quietly disappeared. When Pitak questioned the headman about the missing wood, he fled, implying his guilt in stealing the wood.

4. "Ants": Given their situation of poverty and growing debt, villagers contributed to deforestation themselves. Pitak described individual people who would go into the forest and cut small trees to retrieve later as "ants." At night, they would return on

motorcycles and carry out one log at a time to sell. Even though their level of illegal logging was small compared with the companies or influential people, like ants, their collective impact was huge.

5. Military: Although Pitak listed the military's policies as number five among the causes of deforestation, in Nan Province their actions began the rapid deforestation. Communist insurgents based themselves in Nan because its mountains and forests provided good cover, and its border with Laos gave them a quick retreat. Throughout the 1950s, '60s, and '70s, the Thai military fought the communists in the province. It cut new roads into deeply forested land and up steep mountainsides to access communist hideouts (such as the camp that supposedly existed near Pitak's home village). The roads enabled the military to move quickly into insurgent territories to drive the communists out. They also provided an easy way into a now safe forest for farmers from the lowlands seeking new land.

6. Economic forests: In the name of reforestation, the government developed policies in several parts of the nation to establish "economic forests." While the best-known examples occurred in Isan (such as the Kho Cho Ko program), even the provincial government in Nan had a plan to "green" the province through creating eucalyptus plantations. Deforested areas were to be reclaimed through monoculture plantations that had explicit economic benefits, at least for the government and businessmen who owned them. The Green Nan plan pushed Phrakhru Pitak into the limelight in the late 1980s when a letter he wrote to the governor of neighboring Phrae Province requesting information on why the governor opposed eucalyptus plantations there was published in a national newspaper. Pitak criticized the program as a reforestation plan because, he claimed, it would only plant one tree for every four cut.

7. Firewood: Highlighting the livelihood difficulties surrounding the causes of deforestation, the need for rural villagers to gather firewood for cooking and warmth also contributed to the problem.

Most environmental monks did not detail the causes of deforestation in such depth. Nevertheless, they were aware of the contributions of villagers and other people affected by the economic pressures of a changing economy. Phrakhru Pitak frequently stated that opposing logging or forbidding villagers to cut the forest were not solutions. Alternatives to destructive use of the forest must be encouraged. Following the lead of development monks' agricultural projects, many environmental monks began to promote integrated agriculture. The monks recognize that merely protecting nature is not sufficient if people do not have alternative sources of livelihood to replace cash cropping and clearcutting the forest.

Integrated agriculture (*kaset phasom phasan*), also referred to as mixed farming, sustainable agriculture, or self-sufficient agriculture, encourages villagers not to plant cash crops, but to mix native crops and livestock that mutually support each other, negating the need for chemical fertilizers and pesticides. Many NGO workers had become discouraged in the 1980s by the failures of the Green Revolution with its emphasis on commercial farming to help farmers find a secure livelihood. They sought alternatives that would support rural farmers and protect the environment (Delcore 2000, 245). NGOs began to promote an idealized village community culture and self-reliance; they sought ways to return "back to the roots" (Seri 1986) of village life—an ideal image of village life that tended to downplay difficulties and change over time. Several NGOs, including the Foundation for the Development and Education of Rural Areas (FEDRA), the Coordinating Group for Religion and Society, and the Appropriate Technology Association, encouraged villagers to shift from commercial farming to environmentally sound forms of agriculture that would provide farmers with a sufficient living, help them climb out of debt, and stress village values.

As Delcore (2000, 242; 2004a) points out, the concept and practice of integrated agriculture are dynamic and open to interpretations and the interests of individual actors responding to specific situations. Environmental monks created their own forms of integrated agriculture, using the concept as a concrete link between environmental actions and Buddhist philosophy, particularly the concept of the interdependence of all things (dependent co-arising; *paticca-samuppada,* Pali). In practical terms, the use of integrated agriculture in various forms offered an alternative to cutting the forest, especially in places where it was combined with sustainable use of forest resources, as in Phrakhru Pitak's home village.

Delcore described the ideal concept of integrated agriculture as follows:

> In Thai NGO circles, integrated agriculture refers to the intensive and diversified cultivation of a limited area of land with environmentally

friendly methods and reliance on domestic labor. The goals of the method include decreasing land under cultivation (abandoned fields are ideally allowed to return to forest), use of domestic resources, avoidance of debt, and production of a variety of foods for household consumption with only a secondary emphasis on commercial production. (Delcore 2004a, 37)

I visited many farmers undertaking some form of integrated agriculture during my research. Many of them plant native rice with fish in the flooded paddy fields. Fruit trees surround the paddies, benefiting from the water. Chickens and pigs root among the fruit trees, eating the fallen fruit and discarded rinds, and fertilizing the fields naturally. Peas, beans, and other nitrogen-producing crops are interspersed among the other plants. Crops are chosen based on the nutrients they produce as well as require, creating symbiotic relationships between plants and animals.

Phrakhru Pitak helped one farmer, Dang, to convert his feed corn fields to an integrated and natural agricultural farm. Using funds raised through donations to his environmental work, Pitak helped Dang purchase some fruit tree seedlings and native rice and other seeds. He helped him begin to make the payments he owed to the seed company that sponsored his cash cropping to bring down his debt. Dang attended seminars run by NGOs on integrated agricultural methods, where he received further support to get the farm established. When I visited his farm four years after he switched to integrated agriculture, Dang was managing several acres of land that were covered with fruit trees, natural rice paddies, and herb gardens, and were swarming with chickens and pigs. He claimed that he had paid off his debt and even had a small surplus of funds. He had been able to do this by: (1) not having to buy food (a perennial problem when all of a farmer's fields are devoted to a single crop); and (2) selling the surplus organic crops and livestock. Dang now receives many visitors every year hoping to learn methods of integrated agriculture.

Another environmental monk in Nan Province, Phra Somkit Jaranathammo, also promotes integrated agriculture (Plate 22). Rather than financially supporting individual farmers, Somkit established a model integrated agricultural farm on temple land. On several acres directly behind the village temple, his farm at first appeared chaotic and overgrown to me. Walking through it with him and his brother, who managed the farm, I quickly realized the complexity and beauty of the plan. A fish pond provided water for native dry rice, banana, papaya, and mango trees, and other perennial crops. Pigs and chickens roamed the farm, rooting out weeds and insects and fertilizing the land with their excrement.

At the top of a hill, Phra Somkit proudly pointed out the diversity of plants growing freely. This place, he told me, had been cleared years ago by his father to grow feed corn. The land only supported the corn for a few years before erosion and decreased soil fertility wore it out. At that point, his father donated the land to the temple in order to make religious merit from the gift.

His father's donation of land adjacent to temple grounds motivated Phra Somkit to learn about sustainable or renewable forms of agriculture. He then expanded the notion of the Buddhist practice of *bindabat,* the monks' daily alms rounds for food. In addition to allowing villagers to make merit through giving food, he encouraged them to donate land to be placed under his care and used for the integrated agricultural farm.

Phra Somkit's farm demonstrated the benefits of integrated agriculture to the local farmers (Plate 23). Initially, he encouraged village children to help him, teaching them basics of sustainable agriculture, ecology, and Buddhist teachings through hands-on learning. The children brought their lessons and enthusiasm home, leading their parents to investigate the farm. The high yields, in addition to the regeneration of degraded land, appealed to the farmers. They now volunteer to work on the farm as a new form of merit-making, and to gain the knowledge and skills that are integral to this agricultural approach. By 2006, Phra Somkit claimed that every household in the village participated in some form of integrated agriculture. He received visitors from across Thailand and around the world. He told me that more than a thousand people every year come to see and learn from his farm, including university students from the United States, Europe, and Japan.

The farm, its visitors, and the new ideas it introduces into the village illustrate the ways activist monks serve as intermediaries between village life and the larger world. Through his fastidious Buddhist practice and teaching, Phra Somkit earns the respect of the villagers. At the same time, he uses his position to filter ideas, concepts, and values entering the village, hoping to steer villagers away from models of consumerism and development that he believes incur debt and suffering. Instead, he selects methods and concepts that he hopes will help villagers adapt to and engage the world in ways consistent with Buddhist values, and help them avoid the dangers of uncontrolled economic growth. In 2004, Phra Somkit won the Green Globe environmental award from the Petroleum Company of Thailand (PPT).[9] Several national television shows documented his work, increasing his fame and spreading his teachings to a larger audience.

Despite similar projects and a common grounding in Buddhist principles, environmental monks do not form a single, unified movement. While promoting integrated agriculture, forest conservation, and wildlife conservation are recurrent themes among these monks, their engagement in environmental issues brings them into political debates. The positions they take can vary, even as they remain true to the ideals of relieving suffering at the most abstract level, and protecting nature at the most basic. Some of their work is controversial, as the case of Achan Pongsak Techadhammo and the NGO, the Dhammanaat Foundation for Conservation and Rural Development, demonstrates.

Dhammanaat Foundation—Protecting Nature or People?

The case of Achan Pongsak, one of the first environmental monks, illustrates a debate that has raged across Thailand since the state began to protect forest land through the creation of national parks in the early 1960s. The debate concerns the role of people—particularly ethnic minority mountain peoples in northern Thailand—living in the forest as either destroying or protecting the forest. Most environmental monks tend to support people living in the forest, even if they do not have legal rights to their land. They argue that given sufficient knowledge and support, these people will care for the forest as they have vested interests in its well-being. But Achan Pongsak, and the NGO he co-founded in Chiang Mai with a minor member of the royalty, the Dhammanaat Foundation, adopted a "dark green" approach, joining the ranks of conservation NGOs that "favor a radical separation between people and nature" (Delcore 2005, n.p.). Lohmann (1999, n.p.) describes this approach as a "people-*vs*-trees narrative of forest decline" that blames deforestation and resulting threats to watershed areas on people living in the forests.

Achan Pongsak was one of the most active and well-known monks in Thailand for his conservation work in the 1980s and early 1990s (interview, 3/18/1993; Dhammanaat 1990; Pongsak 1990, 1991a, 1991b, 1991c, n.d.) Like many other "forest monks" who have become engaged in environmentalism, his ecological concerns and actions emerged from his meditation and pilgrimage practice in the forests of Thailand.[10] His ascetic practice provided the base from which he developed his original, yet religiously grounded, ecological interpretations of the dhamma.

It was while on thudong in Chiang Mai Province in the 1970s that Achan Pongsak discovered a small cave deep in the forest of Chom Thong District (interview, 3/18/1993). He settled there to practice meditation, but over the course of only a few years he witnessed severe destruction of the forest environment and watersheds due to logging and human encroachment. As a result, he founded a conservation and development organization, the Dhammanaat Foundation for Conservation and Rural Development, in 1985. The Dhammanaat Foundation worked with people from five Northern Thai villages to protect the watersheds that fed their land and to reclaim deforested and desiccated land for farming, which would prevent further encroachment into forested and watershed areas. This controversial project also included the effort to relocate a Hmong village from a watershed above the valley.[11]

The project brought Achan Pongsak into conflict with local government officials and businessmen who either lost personal benefits they formerly received from logging in the project's area or who wanted to obtain the reclaimed land, which, formerly almost worthless, now had considerable value (interview, 3/18/1993). He received death threats, was labeled a "communist," and was subjected to an attack on his reputation that led him to derobe from the monkhood in 1992 rather than allow the controversy to discredit him, his development organization, or the sangha as a whole. Achan Pongsak continued his work as a devout lay person, wearing white robes, believing it to be not only crucial for the sake of the environment and all the life it supports, but because of its connection with religious practice.

Achan Pongsak takes the dhamma farther than most environmental monks in reinterpreting it in relation to conservation. For him, every aspect of the religion is associated with nature (interview, 3/18/1993; see also Dhammanaat 1990; Pongsak 1990, 1991b, n.d.). Like other activist monks, his main motivation comes from putting the dhamma into practice, teaching people to live according to its principles rather than following selfish desires.

This practice is carried out, according to Achan Pongsak, through a true understanding of *silatham,* one of the basic principles of Buddhism. While silatham is traditionally defined as "morality" (Payutto 1985, 405), Achan Pongsak defines it as "the maintenance of balance with the nature of the individual, the society and the environment" (Dhammanaat 1990, 10). For him it involves attaining a harmony between the natural and social environments and between the physical and mental needs of both individuals and society. Being concerned with only one of these environments or needs leads to imbalance and the rise of selfish aims. Echoing the renowned philosopher monk and his teacher, Buddhadasa Bhikkhu, Achan Pongsak sees the well-being of the forest as crucial to achieving this balance.

> The Balance of Nature in the environment is achieved and regulated by the functions of the forest. Hence the survival of the forest is essential to the survival of *silatham* in our environment. It is all interdependent. When we protect the forest we protect the world. When we destroy that Balance, causing drastic changes in global weather and soil conditions, causing severe hardship to the people. . . . Thus the forest is the creator of environmental *silatham,* ensuring a healthy harmony in people's lives both physically and mentally. (Pongsak n.d., 2)

Achan Pongsak describes forests as our "second set of parents" (Pongsak 1990, 3). They support our life through filtering the air we breathe, acting as water reservoirs, harboring watersheds and nourishing the soil in which we grow our food. They are our first homes, "giving sanctuary to both body and spirit" (interview, 3/18/1993; Pongsak 1990, 3). The forests not only provide the four necessities of life—food, clothing, shelter, and medicine—but also the quiet and peace essential for the well-being of the mind.

The practical application of Achan Pongsak's interpretation of silatham comes from understanding the interdependence between the forests, nature, individuals, and society. Misunderstanding and the resulting "wrong attitudes" lead to both environmental and social destruction. For example, Achan Pongsak said,

> [T]raditionally in Thai society, the forests have sustained the people; the people have sustained society; and the government has been supported by that society. But the government of today acts in the mistaken assumption that they are in charge of the people. They do not know that they are the servants of the people. (Pongsak 1990,2)

Every faction within society, he argues, from the government and businessmen to the farmers and minority groups, has developed wrong attitudes toward the forests. Each of these factions thinks of forests as commodities to be used for personal benefit rather than recognizing their importance for all life. This misconception results in imbalance and the predominance of igno-rance, greed, and hatred.

Like Phrakhru Pitak's use of rituals, Achan Pongsak uses religious con-cepts already familiar to the rural villagers with whom he works, applying them in an innovative way to the tangible problems of deforestation and the lack of water. Far too often, he argues, monks teach the dhamma in an abstract manner, making it difficult for villagers without religious training to comprehend its direct impact on their lives. Achan Pongsak uses his concept of silatham and other Buddhist teachings as the basis of a program to refor-est destroyed land, protect watersheds, and provide villagers with a sustain-able livelihood that will not contribute to further devastation of the forest environment.

It is this two-part purpose that motivates Achan Pongsak's work: to teach the dhamma in a manner that leads to understanding and commitment; and to apply the dhamma to the solution of a problem that causes suffering. In other words, Achan Pongsak is putting the dhamma into practice, finding a balance between its abstract concepts and its tangible application in everyday life. His solution—like those of all environmental monks—contributes, in its efforts to return to a "true" interpretation of the Buddha's teachings, to a radical rethinking of both Buddhism and Thai society; the telltale evidence of the impact of this rethinking is the strong, sometimes violent opposition to Achan Pongsak's work by many people who feel threatened by it.

Achan Pongsak and his supporters favored an interpretation of nature conservation that separated people from the "wilderness." This position was championed by Thai urban elite, who modeled their form of environmental-ism after the U.S. preservationists who advocated the separation of wilderness from people. Thailand established its national parks and wildlife reserves on the notion that the nation's forests survived because of "the relative absence of human influence rather than of human stewardship or commercial inac-cessibility" (Lohmann 1999, n.p.). Pinkaew (2001, 64) argues that even as members of the Thai state adopted North American wilderness thinking in their efforts to protect the nation's forest, they ironically reversed the empha-sis of the underlying concept. She cites Cronon's (1996, 78) description of the "national frontier myth" in the United States that set "wilderness" apart from "the ugly artificiality of modern civilization." In Thailand, the concept of wilderness instead promoted modernization and bringing forested "wil-derness" areas under state control as useful resources. "Most importantly," she says, "this process has been an integral part of the capitalization of natu-ral resources through a 'development' paradigm" (Pinkaew 2001, 65).

Ultimately, Pinkaew concludes that the definitions of nature are fluid, and key elements of the state (itself a multifaceted player in defining the concept and use of "nature") ground their definition through demonizing marginalized, non-Thai people:

> I argue that this particular history [of the formation of "protected areas"] in the context of the modern Thai state often includes the process of creating the "Nature-malicious figures"—the shaping of people and their practices as a source of peril to the designated landscape. Marginalization of peripheral people is therefore an integral part of the process of nature-making in Thailand. Marginalized people, in this process, are not excluded from the domain of the "pristine" landscape; on the contrary, their presence is acknowledged, granted attention, and categorized into a fixed, malign entity overriding their actual history. (Pinkaew 2001, 5)

Dhammanaat Foundation, which Pinkaew describes as "an urban, middle-class conservation group" (2001, 55), represents an interesting case study. On one level, Achan Pongsak and Dhammanaat have won environmental awards, most notably a Global 500 Award from the United Nations Environment Program in 1990 (Lohmann 1999, n. 48; Renard 1994, 661). At the same time, a tension arose between the Buddhist philosophy on which Pongsak's work is based and claims that Dhammanaat's efforts to remove the Hmong from the watersheds amounts to racial oppression (Lohmann 1999). The controversies, as well as the successes, of Dhammanaat illustrate the diversity within the environmental monk movement and the importance of avoiding stereotyping Buddhist environmentalism in sweeping terms.

Particularly controversial were Achan Pongsak's views on the agricultural practices of minority mountain peoples and Dhammanaat's efforts to relocate a Hmong village from a watershed area above the five main villages with which the organization worked. Mountain people primarily live through swidden agricultural practices. As the land in the hills became more crowded and valuable, mountain people had few options for letting their land remain fallow for sufficient amounts of time. Lowland Thais began to blame mountain people for deforestation and degradation of the forest land in northern Thailand. The involvement of many mountain people, especially the Hmong, in growing opium poppies became particularly controversial. Through the support of both the Thai state and the Thai-Norwegian Church Aid Highland Development Project, the Hmong in the Chom Thong region of Chiang Mai Province, where Achan Pongsak worked, shifted from opium production to commercial, chemical-intensive cabbage monoculture agriculture (Lohmann 1999).

Cabbage is a controversial crop itself because of its dependence on both chemical fertilizer and the market. It requires large areas of land to make up for the profits of opium poppies (Plate 24). On the hillsides, cabbage fields quickly contribute to erosion as large areas are clearcut for cultivation. The chemical fertilizers wash downhill, polluting the streams and fields below them. In Chom Thong, the Hmong grew their cabbage in a watershed area. The Thais living below them blamed them for their decreased water and soil degradation problems.

Achan Pongsak agreed that the Hmong, who live in the highest altitudes, contributed to the degradation of vital watersheds. Besides needing to find substitute crops for their opium poppies, he believed they needed to move off the mountaintops and away from the watersheds. The crop substitution program highlights the complexities within the environmental movement. All environmentalists place watershed protection high on a list of priorities, but the consequences of moving the Hmong off the mountains raise questions of methodology and racism.

Academics from Chiang Mai University and abroad, journalists, and other development nongovernment organizations called the Dhammanaat Foundation racist for placing concerns for nature over those for poor, minority mountain peoples (Lohmann 1999, 2000; Paibool 2003). In fact, these sentiments are reflected in comments made by Achan Pongsak when he warned his followers that a

> calamitous drought is spreading across the whole country, withering the land because a small group of people have migrated into Thailand from neighbouring countries. Should anyone insist that human rights take precedence over this law of nature . . . then these people must take responsibility for the destruction of the people of our nation, the land and the life of that land. . . . Which is the larger undertaking—ensuring the survival of our land and our nation or the resettlement of the hilltribes? (Pongsak 1991a, n.p.)

Achan Pongsak's and Dhammanaat's position on the need to prioritize nature and the needs of lowland, Buddhist Thais versus the needs of minority, non-Buddhist and non-Thai people plays on the symbolic rhetoric of Nation, Religion, and Kingship. Twice, Dhammanaat funded lowland villagers to erect a fence in the mountains: In 1986, an eighteen-kilometer, barbed wire fence kept Hmong villagers from the Chom Thong watershed they farmed. Again in 1998, Dhammanaat put up another fence dividing mountain people from "natural" areas. In this case, the fenceposts were painted in the tricolors of the Thai flag: red, white, and blue. As Larry Lohmann (1999, n.p.) points out, "[T]he message was both unmistakable and provocative: those on one side of the fence belonged to the Thai 'nation'; those on the other did not."

Achan Pongsak's emphasis on the value of the forest for Buddhist practice seems at odds with accusations of environmental racism. As the director of Dhammanaat's United Kingdom branch wrote, Pongsak's "consistent reply [to accusations of racism] has been that his duty as a monk is to concern himself with moral issues, and that the health of the forest is vital to the moral, spiritual and physical welfare of all those who live in proximity to it" (Nelson 1990, n.p.). Yet other environmental monks and NGOs criticized Pongsak for insensitivity to the mountain people and a narrow view of Buddhist application.

The case illustrates some of the complexities within Buddhist environmentalism. Leaving aside the scholarly debate as to whether Buddhism is inherently ecological, even when all environmental monks lay claim to a basis in philosophy, the application can take different forms and have diverse social ramifications. More significant is that so many of the monks take similar stances on controversial issues. Achan Pongsak stands out for his unusual position on the question of people in the forest, especially for the racist aspects of his approach. Although not unilaterally in line with state policy, Dhammanaat lines up more closely with government and urban, middle-class attitudes toward marginalized people than most environmental monks. His interpretations of Buddhist principles in support of ecological conservation, however, provide a sophisticated, well-grounded philosophical basis for the work of environmental monks.

❧———☙

One of the major challenges facing environmental monks is conveying the underlying Buddhist principles to the local people and gaining their moral commitment. Development or environmental activities in themselves are not Buddhist. As Phrakhru Manas and Phrakhru Pitak quickly learned, just talking about the connections between Buddhism and nature does not motivate people to change their lives to protect natural resources. The monks needed a means of communicating the moral and spiritual grounding of their work to the laity that would impact people and invest their work with moral authority. Drawing on one of the most powerful and effective aspects of Buddhism in Thai society, they integrated ritual into their grassroots methodology, which quickly formed the core of an emerging, albeit fluid, Buddhist environmental movement.

PLATE 1. Sacred tree at Wat Chedi Luang, Chiang Mai

PLATE 2. Informal tree ordination in Nan Province, performed by Phrakhru Wiboon
Nanthakit

PLATE 3. Formal tree ordination in Nan Province, 1991

PLATE 4. Miss Thailand Universe 2010 contestants performing a tree ordination. Photo provided by Bangkok Broadcasting & T.V. Co., Ltd. with watermark. Copyright 2010

PLATE 5. Phrakhru Pitak Nanthakhun

PLATE 6. Deforestation in Nan Province

PLATE 7. Accepting seedling donations at *pha pa ton mai* ceremony and tree ordination in Nan Province, 1991

PLATE 8. Celebration of Phrakhru Pitak Nanthakhun's ecclesiastical promotion and environmental award at *suep chata* ceremony for the Nan River, 1993

PLATE 9. Monks chanting at a tree ordination holding the *sai sincana,* or sacred cord, connecting them to water, the Buddha image, and the tree being consecrated

PLATE 10. Spirit shrine behind ordained tree in Phrakhru Pitak's village

PLATE 11. Skit enacting blame for deforestation on government policies, performed as part of tree ordination in Nan Province, 1991

PLATE 12. Tree to be ordained in Nan Province, 1991

PLATE 13. Headman drinking consecrated water during tree ordination in Nan Province to seal his pledge to protect the forest, 1991

PLATE 14. Ordained tree, including sign reading, "*tham lai pa khue tham lai chat*," which is translated as, "To destroy the forest is to destroy life"

PLATE 15. Monk drawing a sign for the environmental fair at the *suep chata,* or long-life ritual, for the Nan River, 1993

PLATE 16. Parade for the Love the Nan River Project, 1993

PLATE 17. *Suep chata* pyramid for the Nan River, 1993

PLATE 18. Luang Pu Phutta-poj Waraporn (Chan Kusalo) conducting a ritual to give rural farmers donated buffalos

PLATE 19. Beautiful buffalo contest at Wat Pa Dharabhirom, Mae Rim, Chiang Mai

PLATE 20. Phrakhru Manas Nathiphitak

PLATE 21. Feeding the fish at the fish sanctuary in Don Kaew Village, Nan Province

PLATE 22. Phra Somkit Jaranathammo

PLATE 23. Phra Somkit Jaranathammo at his model integrated agriculture farm, Nan Province

PLATE 24. Cabbage field in Chom Thong District, Chiang Mai

PLATE 25. Monks at seminar on health and environmental issues, Chiang Mai, 1992

PLATE 26. Seminar for monks, "Monks' Roles in Natural Resource Conservation," in the *bot* at Wat Suan Kaew, 1991

PLATE 27. Registration at seminar on "Monks' Roles in Natural Resource Conservation"

PLATE 28. Monks listening to speaker at seminar on health and environmental issues in Chiang Mai, 1992

PLATE 29. Phra Somkit Jaranathammo reporting out from small-group discussion at seminar on health and environment in Chiang Mai, 1992

PLATE 30. Phra Prajak Khuttajitto, 1992

PLATE 31. Phra Somkit Jaranathammo and Phrakhru Pitak Nanthakhun overlooking the integrated agriculture farm at a meditation center in Nan Province, 2010

6

The Movement

If not monks who act, who will? Who else can do it?
—Phra Prajak Khuttajitto, July 19, 1991

Work in certain areas is taken as a model. For example, the work of Phrakhru Pitak and Luang Pho Dhammadilok [Phuttapoj Waraporn] is a good model. . . . Their places become resource centers for monks and the general public to study their work. . . . When these monks started their work, there were no policies to support them. But they experimented, and emphasized the community, and the people who give them alms. They looked at the problems they faced and how to solve these problems.
—Phra Maha Boonchuay, October 18, 2006

MONKS MOVED INTO environmental activism individually. They observed deforestation, lack of water, agricultural problems from intensive monocropping and use of chemicals, and the decrease of wildlife around where they lived and practiced. They sought ways of helping the people around them who were affected by environmental issues that impacted their livelihoods and their ability to meet basic needs, especially water and food. They drew from Buddhist practice and teachings to invest their work with morality and spirituality, using rituals and symbols to create new meanings for the laity, showing ways environmental issues intersected with Buddhist philosophy.

What gave this process its effectiveness was not just the actions of individual monks but the collective impact of a growing number of monks engaging in environmental work and their increasing cooperation, mutual support, and exchange of ideas and experiences. Environmental monks created a movement. Monks engaged in development and conservation came,

167

as Hannerz described a social movement, "together to construct new shared understandings on the basis of shared circumstances" (Hannerz 1992, 153, cited by Tegbaru 1998, 172). They sought out like-minded monks, consciously framing their approaches to the social issues they placed at the center of the suffering of farmers and nature.

I see Buddhist environmentalism as a fluid rather than a linear movement, based more on ideas, values, and constructed social and religious meanings than associations seeking explicit institutional or political change (Gusfield 1994, 64). Even the label "environmental monk" is arbitrary, occasionally self-applied but more often given to various monks by their followers, supporters, or the media. Yet they embrace the implications underlying the label, and negotiate the meanings and responsibilities within it.

Activist monks engaged multiple frames as the movement took shape. They began by defining the problems—from debt and urban migration to loss of natural resources and a sense of community disintegration. Applying Buddhist explanations, monks pointed to what they saw as the root causes of these problems: greed, hatred, and ignorance. This awareness motivated them to take action.

Identifying the problems and their causes is not sufficient to make a movement. Monks began to recognize who stood with them—as Purdue (2007, 7) would say, who could be included as "we" in the movement—and, to a lesser extent, who their adversaries were.[1] Initially, monks joined with other segments of Thai society dissatisfied with the negative consequences of state-led and corporate development on both the natural environment and people's lives as the environmental movement emerged in the mid-1980s. Monks' involvement in public protests against such projects as a proposed cable car up the sacred mountain Doi Suthep, in Chiang Mai, brought a moral element to the debates about economic development. They worked closely with—and needed the support of—development and environmental NGOs, the backbone of the larger environmental movement. Monks concerned with development and environmental issues began to visit each other to observe different projects, learn new methods, and discuss motivations and philosophies. Phrakhru Pitak's approach, for example, shifted from only teaching about environmental responsibilities in his sermons to conducting tree ordinations and organizing concrete projects after he visited several monks already undertaking environmental work. Buddhist environmentalism itself did not emerge until monks began to work with each other, to share ideas and consciously think about what it meant to undertake conservation work grounded in Buddhist principles.

The Buddhist environmental movement is separate from mainstream environmentalism in two ways. First, the monks are motivated to act because they are monks. They hold a unique position in Thai society carrying significant influence and responsibilities. The majority of the sangha enacts this position through serving as "fields of merit," conducting rituals, accepting alms, teaching the dhamma, and meditating. Those who see social justice as a central aspect of their being monks recognize that they are in a minority and that some members of the sangha view their social engagement as inappropriate or too political. They turn to each other for support in making their argument that the primary goal of Buddhism is to end suffering and that that process involves dealing with the social as well as the spiritual context.

Throughout the 1990s, activist monks frequently participated in seminars aimed at supporting those engaged in environmental activities and encouraging those concerned but not yet involved. Regional networks of activist monks emerged, focusing on local and regional issues, such as the Northern Development Monks Network. The Thai Interreligious Commission for Development (TICD) facilitated the formation of a national network of monks concerned about social issues, Sekhiyadhamma. The network sponsored many of the monks' seminars, and produced a newsletter addressing specific issues and sharing individual monks' work. Sekhiyadhamma, the seminars, and regional networks coordinated efforts among individual monks, creating a sense of greater purpose and community among environmental and development monks.

Second, these monks use Buddhism to frame their approach. Buddhism informs their concepts of nature and the human/nature relationship. While activist monks work closely with environmental NGOs, their visions and goals do not always align. The monks' ultimate goal entails helping people make spiritual progress and end suffering. Alternative forms of development and conservation projects are means to that end, not an end in and of themselves.

In her assessment of the origins of the environmental justice movement in the United States, McGurty cites Tarrow to emphasize the centrality of "coordinating, sustaining and giving meaning to collective action" (McGurty 2009, 18). For the Buddhist environmental movement, the construction of meaning occurred on two levels. First, the monks needed to understand the meanings of environmental activism within their Buddhist thinking. Here they drew heavily from the influence of key Buddhist philosophers and "scholar monks" (*phra nangsue*). Only then could they translate Buddhist philosophical meanings for the laity on whom their activism depended, through the use of Buddhist symbols such as themselves as monks and the rituals they performed.

The philosophical interpretations of Buddhism that support an ecological consciousness and, at times, justify environmental actions are formulated by a handful of prominent scholar monks. By far the most influential is Buddhadasa Bhikkhu. Although Buddhadasa did not directly engage in conservation work, his thinking contributed to the involvement, methods, and understandings of many environmental monks, including Achan Pongsak, Phrakhru Pitak, and Phra Prajak. P. A. Payutto's writings similarly provide a religious basis for engaged Buddhist monks. His high standing in the Thai sangha lends credence to the movement even though he, like Buddhadasa, does not engage in activism. The writings of these two leading Thai Buddhist thinkers anchor Buddhist environmentalism as they criticize the materialist directions of Thai society. Even though most environmental monks do not articulate strong philosophical positions, they depend on the ideas and interpretations of Buddhadasa and Payutto. In many ways, the movement began with their thinking.

Engaging the World

Buddhadasa Bhikkhu and P. A. Payutto[2] are the two best-known and most-respected intellectual monks in Thailand today. Even after Buddhadasa's passing in 1993, his philosophy continues to influence countless Buddhist activists, monks and laity, as they wrestle with ways Buddhism can affect the conditions of the world today. Payutto holds a high ecclesiastical position in the Thai sangha, and his writings, especially his extensive tome interpreting the Buddhist doctrine, *Buddhadhamma,* are regarded by many as definitive statements on Theravada Buddhism. Both monks interpret the doctrine in ways that support engagement with the world, while maintaining that ultimately it is spiritual progress and morality that matter most. As such, their thinking provides the philosophical grounding for many activist monks, even when the latter may deviate in practice from some of the core teachings of both senior monks. Other key monks, such as Phra Paisal Visalo, who continue to interpret the dhamma in ways that promote social activism and social justice, are strongly influenced by Buddhadasa and Payutto.

Both Buddhadasa and Payutto argue that Buddhism must be relevant in the modern world. Its teachings offer ways to avoid or deal with social problems that have emerged due to what both monks see as the lack of moral practice. Buddhadasa takes this argument one step farther, pointing to wrong interpretations of religion (and in this he includes all religions, not just Buddhism) (Jackson 2003 [1987], 211). In his critique of religious interpretations and practice fostered by religious institutions, Buddhadasa diverges from Payutto. Buddhadasa rejected any formal role within the Thai sangha organization, choosing instead to live as a forest monk at his meditation retreat in southern Thailand, Suan Mokh. His interpretation of the doctrine similarly rejects formal, institutionally backed approaches.

Payutto took a different path, remaining within the sangha administration, although he did at one point resign as the abbot of a temple in Bangkok to focus on his scholarly research and writing. As a result of his publications, especially *Buddhadhamma,* he was promoted to a high ecclesiastical position. From that position, he is able to further his argument for the application of Buddhist teachings in the world.

Sallie King sums up a key difference in the approaches of the two monks:

The cornerstone of Buddhadasa's spirituality has been the "void" or non-attached mind (*cit-wang*). This has allowed him consistently to "think outside the box" of established Buddhist interpretations and to be uniquely creative in applying Buddhism to the modern world. Payutto, the most eminent scholar of his time, speaks with a scholar's voice, consistently grounding his statements in quotations from scriptures. Buddhadasa liked to bait and provoke others as a kind of skillful means in order to try to get others to see things in a fresh way, to think deeply on matters on which the established understanding had shut off thought. This role as provocateur frequently extended to the realm of politics. Payutto is concerned for the sangha to be apolitical and tends to criticize the most politically engaged elements of the sangha, which makes him appear to support the status quo. When he makes statements with political implications, they tend to be couched in very traditional terms. As a consequence of these traits, Buddhadasa has been much more influential in the development of social and political criticism in Thailand than Payutto. (King 2002, 291 n. 4)

Despite Payutto's affiliation with the sangha administration, Olson argues that his scholarship influences numerous scholars and activists to rethink the place of Buddhism in the world: "this learned monk-scholar's updated and competent applications of Buddhist doctrine started a new wave of writings on the social applications of Buddhism" (Olson 1995, 6). King may see Payutto as less influential than Buddhadasa, but his writings and thinking have provided support and philosophical grounding for many activist monks.

These two most prominent Thai scholar monks in the twentieth century both advocate Buddhism's relevance in the modern world. They both call for a reform of Thai Buddhism through a return to the original teachings. For Buddhadasa, reform includes demythologizing Buddhist doctrine—moving away from the idea of the Buddha as a figure of reverence who could intervene in the world, and away from merit-making as the predominant form of Buddhist practice in Thailand. For too long the emphasis in Thai Buddhism has been improving the individual's position in a future life, rather than working for spiritual progress and enlightenment in this life. According to Jackson,

> The systemic demythologization of Buddhist doctrine is paralleled by Buddhadasa's pervasive concern to give religious value to action in the material world. His reinterpretations of the religion's teachings are characterized by a shift of the theoretical focus of Buddhist doctrine from the transcendent to this world here and now. Buddhadasa effects this shift by redefining the notion of Buddhist salvation as being a condition of life in this world, and then using this new definition to develop a more explicitly social thrust to Buddhist doctrine. (Jackson 2003[1987], 33)

Jackson (2003[1987], 5) argues that Buddhadasa's concern with the social relevance of Buddhism emerged from the social changes occurring in Thailand as a result of modernization in the twentieth century. Buddhadasa was aware of the socioeconomic environment in which he lived, and was concerned with the effects of these changes on people's interpretations of religion and religious practice. Rather than rampant development based on individual greed, which he felt defined capitalism, Buddhadasa called for socioeconomic development based on Buddhist teachings. In the process, he emphasized the good of the whole (society) over the individual (King 2002, 290), and criticized the "traditional" interpretation of doctrine by both the official sangha administration and Thai elite (Jackson 2003[1987], 52).

In examining the links between the individual and society, both Buddhadasa and Payutto critique the current state of Thai society, especially its dependence on capitalism and consumerism. Capitalism is not, for either scholar, the root of social problems in and of itself, but a symptom of the lack of morality in society. Desire (tanhā, Pali), particularly the desire to consume, leads people to exploit and oppress others, resulting in the suffering of poverty (and further desire for material goods). Buddhadasa explicitly blames religious institutions for wrong interpretations, creating the desire for materialism:

> Because of wrong interpretations people fail to apply themselves to religious practice so that their so-called "religion" ceases to be an effective device for solving the problems of everyday existence. Only when a religion has failed to do its duty does materialism come into existence in the world. . . . [I]f religious institutions interpret the tenets held by them correctly, especially the tenets expressed in the language of *Dhamma* [i.e., *phasa tham*], then religious practice itself will prove to be the "decided opponent" of materialism in all its forms. (Jackson 2003[1987], 211)

The underlying cause of this failure is not maintaining *chit wang,* or detached mindfulness. Without chit wang, people develop self-centeredness: "Self-centredness is the basic cause of suffering, both individually and socially," Buddhadasa wrote (Jackson 2003[1987], 210). Self-centeredness leads people to desire material objects, believing they can be possessed. This belief further leads to hoarding and economic imbalance in society. Those who are poor rebel against a socioeconomic system that oppresses them, resulting in conflict and violence (Jackson 2003[1987], 236). Self-centeredness is central to what Buddhadasa refers to as the "wrong view":

> [The w]rong view takes the position, "Eat well, live well." But the right view asserts, "Eat and live only sufficiently." These perspectives differ greatly. Those who hold the, "Eat well, live well," view do not have any limits. They are always expanding until they want to equal the gods (devata). Those who hold the "eat and live only sufficiently" view represent moderation: whatever they do, they do moderately. This results in a state of normal or balanced happiness (pakati-sukha). They will have no problem of scarcity, and there will be no selfishness. If people are overly ambitious, they become selfish. Those who limit their ambition are not selfish. They are not consumed by the fires of desire. The values represented by right view

and wrong view differ. The one leads to appropriate consumption. The other to excessive consumption. In the most basic sense the wrong view will see very little or no value to morality; the right view, however, will consider morality to be very important, valuable, and of great interest. (Buddhadasa 1989, 162)

Selfish desire (tanhā) lies at the root of social as well as individual problems in Payutto's thinking as well. The Buddha defined this kind of desire as "a desire to consume and lavish things upon yourself." Such desire, in Payutto's view, "raises problems for development, such as deceitfulness, laziness and elusion, and looking for personal gains by taking short-cuts" (Payutto 1987, 62–63). In contrast, another kind of desire articulated by the Buddha is *chanda*, a "desire for knowledge and action which is correct and excellent" (Payutto 1987, 62). Payutto describes chanda as "a desire which is necessary for solving all types of problems. . . . If we translate it very simply, it can mean desire in dhamma or with regard for dhamma. . . . Chanda, in this sense is, therefore, related to truth; thus we can translate the desire for knowledge or an interest in knowledge as a desire to know the truth" (Payutto 1987, 63–64). Such a desire counteracts tanhā as one develops the knowledge and understanding of the problems of selfishness and its impact on others. Payutto summarizes as follows:

[C]handa can be translated as the desire for knowledge, an interest in knowledge and wanting to do, or taking an interest in doing what is correct and excellent. I believe that *chanda is the axis of development,* it is the thing which education must instill, and then we will not have the problem of desiring or not desiring, and we can stop talking about it altogether. (Payutto 1987, 64; emphasis in original)

Buddhadasa describes the relationship between the kinds of desire in different but similar terms, expanding them to consider their impact on society:

Nature would have each of us use no more than we actually need. For years people have failed to heed the way of nature, competing with one another to take as much as they can, causing the problems that we live with to this day. If we were to take only what is enough, none of these problems would exist, because then people would not be taking advantage of others and oppressing them. (Buddhadasa 1989, 174)

He continues,

> What is needed is an approach that emphasizes not taking more than is needed and at the same time is in accordance with the laws of nature, for then people would share whatever extra they had out of *metta-karuna*—compassion and loving kindness. People would set aside for themselves only what they needed; anything in excess of that would be left for society. (Buddhadasa 1989, 174)

Buddhadasa and Payutto both emphasize that spiritual and material progress must occur together, an idea that development monks in particular uphold. Buddhadasa said, "Solving problems materially is inadequate; problems must be solved mentally as well" (in Jackson 2003[1987], 203). Swearer describes how Buddhadasa sees this process working on both the individual and social levels:

> Buddhadasa's vision of the good and just society coincides with his view of an original state of nature or an original human condition, one of mutual interdependence, harmony and balance. By its very being this state of nature is selfless—individuals are not attached to self for its own sake. But with the loss of this state of innocence, individuals are subject to the bondage of attachment (*upādāna*) and unquenchable thirst (*tanhā*). Consequently, sentient beings need to find ways to return to or restore this condition of mutual interdependence and harmony, love and respect. On the personal level, the attainment of wisdom through the methods of awareness (*sati*), continuous attention (*sampajañña*), and focused concentration (*samādhi*) serve to break through the conditions of greed, ignorance and defilement (*kilesa*), while on the social level those in positions of power promote economic and political policies which after meeting basic physical needs promote a balanced development in which matters of spirit (*citta*) assume their rightful dominance.
>
> His vision serves as a critique of both capitalism and communism and provides the basic principles for a political philosophy with the potential to help guide Buddhist Thailand to a more just and equitable social, political and economic order. (Swearer 1989, 7)

Jackson points out that for Buddhadasa, the relationship between spiritual and material progress revolves around the inability of the poor to have the resources to devote themselves to spiritual affairs. Spiritual attainment, in his philosophy, should be a universally accessible goal in the here and now, regardless of one's economic status (Jackson 2003[1987], 207). Much of Buddhadasa's writing on socioeconomic and political issues involves working toward the spiritual salvation of the populace. Liberation from suffering does not only entail overcoming one's own desires, but also the oppressive conditions in the world. In this way, Buddhadasa argues for Buddhist-based activity to improve the well-being of others to change or get rid of the external causes of suffering so that people can concentrate on achieving spiritual liberation. In fact, he sees it as a responsibility of a religious person to work for the greater good:

> Religion doesn't only mean the actions of individuals to pass beyond suffering. We must still help others to pass beyond suffering also. That is, we must have loving-kindness (*karuna*) towards our fellow man and towards all sentient beings, because if we are completely without loving-kindness we will be a self-centred person. . . . As is said in the Pali words of the Lord Buddha in the *Nipata Sutta* of the *Khuddaka Nikaya* . . . , "A person who only has wisdom in seeking out his own benefit is an impure human being . . . " Hence a religious person must assist others as one type of necessary human duty, or else it will be to have a religion in words only. (Jackson 2003[1987], 223)

Payutto parallels Buddhadasa in articulating the moral value of eliminating suffering in the world on both the spiritual and material levels. This entails development on both the individual and social levels, involving moral and material development. People who have achieved these levels of development should work with others for the good of society:

> According to Buddhist principles, people who are already developed are those who can help solve problems and develop society along with developing themselves; that is, developing yourself goes right along with other kinds of development. These kinds of people have four characteristics—monks use the Pali word bhāvita: 1) bhāvita-kāya, 2) bhāvita-sīla, 3) bhāvita-citta, and 4) bhāvita-paññā. Translated very simply **bhāvita-kāya**—means having made bodily or physical progress and development; **bhāvita-sīla**—means having morality and discipline which is advanced and developed; **bhāvita-citta**—means having a heart-mind which is developed and has made

progress; **bhāvita-paññā**—means having developed wisdom and intelligence. (Payutto 1987, 71; emphasis in original)

Payutto elaborates on the meanings of the four kinds of development, showing how the individual and social aspects are interrelated. In the process, he provides a deep philosophical base for activist monks who undertake community development. In fact, from his position at Mahachulalongkorn Buddhist University in the 1970s, Payutto was a strong advocate for the creation of community development courses for monks that would enable them to assist rural communities.

Payutto bases his support of monks undertaking community development work in both his ideas of spiritual and material development and in rebuilding and retaining the relevance of Buddhism and the sangha in a changing world. He believes that as Siam modernized at the end of King Chulalongkorn's reign (1868–1910), modernization on the part of the sangha declined. The kingdom secularized its education and development process, leaving the monks on the sideline. Most monks took on ritualistic roles as a result, emphasizing traditionalism and merit-making (Payutto 1984, 106). Thailand has been described as undergoing modernization without development, which Payutto blames at least in part on the absence of the sangha in the process. The spiritual, moral aspects of development were ignored, allowing the rise of tanhā and greed described above.

To counteract this process, Payutto calls for monks to engage in society by getting a full education on which they can draw. He argues that they could work for social change from within the system, where they would hold the respect of the laity. They could work with Thailand's intellectuals to effect social change based on Buddhist concepts of loving-kindness (*metta*), compassion (*karuna*), sympathetic joy (*mudita*), and equanimity (*upekkha*). The sangha could take spiritual leadership in society again, working toward the joint goals of moral and social development. Monks need to remember the Buddha's statement to his followers to go forth out of compassion for the happiness and well-being of the people in the world (Payutto 1984, 114). While this call is interpreted conservatively to refer to spreading the Buddha's teachings, Payutto incorporates helping with the welfare of the laity as one of a monk's duties:

It is not that we are trying to secularise the Buddhist monk. Rather, we are attempting to restore his traditional place as religious leader and guide of the people. . . . Besides their own peculiar duties towards the goal of self-enlightenment, monks are bound with many social obligations to serve their community and to render reasonable services for the benefit of the layman's society. (Jackson 2003[1987], 217)

At the same time, Payutto is critical of monks merely supporting government programs or becoming involved in political agendas. Doing so makes the sangha followers of the secular government. "Thus, usually, [the sangha] readily joins or cooperates in the programmes and activities that are operated or supported by the government or government agencies, although such undertakings might have a tone of some modern social or even political ideologies" (Payutto 1984, 115). He includes the well-known government-run sangha projects Thammacharik and Thammathut, implying that the motivations underlying the projects are not sufficiently spiritual. He is more positive about monks, even some sangha administrators, who initiated their own community development and health projects.[3]

Similarly, Buddhadasa invoked the Buddha's admonition to monks to go forth and engage with people:

Buddhist monks are wanderers, not hermits. That is to say, they wander about in order to be involved with people who live in the world, rather than living in the forest cut off from social contact. Their duty is to help the people of the world in whatever way is suitable so that they do not have to suffer or, in the words of a Thai proverb, so that they can know "how to eat fish without getting stuck on the bones."

Buddhist monks, with the Buddha as their head, are always involved in society in order to teach people about the true nature of the world, to overcome suffering and avoid choking to death on the bones of life. Buddhism wants people neither to escape from the world nor to be defeated by it, but to live in the world victoriously. (Buddhadasa 1989, 83)

The main difference in Buddhadasa's call is that he believed monks must remain as spiritual guides rather than actively doing any form of development or social work, or especially direct political involvement. As the laity takes on a greater spiritual role in Buddhadasa's vision, able to achieve enlightenment in the here and now with proper moral practice, he saw the sangha's role as providing the moral guidance necessary to do so. An informed and educated—and spiritual—laity would then take up social welfare concerns.

Buddhadasa's approach complements that of Payutto. Together their philosophical interpretations provide a solid grounding for engaged Buddhists. They have each earned a national reputation for well-thought-out and carefully supported interpretations of the dhamma—Payutto as a high-ranking, highly educated Buddhist scholar who bases his work firmly on readings of scriptural texts and historical traditions; Buddhadasa as an independent, innovative meditation practitioner and teacher who rejected a monastic career, and draws from experience to create an ontological, active interpretation of the dhamma. Public recognition of their theological prowess and their sacredness gives both of these monks positions of influence and power within the Thai Buddhist world. Their interpretations of the dhamma as central to dealing with current social issues lend legitimacy to the activist monks who apply them to immediate and particular situations. In each of these senior monks we see a conscious interpretation of Buddhism in ways to make it applicable and relevant in contemporary society. It is left to the individual monks who choose to take up the call to social action to determine how to implement these philosophies.

Some monks began to apply these philosophies on their own, but soon discovered the difficulties of working alone. Others looked at the larger issues faced by Thais and realized the value—and urgency, in their minds—of grounding calls for change or challenges to economic development projects in Buddhist principles in order to avoid the kinds of social problems raised by Buddhadasa and Payutto. Neither Buddhadasa nor Payutto formally called for a social movement of monks in environmental or development work. They both eschewed direct political engagement by monks, seeing their responsibility as providing moral guidance for laity's involvement.

Drawing on and implementing their ideas, activist monks took their philosophies into the political realm. Even as common understandings of Buddhism's relevance in contemporary society and the shared meanings underlying their actions emerged, debates arose over methods and the extent of political activities. As with all social movements, the process was not always smooth nor homogenous. These monks did agree, though, that the state of Thai society necessitated intervention and that as monks they had a responsibility to act.

Sacred Protests

While the 1970s saw a growing movement for alternative development that evolved into a rich and complex environmental movement in the late 1980s, one incident stands out as marking the entry of Buddhism into environmental debates in Thailand. Prior to 1985, a small number of monks engaged in rural development work, and an even smaller number quietly introduced issues of environmental conservation into their local development projects. All this changed when the Tourism Authority of Thailand proposed to build a cable car up Doi Suthep, the sacred mountain that overshadows Chiang Mai city.

No one knew the term *environmental monk* at that time. Connections between economic development and environmental problems were only beginning to grab public attention as the international environmental movement made inroads into the Thai landscape. Even with earlier specific causes and actions, the environmental movement only emerged as a powerful force with the successful protest against the construction of the Nam Choen Dam in Kanchanaburi Province in 1988 (Rigg 1995, 13). The campaign against the cable car up Doi Suthep set the stage for this movement, and placed monks as environmental activists in the public eye for the first time.

Doi Suthep stands high above Chiang Mai city, a constant reminder of the city's history and the omnipotence of Buddhism. Chayant describes the importance of the site for Northern Thai Buddhism:

> Doi Suthep is a mountain lying at the outskirts of the town of Chiang Mai, named for a seventh-century Lawa chieftain who converted to Buddhism, became a monk, and retreated from the world to the mountain which now bears his name. It is the location of an important Buddhist monastery, Wat Pra That, which houses a relic of the Buddha. Local people revere the mountain temple as a destination of spiritual significance for Buddhists. Since the construction of the temple in the fourteenth century, Doi Suthep has been an important pilgrimage site. (Chayant 1998, 265–66)

In 1934, the charismatic abbot of Wat Phra That, Khruba Sriwichai, organized his followers to build a road up the mountain so that pilgrims could more easily reach the site.[4] People came from across the region to contribute time and labor as acts of merit making to build the road that still winds up the sacred mountain. In the 1980s, Chiang Mai began to look for ways to improve its tourism, a major source of revenue for the city, including emphasizing its Buddhist temples and Doi Suthep. The then abbot of Wat Phra That concurred with city officials and the Tourism Authority of Thailand that the road up the mountainside was outdated and dangerous. The most efficient way of getting pilgrims and tourists to the temple would be via cable car (Chayant 1998; Swearer et al. 2004, 33–35).

The idea of building a cable car up the mountain to Wat Phra That and developing it as a commercial tourist site offended the religious sensibilities of most Chiang Mai people. Not only would the cable car cut through the Doi Suthep-Pui National Park that encompassed the temple, a royal palace, and the surrounding forested mountainside, but it endangered the peace and sanctity that the temple and mountain, as sacred sites, embody. It also threatened the identity and well-being of the people of Chiang Mai. As Swearer et al. (2004, 35) put it, "The reverence for Doi Suthep in the cultural imagination of northern Thais is unique. . . . If Doi Suthep and the mountains of northern Thailand degenerate into a terrain to be exploited for commercial value, more than trees and spectacular views will be lost; the morality and spiritual well-being—indeed, the very identity of a people—will be jeopardized as well."

Opposition to the cable car project emerged as soon as the government made the proposal public. Reflecting the emerging environmental movement as a whole, opposition included students, people's organizations, social action groups, local media, and the general public of the city. Buddhist monks joined the protests as the cause gained publicity and the full ecological and cultural impacts of building the cable car became apparent.[5] Concerns were raised over the deforestation of the mountainside, especially through the national park, which contained diverse plant, bird, and animal species. The combined efforts resulted in the project being withdrawn in 1987 (Chayant 1998, 267).[6]

Arguments focused on environmental conservation versus economic development, but the monks mostly framed their involvement in terms of sanctity and the threat to a sacred Buddhist heritage site. They responded to a local social and historical situation more than to an ecological issue; the threat to the sacred sites of Doi Suthep and Wat Phra That should not be underestimated as a powerful motivation for monks to move into political activism.

One monk in particular, the late Phra Phothirangsri, then assistant ecclesiastical governor of the Chiang Mai Province and highly revered abbot of Wat Phan Dong, took a leading role in the fight against the cable car (Swearer et al. 2004, 34). He articulated a link between Buddhism and preserving trees and the forest, beyond the immediate religious concern for a pilgrimage site. He argued that Buddhism and the forest cannot be separated. Phra Phothirangsri stood out as one of the first monks to articulate an environmental ethic publicly, and in a political debate. He later claimed the sangha administration bypassed him for ecclesiastical promotion as a result (personal communication, 9/5/1992).[7]

Phra Phothirangsri's willingness to speak out and lend the power of his name and reputation along with other monks to the anti-cable car movement contributed to the success of the protests. The case symbolized the connections between ecological and religious, cultural concerns about the direction of economic development in the kingdom. While most situations in which environmental monks engage do not explicitly involve a sacred site, the cable car case enabled monks to move into environmental activism explicitly through Buddhism. The public support for the anti-cable car movement encompassed the monks involved, despite criticisms from the sangha hierarchy. The explicit Buddhist connection in the Doi Suthep case laid the groundwork for eventual acceptance of monks' environmental engagement. With each event, even while controversy swirled around some monks, the public became more aware of their activities and motivations, and the larger impacts of the projects and policies to which the monks objected.

Environmental Monks and Civil Society

Key to understanding the emergence of Buddhist environmentalism as a movement is the relationship between activist monks and NGOs, a major component of Thai civil society. NGOs often supported and coordinated with environmental monks to enact their social and political goals of raising awareness and encouraging local engagement. The relationship between environmental monks and NGOs, at both national and local levels, demonstrates some of the ways civil society—the major site of opposition to state hegemony and state-led development—responds to social expectations and public reactions to the activities of prominent religious figures.

Maina's "activity view of civil society" (1998, 139), developed for an African context, offers a framework for understanding the potential of environmental monks' work with local people and NGOs. An activity view goes beyond defining civil society through organizational forms and institutions:

> Much that is both interesting and transformative in the [African] continent occurs outside or at the periphery of formal organizational life. Spontaneous protests, laxity and lack of discipline and active non-cooperation with the State are important civic activities that take place outside of formal organizations. Spontaneous,

non-confrontational methods such as these are safer ways of register-
ing one's disagreement with the government than more robust public activities such as protest marches, placard-waving and burning
effigies. (Maina 1998, 139)

Adapting Maina's concept to the situation of the Thai environmental
monks, their resistance to the government's push toward economic development and industrialization through working with rural farmers can be
incorporated into a deeper understanding of the complexity of the nation's
evolving civil society. For environmental monks, the nonconfrontational
methods used included helping rural people resist the government's push
toward capitalist economic development, particularly framed through the
performance of rituals such as tree ordinations. While their involvement in
protests and public actions brought environmental monks into the public
eye, their grassroots efforts together with various NGOs integrated their
approach with those of other elements of the Thai environmental movement.
This relationship led to mutual legitimation—lay environmentalists benefited
from the moral presence of activist monks, and the monks gained acceptance
from the growing segment of Thai society calling for social change as they
participated in key nonviolent protests and actions.

As they engaged in grassroots projects, these monks recognized the limi-
tations of working alone: a monk cannot organize people and handle all the
logistics of an environmental conservation project by himself. Drawing from
the relationship built through cooperation in protests, monks often turned
to NGOs—both local and national—for support, either joining with existing NGOs or, in a few cases, creating their own organizations. In many cases,
NGOs such as TICD or the Wildlife Fund Thailand (WFT) approached
monks to encourage or support their entry into conservation work. Key
examples of monks who established or coordinated NGOs include Achan
Pongsak and the Dhammanaat Foundation, and Phrakhru Pitak and the
Love Nan Province Foundation.

The cases of Phrakhru Pitak and Achan Pongsak demonstrate two models of monk-NGO cooperation, and monks' involvement in the public
sphere. For Achan Pongsak and the Dhammanaat Foundation, the model
shows an activist monk who established an NGO to promote his teachings
and undertake the majority of the actual work on his project. He served as
an advisor and director, as well as working closely with the villagers to help
them understand his philosophy, the urgency of protecting the forest, and
how both could improve their lives.

The story of the community forest project that Phrakhru Pitak under-took in 1991 demonstrates the dynamic nature of NGO-monk cooperation in environmental projects and the ways in which NGOs encouraged the Buddhist environmental movement. Begun a year earlier as one monk's efforts to deter the deforestation he witnessed in his home district, the project grew to be a showcase of Buddhist environmentalism and the growing push nationwide for government recognition of community forests. The community forest movement within the broader Thai environmental movement challenged the predominant government claim that people living within forested land could not adequately protect it. Many environmental NGOs argued that forest dwellers are the best defense against deforestation because their livelihoods depend on the forest resources.[8] Formally recognizing community-maintained forests, they argued, would help protect the remaining forest in Thailand (Local Development Institute 1992; Saneh and Yos 1993; J. Taylor 1994).[9]

National environmental NGOs saw the case of a Buddhist monk working with local people as an excellent opportunity to promote their efforts nationally to conserve the diminishing Thai forest. The "Citizens Love the Forest Program," a coalition of academics (predominantly social scientists from Chiang Mai University) and NGOs, took up Phrakhru Pitak's project in 1991 as one of several they supported across northern Thailand.

Phrakhru Pitak's work is less focused on one person's philosophy and guidance, but rather more closely resembles the model established through the cable car protest. Although his work is not in direct opposition to a specific project, it involves cooperation among several different groups with urban and middle-class allies concerned with the condition of the forest, the livelihood of the people living there, and the impact on both by government economic development policies. The space this cooperation creates represents an example, following Maina's activity view (1998, 139), of "civil society" in Thailand—how a coalition of people from a variety of backgrounds and classes spontaneously comes together surrounding a specific policy that they want the state to change. It also illustrates a shift from the spontaneous actions against the Doi Suthep cable car in the mid-1980s to a somewhat more organized, yet not fully systematic, approach to challenging government policy.

Both Phrakhru Pitak's and Achan Pongsak's examples reflect close cooperation between activist monks and particular NGOs. Early in the environmental movement, all factions involved stood to gain from working together, regardless of the differences among them concerning goals, methods, and ideologies. While the environmental movement in Thailand was never completely unified, at its height in the late 1980s and early 1990s diverse people and organizations joined together with a common cause of raising awareness in society and government, and initiating environmental action and reform.[10]

This momentum and cooperation within the environmental movement were hard to maintain over the long term. As more causes arose, the numbers of players grew and tensions between rural and urban interests emerged. Nevertheless, the early successes pointed to the benefits of putting various ideological and methodological differences aside to accomplish specific aims. Besides stopping the Doi Suthep cable car, at least for the present, a coalition of environmentalists, NGOs, people's organizations, monks, and students also halted the construction of the Nam Choen Dam in Kanchanaburi in 1988 (Rigg 1995, 13), and helped convince the government to establish a nationwide ban on logging in 1989 (Pinkaew and Rajesh 1992).[11]

In the context of the global environmental movement, one aspect of the movement in Thailand that these early cases demonstrate is the importance of framing environmental action in culturally relevant concepts (Rigg and Stott 1998).[12] Making the movement "Thai" rather than "Western" helped to gain support of people skeptical of foreign intrusion and change. An argument I frequently heard from NGO workers was that alternative development and environmental activism should be based in "Thai" concepts and culture, or—even more important—local understandings and practices of these concepts and cultures. Using Buddhist principles as the basis of such work was one frequent form of this approach (Seri 1986, 1988; Sulak 1992). Although not all environmental NGOs—either local or national—worked with activist monks (the Project for Ecological Recovery being the most prominent example), those that did gained from the relationship.

Monks' participation in NGO projects encouraged cooperation from lay people, especially in rural areas, because of the high esteem villagers held for monks. Villagers saw them as community leaders as well as spiritual leaders. When NGOs, especially those based in the capital or provincial cities, entered a village with the aim of getting the people to help protect the forest, watershed or other natural resources, villagers were more likely to listen to them if a local or famous monk supported the effort.[13] The image of Buddhist monks engaged in protecting the forest (especially through the action of ordaining trees) became invaluable social capital for NGOs to boost their reputation and gain the sympathy and cooperation of people nationwide.

NGOs helped the monks with funding, provided logistical and organizational support, and publicized their activities. Although only a handful of monks established their own NGOs, as in the case of Achan Pongsak and the Dhammanaat Foundation, or became as closely connected with a specific local organization as Phrakhru Pitak did, few undertook environmental activism without at least some support from an NGO. In addition, working with NGOs pulled the monks into the broader environmental movement, furthering public acceptance of their activism in this arena.

A less obvious indication of the benefits both monks and NGOs gained from their cooperation were seminars for monks interested or already engaged in environmental activism organized by some national NGOs, most often TICD and WFT. These NGOs reached out to monks in order to provide training for and facilitate dialogue and networking among activist monks. TICD helped organize Sekhiyadhamma, a network among activist monks that sponsored seminars and put out a regular newsletter about their work. In the case of WFT, most of the funding for their Buddhist project came from the Hong Kong–based Buddhist Perceptions of Nature Project initiated by Nancy Nash and inspired by the Dalai Lama (Davies 1987; Chatsumarn 1987b, 1998). The monks gained from these seminars in terms of building a support network among the sangha and learning new techniques and knowledge relevant to their work. The seminars increased public awareness of the activities of environmental monks, strengthening the impact of these projects as aspects of Thai civil society.

The most important aspect of these seminars came from the dialogue among environmental monks. Through the seminars, environmental monks defined themselves as distinct from the larger environmental movement. They discussed the meaning of using Buddhism for environmentalism in terms of methods, philosophies, and implications. Ultimately, coming together to share experiences, understandings, questions, concerns, and approaches led to the creation of a more cohesive movement among the monks themselves (Plate 25).

Imaging A Movement

A delicate light filtered through the branches illuminating the monks sitting below. The trees surrounded the sacred space of the *bot*, the consecrated assembly "hall" of the monastery, their branches meeting high above the tiled floor to form a natural roof. A moat surrounded the raised floor of the bot and contained the eight *sima,* consecrated boundary stones that marked the sacred area. Most bot across Thailand are elaborate buildings, often with dark interiors, where key rituals such as ordinations occur. Here there were no walls, just the trees framing the space.[14]

On this particular morning, the bot filled with monks who had come together to discuss their involvement in nature conservation (Plate 26). The setting was ideal for the subject matter, creating a calm, cool, peaceful environment in which to contemplate how to protect far larger stretches of forest and water under threat. The symbolism of the tree-lined bot emphasized the solemnity of the issue. The underlying urgency and contentions seemed muted in such serene surroundings.

More than two hundred monks attended the three-day seminar, entitled "Monks' Roles in Natural Resource Conservation." Co-sponsored by TICD and WFT, with support from twenty-one other NGOs, the conference offered insight into how these seminars worked to promote Buddhist environmentalism and to include new monks into the movement. The year was 1991, and the movement was in its early phases, in which only a few monks ran grassroots environmental projects, establishing wildlife sanctuaries, village forest conservation committees, and integrated agriculture projects. Even fewer conducted rituals such as tree ordinations or long-life ceremonies for waterways in conjunction with such projects. Fewer still were known outside of their communities. The best-known environmental monk at the time was Phra Prajak Khuttajitto because of his first arrest for allegedly trespassing in Dong Yai forest reserve. His radical actions highlighted deforestation and instigated debate across the country. At the time, the general public thought of controversy when environmental monks were mentioned because of the media attention surrounding Phra Prajak and the questions surrounding tree ordinations.

The NGO organizers invited all the monks they knew who were undertaking environmental work to discuss the activities of various monks and the future of the movement. They invited more than three hundred monks, but based on prior experience organizing such gatherings, they anticipated only about sixty would attend the three-day event. As registration the first day opened, the organizers were shocked as monks—including many who had no prior experience in social engagement—continued to arrive (Plate 27).

The seminar was held at Wat Suan Kaew outside of Bangkok, the temple of a well-known and outspoken abbot, Phra Payom Kanlayano. It is possible many monks attended out of curiosity because the conference occurred at Phra Payom's temple. His weekly dhamma radio shows incorporated commentary on social events and politics, and he was often openly critical of the sangha as a whole. The choice of his temple as the location for the seminar, however, had little to do with him personally—in fact, the organizers were aware of possible negative repercussions through associating the movement with him. The convenience and capacity of the temple compound lent itself to such a gathering.

More likely, the media attention given Phra Prajak drew many monks unfamiliar with the work of environmental monks. Many struggled to understand the tensions between activist monks and the state surrounding the goals, methods, and effects of the development process. A major theme throughout the seminar focused on the relationship between the sangha and the state, an issue highlighted in Phra Prajak's case. Monks not yet engaged in conservation work came to learn more—some wanting general information about the budding movement, others seeking more in-depth ideas and understanding of environmentalism. All brought concerns about keeping the movement grounded in Buddhism and building its relevance in society.

The seminar followed a pattern common to most that I attended throughout the 1990s. The organizers, together with well-known monks, introduced the main themes and questions for the gathering. They presented several informational talks that outlined the problems to be addressed, such as the environmental conditions in different regions of the country or the specific location for the seminar. Leading environmental monks presented their experiences, offering their stories to inspire other monks. Phrakhru Pitak spoke regularly at such seminars, including the one at Wat Suan Kaew, telling and retelling how he first became aware of and concerned about environmental issues (the story of the baby langur being a popular tale), the challenges he faced, and how and why he persevered. His story varied little from time to time. Phrakhru Pitak related a set version of his life story. Thinking carefully about his audiences and potential impact, he crafted a story that captivated and motivated listeners.

Through retelling, often to the same audience, the monks' stories became reified and almost turned into legend. Monks could tell other monks' tales, especially the more dramatic events. Phra Prajak's encounters with illegal loggers and his arrests quickly became popular lore among environmental monks as he grabbed society's imagination in 1991.

Phra Prajak's story structured much of the Wat Suan Kaew seminar. His conflict with the state occupied the minds of many environmental monks, concerned about the implications of the case for the sangha as a whole, the work of environmental monks, and their own situations. Another monk facing eviction from an illegal monastic residence on National Forest Reserve Land spoke at the conference together with Phra Prajak, further emphasizing the legal challenges with which forest monks in particular, but potentially all environmental monks, must come to terms. A main theme that emerged from the three days of talks, discussions, presentations, and meditations was political, not ecological or religious. Over and over again, monks and lay experts (primarily academics and social critics, including Sulak Sivaraksa and Dr. Prawase Wasi, two well-known spokesmen for social justice based in Buddhist teachings) raised the issue of how monks could engage in moral social and environmental work within a charged political setting and hierarchical society.

Speakers emphasized the challenges faced by the sangha in its relationship with the government concerning conservation issues. Phra Prajak's case took center stage, raising the debate whether monks protecting the forest, especially from state-led development programs, were breaking the law. Speakers used his case to explore the roots of forest destruction in the economic policies of the state. Sulak Sivaraksa, for example, offered a critique of Western influence in the nation's development and the state's policies, particularly through creating the desire for material goods. Such desire, he argued, changed people's relationship with nature, leading them to see natural resources as things to be possessed and used rather than as something to be valued and protected. Monks were in a unique position to affect local people's behavior, as role models and teachers. The challenge inherent in this process lay in confronting powers that stood to benefit from the material exploitation of nature. This confrontation formed the core of Phra Prajak's case, complicated by debates surrounding the evolving place of monks in Thai society.

Activist monks coalesced around Phra Prajak. He told the story of his arrest publicly for the first time at the Wat Suan Kaew seminar.[15] His charisma and dynamism captured the audience's attention and empathy. Despite the uncertainty of his case and the lack of comments and support from the sangha administration, most environmental monks were drawn to him, seeing him as a leader willing to take the risks necessary for the better good.[16]

In his talk, Phra Prajak underplayed his arrest. He spoke instead about the urgency of taking action, and the Buddhist concepts that motivated him. He adapted Buddhadasa's ideas, translating his more abstract philosophy into concrete terms to encourage other monks to engage the problems before them. Phra Prajak described the forest as a "world university" and "our second mother." The forest provides medicine and food, and serves as our teacher. The forest environment helps our chitchai, our heart and mind. As a forest monk, Phra Prajak followed in the tradition of seeing the forest as challenging and providing an environment conducive to meditation practice (Kamala 1997; Tambiah 1984; J. Taylor 1993a). He extended these benefits beyond the monks who retreated to the forest, recognizing what it gives to everyone. Everyone carries the responsibility to care for it, not just the Royal Forest Department officials, he argued, placing his concerns in the immediate context of crisis. Tree ordinations, which he first performed in 1989, preserved the few remaining large trees and emphasized the value of the forest. "The Buddha said the forest is our home. We should love it and care for it," he said. When he saw the forest being destroyed, he wanted to do something. "If not monks who act, who will? Who else can do it?" (seminar presentation, 7/19/1991).

Phra Prajak offered support and contributed to the creation of shared meaning among environmental monks. His situation inspired monks to move cautiously, thinking through the complex social and political webs surrounding their work. For example, Phrakhru Pitak deliberately held his first suep chata ritual on military land in 1993 and invited the governor to open the ceremony in order to pull both military and government officials into the project before they objected to any aspect of it. Although not articulated publicly at the Wat Suan Kaew seminar, I heard some monks quietly criticize Phra Prajak's rashness and inattention to the broader implications of his actions. Creating enemies within the state, military, and business worlds raised potential obstacles to achieving the objectives of protecting the forest and its natural resources and relieving the suffering of the people affected by deforestation. Prajak's approach was seen by some as creating dualism, while Buddhist teachings emphasize nondualism. At the same time, his case provided a rallying point for activist monks, and the seminars became a venue for working through reactions and articulating public responses.

Another key theme at the Wat Suan Kaew seminar examined the "greening of Thai Buddhism." Again, speakers, both sangha and lay, related the process to the changing relations between the state and the sangha over environmental issues. The discussion on how Buddhism could be used for nature conservation in the Thai context—political, social, and economic—led to an explicit consideration of the formation of a social movement. Beyond exchanging experiences and supporting each others' work, such seminars brought monks together to think about the broader implications and meanings of their activities. Along with rethinking rituals to promote social change, the seminars contributed to the construction of new knowledge of Buddhism's position in society and ways in which monks could impact social thinking and behavior. Like Phra Prajak, monks often invoked Buddhadasa's philosophy to support their work and give it meaning. In their rituals and projects, individual monks wrestled with immediate situations and ways of relieving suffering and investing social action with moral meaning. Sangha seminars gave them the opportunity to discuss these meanings and create new approaches.

From 1991 to 1993, I attended seven seminars for development and environmental monks, only a fraction of the number of such seminars held during that time (Plate 28). The seminars ranged from a small gathering of twenty monks in Prachinburi Province to discuss challenges and problems, to the seminar at Wat Suan Kaew that drew more than two hundred monks to discuss environmental problems and Buddhist approaches. In the early 1990s, monks who came together consciously built on the networks created by development monks and debated how to construct similar organizations for environmental monks. A month before the seminar at Wat Suan Kaew, development monks in southern Isan met to discuss issues immediately relevant to their area. They established a network of Southern Isan Development Monks that would concentrate on both development and environmental issues, meeting regularly to support each other and respond to specific problems. At Wat Suan Kaew, monks debated whether environmental monks should form a new organization or expand the focus of Sekhiyadhamma to include conservation along with development issues. They set up an environmental section of the network, with volunteers to represent the regions of the country. They selected Phra Prajak, despite (or because of) his ongoing legal struggles, as the representative for southern Isan.

During this time, regional networks of monks formed to examine issues specific to their areas, such as the Southern Isan Development Monks Group, the Northern Development Monks Network, and the environmental monks' network of Surat Thani Province in the south. Each group discussed how they should focus their efforts, and whether to integrate environmental and development issues. Most agreed the two could not be separated, as environmental change involves economic and livelihood issues. How they would represent their projects and their groups varied regionally. In the north, the first development monks' organization arose after fourteen monks visited the Isan Development Monks Group (before it split into two sections, north and south) in 1989. Returning to northern Thailand, they held a meeting at Wat Pa Dharabhirom outside Chiang Mai. With Luang Pu Phuttapoj's encouragement and support, they formed the Lanna Development Monks' Association.[17] The first president of the group, Phrakhru Saokham of Chiang Mai, stressed the importance of the support of high-ranking members of the sangha, such as Luang Pu Phuttapoj. "If they agree with the work, it's easy," he told me. "If not, it's difficult or impossible" (personal communication, 6/20/1991). The group expanded as additional monks wrestling with similar concerns, including Phrakhru Pitak, joined. While this group eventually reformed into the Northern Development Monks Network, it maintained the dual concern about development and environmental issues.

While the regional meetings tended to be organized by monks themselves, most of the seminars were sponsored by NGOs. Occasionally NGOs paired with government organizations to provide monks with training and information, such as a seminar at Wat Palat outside of Chiang Mai city (Plate 29). In this case, the Ministry of Health teamed with the NGO Coordinating Committee of the North, a coalition of several NGOs, to educate northern monks about health and environmental issues. More often, cooperation between NGOs and government officials to train monks occurred at the provincial or district level. Several such trainings took place in Nan Province, almost always drawing on Phrakhru Pitak as a main speaker.

The seminars reified the concept of "environmental monks." Monks long engaged in environmental work, those just beginning, and those with interest but no ideas how to commence all interacted, exchanged approaches and concepts, and discussed what it means to engage in "Buddhist environmentalism" or "Buddhist development." Although they did not always agree on the details, through the process a movement took shape and spread among the sangha. The stories, experiences, discussions, and presentations at these seminars contributed to the evolution of a common discourse among environmental monks. The networking organizations similarly provided structure and support as the monks reached out to each other and to the larger society to spread their message and work beyond their immediate locales.

Dhammayatra

In 1996, monks from Sekhiyadhamma and lay supporters organized a Dhammayatra, a "dhamma walk," around Songkla Lake, the largest in the nation, to raise awareness of environmental threats to the lake's ecology and the livelihood of the people around it. Dhammayatra were first run in Cambodia by Samdech Maha Ghosananda in the early 1990s as peace walks.[18] The leading Cambodian monk led hundreds of monks, nuns, and lay supporters in a walk through some of the most dangerous areas of the country, due to minefields and insurgents, to the capital, Phnom Penh. The walk involved meditation and chanting, while spreading a message of peace among the people encountered along the way.

In southern Thailand, the Dhammayatra held an ecological focus, although unifying people in the region formed a secondary objective. Santikaro Bhikkhu, one of the original organizers and a disciple of Buddhadasa Bhikkhu, listed three primary goals for the first walk: First, they aimed to highlight the ecological and related socioeconomic problems surrounding Songkla Lake. In the process, he said, "we wanted to establish a middle way between protest marches and apathetic silence. Some of us see ever more violent clashes over natural resources in Siam's future and hope that Buddhist leaders can help mediate just and peaceful resolutions" (Santikaro 2000, 207). Second, the organizers sought to establish a people's network around the lake, bringing together people from different classes, ethnic groups, and religions that all faced the same problems due to development in the area. The third goal was to identify and encourage local monks to participate in socially engaged work.

Unlike in the work of most environmental monks, nonlocal monks organized the first Dhammayatra. The idea emerged from members of Sekhiyadhamma, which Santikaro (2000, 206) describes as "a small but growing network of grassroots monks struggling to integrate the study and practice of Buddha-Dhamma with responsibility for the communities, culture, and society crumbling around us." The monks from Sekhiyadhamma worked with southern NGOs, village leaders, and some government officials to plan the walk, but few people from the immediate area were involved. The Sekhiyadhamma monks let local people take the lead and responsibility for organizing the second, third, and later walks (held annually), realizing the importance of local involvement and commitment. The major issues concerning the lake—loss of fish and wildlife, bad quality and reduced levels of water, loss of land to housing and other development, and the breakdown of community (Santikaro 2000, 208–209)—reflected the kinds of ecological and socioeconomic problems occurring across Thailand. Yet the problems and related policy decisions must first be recognized and dealt with locally in order to have a greater impact nationally in searching for solutions.

Dhammayatra organizers were deliberate in their coalition building, with local villagers, leaders, government officials, and activist monks. The idea came from discussions among monks already engaged in development and conservation work and aimed to encourage other monks to join. In this way, the Dhammayatra represented a self-conscious movement as monks and supporters came together to act on the particular issues concerning Songkla Lake. As Santikaro pointed out, the organizers aimed to find a middle ground between protests and silence, yet the walk raised questions about the direction of economic development and state policies in the region. Not only was good land taken over for housing and the expansion of towns, such as Had Yai, but outsiders (government and corporate) encouraged farmers to turn forests and mangrove forests into rice paddies and shrimp farms. Even though the Dhammayatra participants avoided taking sides, instead trying to listen to the concerns and needs of local people, the walk highlighted the same problems with economic development and consumption that environmental monks across Thailand critique. Theodore Mayer, an anthropologist who chronicled the early walks, summarized the balance between focusing on an immediate problem and outreach through this project: "The 'dharma walk' was intended as a way to respond to an important environmental and social problem. However, it was also seen as a way to promote education, popular participation, and build a network of monks" (Mayer 1996, 61).

Santikaro (2000) noted several challenges faced by the participants. The majority of local participants and people who greeted the walkers were older, as the youth left the area each day to work in towns or factories. As the organizers hoped to encourage young people to care for the lake's environment and the people and lifestyles around it, the lack of youth witnessing or participating in the walk disappointed them. Still, they garnered considerable attention, and enough enthusiasm for local people to volunteer to organize future walks. Gaining the cooperation and attention of Muslims in the region emerged as a significant issue, as monks not only led the walks but participants engaged in Buddhist practices and rituals along the way (Santikaro 2000, 211).

The involvement—or lack thereof—of Muslims highlights a tension within aspects of the Buddhist environmental movement. While the majority of Thais are Buddhist, the problems of environment destruction and economic inequities extend beyond the Buddhist population. Activist monks vary in their efforts to reach non-Buddhists (Muslims in the south, ethnic minority groups in the mountains in the north being the major groups) with their message or to incorporate their concerns. Violence between Muslims and Buddhists in southern Thailand has become a crisis, challenging the focus of activist monks on the state of the environment rather than promoting peace.[19] In 2006, the Dhammayatra took on more of an aspect of peace and community building, as religious and ethnic tensions in the south had worsened considerably since the first walk (Phra Paisal Visalo, interview, 10/6/2006).

In the north, environmental monks pay somewhat more attention to relations with non-Buddhist minorities. I attended a seminar in 1991 entitled "Mountain People's Ecological and Conservation Attitudes and Adaptations," organized by an NGO that focused on the minorities in northern Thailand. Although the majority of the mountain people are not Buddhist, the second day of the two-day seminar included several activist monks, including Phrakhru Pitak and Phrakhru Manas, both northern monks who work with mountain peoples as well as Northern Thais. The organizers placed the problems facing the minorities within broader social issues, including discrimination against them by the Buddhist majority, through inviting the monks to speak. At the same time, they highlighted the increasing recognition of environmental monks as central to the environmental and social justice movements. Nevertheless, tensions exist here, too, between the Buddhist majority and the minority peoples, including within the environmental movement. Achan Pongsak has even been called racist because of the actions against the Hmong by the Dhammanaat Foundation (Lohmann 1999, 2000).

The Dhammayatra reoccurred many times, including a tenth anniversary walk in 2006 (Phra Paisal Visalo, interview, 10/6/2006). As Santikaro predicted (2000, 212), "the Dhammayatra is now set to be accepted as a legitimate form of social statement in Siam." Other environmental monks used Dhammayatra elsewhere to bring awareness for specific issues, such as walks arranged by Phra Kittisak Kittisophano to protest dams along the Mekong River in the north (interview, 10/8/2006).

The Dhammayatra for Songkla Lake reflected the efforts of monks working together to define their movement. It put them in the public eye, together with other segments of society calling for environmental action and reform. Connections with academics, students, NGOs, and other civil society groups made them part of a larger movement, softening the criticisms that such actions were not appropriate for members of the sangha while familiarizing the public with their activities. Through such public actions, engaged monks created a public definition and awareness of Buddhist environmentalism, and established it as part of a broader growing environmental movement in Thailand.

❦──────❦

From individual monks working to relieve suffering at a local level, the collective process evolved to articulate a Buddhist frame, catch the public's attention, make people aware of the urgency of environmental problems, and provide the means for changing behavior. Together, environmental monks challenged the status quo of state and corporate development that neglected both the people (especially the rural poor) and the natural landscape. They drew from the teachings of thinkers such as Buddhadasa Bhikkhu and P. A. Payutto and the precedents of independent development monks like Luang Pu Phuttapoj Waraporn as they created a movement concerned with people's spirituality, livelihoods, and the well-being of the natural environment in which they lived.

This process was not without problems, as these activist monks directly and indirectly threatened people with power. The engagement of monks in such political issues raised questions about the appropriateness of their behavior and the authenticity of the monks' interpretations of Buddhism. Such efforts to change both social and religious institutions provoked strong responses, despite the monks' high status in society, to which I now turn.

7

The Challenges

I don't know whether monks have crashed into the world, or the world has
crashed into the monks.

—Phra Sunthorn Yannitsaro, July 19, 1991

ON JUNE 17, 2005, the Thai monk, Phra Supoj Suvacano, was murdered.
He was an active member of Sekhiyadhamma and was trying to protect the
land around the meditation center where he lived in Chiang Mai Province
from being converted into a tangerine plantation. At first glance, the case
seems to be a straightforward instance of land conflict. Put into the broader
context of the number of monks engaged in environmental activism and the
strength of the Thai environmental movement, Phra Supoj's assassination
can be seen as evidence of complex tensions between engaged monks, the
state, and society's image of how a monk should act in the modern world.
His case raises questions of the relations between monks as well, especially
between activist monks and the sangha authorities, as sangha authorities
often do not approve of the political aspects of environmental monks' work.
His murder was the most severe of the kinds of conflicts and tensions surrounding environmental monks.

When Phrakhru Manas Nathiphitak first ordained a tree in the name
of environmental conservation in 1988, the media labeled him as "crazy"
and called for him to derobe (personal communication, 9/30/2006). Super-
ficially, the criticism indicated that society was unfamiliar with the use of
rituals for sociopolitical purposes. Yet a few development monks had organized pha pa rituals, the giving of the forest robes, as a means of fundraising

197

for development projects more than a decade earlier and the practice had spread across the nation. Given Phrakhru Manas's suspicion that the newspaper critical of him had been influenced by loggers who stood to lose if he was successful in protecting the remaining forest in his district, a different analysis of the criticism emerges. The label as "crazy" and the call for him to derobe indicated the potential effectiveness of the ritual: the powers that benefited from the logging may have felt threatened enough to try to undermine Phrakhru Manas's project.

As more monks entered the environmental movement over the years, the criticisms, risks, and even attacks on activist monks increased. The rise in such responses further signified the impact the monks' actions had on those in power. Not only did protests in which monks participated succeed in halting large-scale development projects such as the Doi Suthep cable car and the Nam Choen dam, but developers apparently feared the potential success of monks' grassroots efforts as well. If farmers stopped growing cash crops and began feeding themselves through integrated agriculture, and if local people took on the responsibility to monitor forests and protect them from all forms of logging, powerful people and companies could lose significant income.

Several examples of responses that attempted to discredit or intimidate environmental monks occurred in the late 1980s and early 1990s. Activist monks were overlooked for ecclesiastical promotion, arrested for opposing government development schemes, accused of scandal, and received death threats. On one hand, these negative responses pressured environmental monks to hold themselves to a stricter standard of moral behavior as their every action was watched and critiqued. They learned to negotiate tensions with the sangha administration, local, provincial and regional government officials, powerful businessmen, media, representatives of civil society, NGO workers, and even villagers, all looking for ways of manipulating the work of the monks for their own ends.

On the other side, such tensions and pressures demonstrated the social capital of the monks' involvement in environmental activities. The moral framework they provided lent greater legitimacy to projects and increased the potential for success. Some people apparently felt threatened by the monks' work and attempted to weaken their moral authority.

This chapter examines the challenges to both individual monks and the Buddhist environmental movement. The difficulties environmental monks face fall into two types. First are the personal risks and conflicts that arise as they undertake environmental conservation work, ranging from tensions with sangha authorities over the appropriateness of their involvement, to dealing with the fame that comes with successful and innovative work and scandals that erupted surrounding well-known environmental monks, to death threats and the murder of a colleague. Activist monks question what society thinks the role of a monk should be as they respond to the new problems, issues, and interpretations people must wrestle with in the modern world. As a result, they face new kinds of obstacles and struggles that jeopardize their continued work.

Second, emerging from the success of Buddhist environmental projects and their growing popularity, mainstream society, including NGOs, businessmen, and the government, appropriated the methods, discourse, and symbolic capital—especially tree ordinations—of the movement. In the process, they diluted its impact. Tree ordinations became commonplace and society began to expect monks living near forested land would work to conserve it. Monks' engagement in environmental conservation and adaptation of rituals no longer startled people into thinking deeply about the environment or changing their behavior toward it. As Lee and So (1999b, 122) note, there was a shift in Thailand from a "robust environmental movement from below" in the 1970s and '80s that emphasized local, grassroots, and livelihood issues, to an "environmental movement from above" dominated by big business and state bureaucrats concentrating on "lifestyle and 'cosmetic' issues" by the 1990s. As the environmental movement as a whole became popular and was co-opted by dominant corporate and government powers, Buddhist environmentalism itself was co-opted by the same powers the monks criticized. Even more than the physical and personal threats, the appropriation and consequent reframing of the symbolic capital of the movement hold the potential for derailing it from its forward momentum and impact.

Ecclesiastical Invisibility

The first personal challenge to an environmental monk occurred before the movement emerged and coalesced. The proposed cable car project on Doi Suthep in Chiang Mai first placed Buddhism and Buddhist monks on the national stage as opposing development in the name of conservation of both the religion and the natural environment.[1] The case also highlighted the conflicts between environmental monks and sangha authorities. One of the leading monks to oppose the cable car was Phra Phothirangsri, assistant ecclesiastical governor of Chiang Mai Province and abbot of Wat Phan Dong, located in the center of the city. Phra Phothirangsri spoke publicly against building the cable car because he feared it would bring too many people to the mountaintop temple, which would disturb the peace of the sacred site and disrupt the forest surrounding it.

Phra Phothirangsri's position challenged that of the abbot of Wat Phra That, himself a high-ranking and influential monk. The abbot hoped that the cable car would bring more visitors to the temple, strengthening its economic base (Chayant 1998). Phra Phothirangsri told me several years afterward that he believed he was passed over for ecclesiastical promotion because of his position on the cable car issue. His influence among the northern sangha diminished, despite the success of the opposition to the cable car (personal communication, 9/9/1992).

Phra Phothirangsri acted based on his beliefs of the dangers of building the cable car to both the religion and the natural environment, articulating the intertwined relationship between the sacred mountain, the people and city of Chiang Mai, and Buddhism (Swearer et al. 2004, 35). His actions entailed speaking out in support of the opposition, bringing legitimacy to the coalition through the backing of a well-known and high-ranking monk. At this point, monks performed few rituals in conjunction with the movement—the first tree ordination had not yet been performed. The involvement of monks in the opposition, especially when another leading monk was a proponent of the cable car project, marked a critical moment when the mundane environmental movement incorporated a spiritual and moral argument. This involvement also opened activist monks to intense public scrutiny and made them potential targets of opposition.

Phra Phothirangsri did not suffer any direct attacks because of his environmental work. He remained abbot of his wat, and continued to advise other monks engaged in social and environmental activism, even as his overall influence waned. His ecclesiastical career was slowed as he was not promoted for years. Already old, he resigned himself to this fate, accepting that his role was to continue to support environmental conservation and work to keep Buddhist principles at the forefront of economic development planning. The immediate risks he faced were personal and low key. His case highlighted tensions within the sangha over the activism of monks, and marked the beginning conflicts between environmental monks and powers that favored economic growth. Already it was apparent that environmental monks must hold themselves to a higher standard of personal morality and behavior than the average monk.

Charismatic Conflict

The only monk in the history of Thailand
ever sent to prison,

Imprisoned for trying to save the virgin forest
of Buriram [Province],
A monk who has come to save the forest he lives in,

Imprisoned by the very officials responsible for
saving the forest,

This is our story, our story,
The story of Phra Prajak,
Buriram, Thailand,
Phra Prajak, Buriram.

(Popular Thai song "Luang Phor Prajak," by songwriter and singer
Yeunyong Ophaakhun (alias "At Carabao"; quoted in and translated by J. Taylor 1993b, 3)

In July 1991, the popular Thai folk singer At Carabao released a new song
entitled, "Luang Phor Prajak."[2] In keeping with the band Carabao's usual
focus on contemporary social issues, this song took a stand on the recent
arrest of Phra Prajak Khuttajitto, a forest monk and meditation teacher, for
trespassing on National Forest Reserve Land in Buriram Province. The song
celebrated Phra Prajak as a folk hero for standing up to the government in
order to save "the last virgin forest" in Buriram, noting (incorrectly) that
Phra Prajak was the only monk to have been imprisoned in Thailand. He was
fighting for his home in the forest, the rights of the villagers, and the preservation of the forest against the government's policy to relocate people out of
forest reserves (Plate 30).

In his early fifties, Phra Prajak was the best-known environmental monk
in Thailand in the early 1990s. A forest monk living in the woods of northeastern Thailand (Isan), Phra Prajak emerged onto the public stage in 1991
(J. Taylor 1993b, 1994, 1996, 39–46). Through his practice and life in the
forests of Isan, Prajak became aware of negative social and environmental
effects of government- and military-sponsored development schemes. His
controversial efforts to protect forest reserves and help villagers impacted by
those schemes led to him twice being arrested and imprisoned for allegedly
violating state laws.[3]

The significance of Phra Prajak's arrests was not that a monk was arrested. This had happened before. In Prajak's case, he was not defrocked before the arrests. In other cases of monks who were arrested, their robes were removed and they either wore white lay robes or lay clothing, as their misdeeds were seen by the public and the police as having been carried out by them as men, not monks.[4] Pictures of Prajak in his robes being detained by police brought into sharp relief that he was being arrested because of his actions *as a monk*. I believe the authorities arrested Prajak in his robes as a warning to other activist monks. The high visibility of the case brought the tensions between corporate and development interests and socially concerned monks to the forefront in Thai politics and society. Phra Prajak became a pawn in this tension.

Phra Prajak led villagers in tree ordinations to protect the forests of Dong Yai national forest reserve in Buriram Province, which was threatened by illegal logging, and promoted alternatives to commercial use of forest resources. He was first arrested for allegedly trespassing in Dong Yai when he established a meditation center deep in its forest. As a forest monk, Phra Prajak emphasized the value of remote, wild sites for meditation practice. Other monks had meditation centers and illegal residences on national land, but they tended to keep their activities and environmental concerns local. Phra Prajak challenged a national policy, and openly accused the military of illegal logging in the reserve.[5] The creation of his meditation center served to highlight his belief that the national forests needed to be protected for the good of the Thai people and their spiritual and economic well-being. His methods of bringing his opinion forward led to a national debate on monks' roles in political debates.

Phra Prajak photographed what he claimed was evidence of illegal military logging in the forest. He connected the activity with the financial benefits he claimed the military and big business got from relocating poor farmers from their land to make way for "regenerating" degraded land through establishing economic forests, such as eucalyptus plantations, the core of the government's Kho Cho Ko program. Kho Cho Ko was based on the idea that people and forest cannot exist together. As Jim Taylor describes it, "This scheme, ostensibly to protect reserved degraded state forests from intensified encroachment, actively promoted the establishment of monoculture commercial tree-farming" (1996, 39). Many environmental monks such as Phra Prajak saw this approach as a means of removing local people in order to ease efforts to develop forest land.[6] The government arrested Prajak for illegally occupying the forest reserve, although he was soon released on bail.

A few months later, villagers of nearby Khorat Province invited Phra Prajak to assist them in their protests against resettlement through Kho Cho Ko. Unfortunately, a scuffle occurred during a protest march led by the monk, and he was arrested a second time for allegedly hitting a police officer. The details of the two arrests took a back seat to the fact that he was arrested wearing his robes. Phra Prajak commented to an American reporter, "When people can become so greedy and power-hungry as to arrest a monk in the forest who's not harming anybody, it's a sad state of affairs. People are so busy trying to control others because they can't control themselves" (quoted in Magagnini 1994, 13). For two years, the Thai public equated the environmental monk movement with Phra Prajak and his controversial methods. At the same time, general opposition to Kho Cho Ko grew, and the government cancelled it in 1992.

Phra Prajak taught environmental awareness and the relationship between Buddhism and nature. He often participated in seminars and conferences for ecology monks and lay environmentalists. Along with his forest meditation center, he frequently led both monks and lay people on thudong, going into the wilderness to focus on meditation practice, in order to experience the value of the forests for peace of mind.[7] Like other environmental monks, Prajak stressed an updated interpretation of the dhamma that not only supports conservation activities but also demonstrates the necessity of reinterpretation and its derivative social action to the maintenance of the religion's relevance in contemporary life. Helping relieve villagers of suffering and providing them with means to help themselves are examples of how environmental monks put their interpretations of ending suffering (dukkha) into practice. He taught meditation as a means of realizing a simple life, shifting people away from consumption in the process.

While few monks questioned Phra Prajak's sincerity or motivations for preserving the forests of Thailand, or the effectiveness of his work in Buriram to protect a large forested area, many disagreed with his methods. First, his direct confrontation with the government clearly overstepped the ideal of the sangha remaining aloof from political affairs in the minds of most monks and lay people. Second, they criticized him for unintentionally disturbing the peace of the forest where his meditation center was located. Achan Pongsak Techadhammo of Chiang Mai, among others, pointed out the impact of noise from cars and buses bringing people to see Phra Prajak and from a loudspeaker system at the center (personal interview, 3/18/1993; Pongsak 1991c). That Phra Prajak drew a large, predominantly urban following even as he advocated protecting the peaceful environment of the forest was reminiscent of some of the famous forest monks of Isan, such as Achan Cha.[8]

Phra Prajak's popularity and the respect many Thais (among both the sangha and the laity) accorded him stemmed from his sincerity, his strict religious and meditation practice, and his charismatic presence. In December 1992, I participated in a seminar for environmental monks in Prachinburi Province at which Phra Prajak was one of the main speakers. During an overnight "Dhamma Walk" in the forest, I experienced the power of Phra Prajak's charisma and witnessed the esteem with which other activist monks held him. As more than twenty people (mostly monks) spread out through the rough, mountainous terrain, Prajak's voice and contagious laugh reverberated through the forest as he maintained an ongoing lesson on dhamma and nature. In the evening and again early morning, he led a fireside discussion on the challenges faced by environmental monks in balancing their religious practice and social activism. Besides his arrests, he talked about the tension between consumerism and Buddhist teachings. Even the sangha succumbed to consumerism as temples advertised rituals and Buddhist holidays through large billboards. Prajak and the other monks at this seminar raised concerns about the direction of Thai Buddhism. The Thai sangha, they bemoaned, seemed to follow social trends rather than providing moral guidance to avoid them.

Despite the controversy that surrounded him, Phra Prajak epitomized the personal qualities that are characteristic of the most influential among both forest and environmental monks. Primary among these characteristics is *barami*. While succinctly translated as "augustness" or "grandeur" (So 1989, 166), this is a complex Buddhist concept (as seen in the discussion of Luang Pu Phuttapoj in chapter 4). The canonical qualities themselves do not thoroughly define barami as a popular concept. In practice, barami is a social quality that exists because it is recognized by others. Worsley's discussion of charisma could easily be applied to the concept of barami in the Thai context:

[C]harisma . . . can only be that which is recognized, by believers and followers, as "charismatic" in the behaviour of those they treat as charismatic. Charisma is thus a function of recognition: the prophet without honour cannot be a charismatic prophet. Charisma, therefore, sociologically viewed, is a social relationship, not an attribute of individual personality or a mystical quality. . . . Followers . . . do not follow simply because of some abstracted "mystical" quality: a leader is able to magnetize them because he evokes or plays upon some strand of intellectual or emotional predisposition, and because—more than this—he purports to offer the realization of certain values in action. (Worsley 1986, xii)

Barami is a virtue attributed to the most highly revered members of the sangha by other monks and lay people. Beyond its usual application to forest monks, I often heard monks refer to the more active and influential monks involved in conservation work as possessing barami. In applying the canonical concept of barami to the social qualities of activist monks, the concept is secularized[9] and provides a bridge across the gap between the ideal of renunciation of forest monks and the social involvement and fame of environmental monks.

In many ways Phra Prajak followed in the tradition of the forest monks of Isan. He practiced thudong, led meditation retreats, and followed a strict moral standard of behavior. His morality, teaching, and perceived quality of barami attracted a large lay following and contributed to his reputation and fame. Yet Prajak became a folk hero across Thailand, an image antithetical to the forest monk ideal. This reputation was most clearly seen in At Carabao's song, emerging from the monk's confrontations with the government and the popular position he took on conservation.

Phra Prajak was outspoken, charging many public figures and institutions with wrongdoing through carrying out public policies that harmed villagers' livelihoods and damaged the forest. Such accusations did not win him any supporters from within the political hierarchy or business world. Nor did the sangha hierarchy speak out in support of him. Instead, the sangha distanced itself with silence, leaving him to fight his legal battles on his own.

Phra Prajak's cases quietly faded from the public eye. In August 1993, he was found guilty in the first case on two counts of encroachment on national park land. Yet, according to journalist Steve Magagnini (1994, 14), the judge suspended his eighteen-month sentence on the grounds that he had helped the country. "He has never done anything wrong before this," the judge stated. "He has a clean record. He helped villagers grow plants, grow trees" (quoted in Magagnini 1994, 14). Despite the judge's praise, Prajak's suspended sentence received little media attention, especially compared with the coverage of his arrests. Few noted his quiet decision to derobe, the loss of lay support, or his going into hiding to avoid media attention.

Few among the Thai public seem to remember his case or his cause today.[10] In 2007, I found a short article about the dismissal of one of his cases in *Seeds of Peace,* the newsletter for the International Network of Engaged Buddhism ("Phra Prajak Khuttajitto" 2007, 25). A search through archives of Thai newspapers located only one brief mention that Prajak had recently reordained. From being the center of an emerging, popular, and controversial movement in the early 1990s, conflict and arrest forced Phra Prajak to give up his activist work.

Phra Prajak influenced the growth of the Buddhist environmental movement in the early 1990s. He spoke often at monks' seminars encouraging other monks before the pressure of his cases overwhelmed him. Talking about his difficulties and motivations furthered discussion about how and why monks engage in social and political projects, and what the implications of such work are. At the seminar in Prachinburi, Prajak described the "role of monks" to serve as a "bridge" between the wealthy and the poor. While lay leaders such as doctors and teachers can influence the elite's attitudes toward the poor, he believed monks were in a position to be most effective in this effort (seminar presentation, 12/18/1992). Many monks perceived his arrests as warnings to activist monks for their engagement in politically sensitive issues. Monks such as Phrakhru Pitak learned from Phra Prajak's approach, and worked to engage public figures before they could criticize the monks' work. Prajak's case highlights many concerns of environmental monks, leading to extensive discussion and care among them to avoid the kinds of problems and conflicts that he faced. Despite his perceived barami, Phra Prajak was vulnerable to legal actions and media pressure.

Purity, Practice, and Politics

Phra Prajak's case represented an extreme example in the conflict between the government (and secular law) and environmental monks. Key to his case and many others, especially across Isan, was the problem of informal, unofficial forest monks' residences, or *samnak*. As with Phra Prajak's meditation center in Dong Yai forest, many forest monks in Isan set up small residences for their meditation practice in the few remaining forested areas. Most of these areas were in National Forest Reserve Land (NFRL). The government, especially the Royal Forestry Department, considers these sangha residences illegal. The monks view such forested land as ideal for meditation practice, as it is quiet, peaceful, and isolated. Following the forest monk tradition, they seek sites that are far removed from society where they can concentrate and face the challenges presented by the wilderness (Kamala 1997).

In 1992, one such forest monk, Phra Sunthorn Yannitsaro, lived in an illegal samnak in Prachinburi Province. He hosted a seminar that December, facilitated by Sekhiyadhamma and the Thai Interreligious Commission for Development, for activist monks trying to maintain their practice in the face of social and political obstacles. Twenty monks traveled to his remote residence deep in the forest on the Thai-Cambodian border to participate in the five-day seminar. Three NGO workers from TICD attended to handle logistics. Three *mae chi,* unordained nuns, cooked for the monks, NGOs workers, and me.[11]

The seminar emphasized finding a balance between activism and meditation practice. Much of the discussion dealt with the concept of purity—how monks could engage in worldly and political issues while remaining committed to their religious practice. Action, the monks stressed, must be informed and motivated by meditation practice grounded in the dhamma. They noted, especially when discussing cases such as that of Phra Prajak and a series of scandals affecting well-known monks (including a couple of environmental monks, discussed below), that the reputation of the sangha can easily be tainted in the public eye by the behavior of a small number of monks. Yet monks are only human and must constantly face and negotiate temptations.

As the discussion continued, several monks corrected the word *reputation* to *purity* (*borisut*). Their concern involved purity of mind as much as— or even more than—behavior. The ideas of intention and motivation inform whether a monk is considered to lead a holy or chaste life (*phramachan,* Thai; *Brahmacariya,* Pali; Payutto 1985, 394). The concept of living a holy life, as with barami, is difficult to assess, dependent on how people perceive the behavior of individual monks. Intentions and motivations are not visible, and must be shown through behavior.

Three specific issues that activist monks confront formed the focus at the seminar as embodying the tensions between practice and behavior: handling money; dealing with fame; and relations with women. Most of the monks present considered themselves as *nak patibat,* or "practice" or meditation monks. These are monks who devote themselves to meditation, and are often forest monks. Meditation monks usually embody barami and serve as ideal models for the laity for interpreting and practicing the dhamma. Engaging modern social problems, such as environmental degradation and social demise caused by consumerism and material development, forces monks to encounter situations that meditation monks would ideally avoid, particularly those involving money, fame, and women.

Phrakhru Suthachanawan from Yasothorn Province emphasized the urgency of using the dhamma to deal with problems in society. "The role of monks," he stated, "as inheritors of the Buddha's teachings, is to solve social problems." The key to this process, he continued, is purity in actions and intentions. Monks can no longer teach the dhamma as they did in the past; preaching alone is not effective. They must teach through their actions and example. They must avoid only serving rich, powerful people or government officials; ignoring the problems of the poor has led to the diminishing influence of monks in society. "Dhamma builds social values," he concluded, stressing the importance of monks' holding onto this concept for themselves as well as the people with whom they work (seminar presentation, 12/14/1992).

Money

Working with the poor requires funding. Yet monks are not supposed to handle money. While many monks in Thailand do not pay attention to this precept, given the increased scrutiny that environmental monks face they must be wary of any action that could be interpreted as violating a monk's ideal behavior in the eyes of the laity. Activist monks must therefore find ways to handle the financial aspects of social engagement without appearing to be overly concerned about money.

Society's sensitivity to the sangha's approach to financial issues became clear during the Asian economic crisis in 1997–98, which began with the collapse of the Thai baht. Monks and temples struggled to meet basic needs as donations decreased and people turned to temples for support in the forms of fortune telling, requesting lottery numbers, receiving free meals, and looking for solace in time of need. Monks complained that while the numbers of people coming to them increased during the economic crisis, financial support had dwindled, making it difficult for them to survive, let alone help all those who ask for it. Monks needed to find new methods of supporting themselves and maintaining temples. Many used the increasing requests for ritual services to gain funds for the temples—performing more funerals, Buddha image consecration ceremonies, fortune telling rites, and other rituals.

In 1998, the Department of Religious Affairs criticized the sangha's management of funds and temples since the beginning of the economic crisis. In May 1998, a poor fruit vendor claimed that a Bangkok temple refused to hold funeral services for her father because she could not pay the high fees they demanded. This incident prompted an investigation and a call by the Religious Affairs Department to the Sangha Supreme Council to issue a clear-cut guideline on funeral services to curb overcharging by Buddhist temples. The claim was that many monks provided funeral services and other rituals, such as blessing new houses, on a commercial basis, making large sums of money (Kamolthip 1998).

Two prominent monks, Phra Payom Kalayano (a well-known and controversial monk based outside of Bangkok) and Luangta Maha Bua Yanasampanno in Udon Thani Province, took a different approach. They each planned a fundraising scheme to help the government with its dwindling foreign reserves. In December 1997, Phra Payom Kalayano urged Buddhists to stop building religious buildings for the next three years, and to donate funds instead to bail out the government. He emphasized that through giving to his fund people could make religious merit and help the country at the same time.

Four months later, in April 1998, Luangta Maha Bua began his "Help the Country Project." His aim was also to help build the nation's foreign reserve, but his targets were more ambitious than Phra Payom's. He requested his supporters to donate at least Bt 4,000 each for his fund. By July, his fund gave U.S.$1.2 million and 400 kilograms of gold to the Bank of Thailand, with reportedly another 563 million baht and 191 kilograms of gold collected to be handed over at a later date. In a controversial move, that October Luangta Maha Bua threatened suicide if his followers didn't raise an additional 336 million baht by the middle of the month. In response, the Government Lottery Office donated 100 million baht to the fund, and the head of Krating Daeng, the popular drink company, promised another large donation.[12]

The question that emerged was whether this is an appropriate role for monks. Particularly through threatening suicide, Luangta Maha Bua changed the terms of giving from one of *dana,* a selfless act of generosity, to one of coercion. Even while funds came in, the monk was criticized publicly for devaluing the true meaning of Buddhist teachings and dana. People raised the concern of the potential for misuse or corruption, drawing further criticism toward the sangha for potential mismanagement.

The implication of the Department of Religious Affairs' actions toward the sangha during the economic crisis was that there was increasing ritualization and profiteering by the sangha. The practices were, in many people's eyes, not "true" Buddhism. While the sangha weathered the crisis along with the nation, the criticisms raised concerning fundraising, use of rituals, and the "proper" role of monks reflect the importance of activist monks' concerns about handling money and how they are perceived by the lay public. Arguing that social engagement is part of a monk's responsibilities, activist monks need to tread carefully to avoid undermining their work due to mishandling funds.

Phrakhru Pitak established Hak Muang Nan Foundation (HMN) partly to assist him in dealing with the financial component of his work. HMN, as a coalition of NGOs, civil society organizations, and provincial officials, keeps careful records of donations and grants for the foundation's projects. Lay staff, in the office located at Phrakhru Pitak's temple, Wat Aranyawat, monitor income and expenses along with planning the foundation's activities.[13] Phrakhru Pitak is officially an advisor to the organization, which removes him from directly dealing with financial issues. No major decisions are made, however, without his input.

While a handful of environmental monks such as Phrakhru Pitak established NGOs to oversee their socially engaged work (including Achan Pongsak, who founded the Dhammanaat Foundation in 1984), most activist monks work on their own directly with villagers. Depending on the size of the temple and the village it serves, many monks do handle the funds for their basic needs and temple upkeep. Most temples have a lay committee that assists the monks with such mundane matters. As monks move into socially engaged activities, the amount of funds they use increases, and it becomes more challenging to handle money without people raising suspicions about the monks' motives. I have never heard any accusations of environmental monks mishandling money, but the focus on this issue at the Prachinburi seminar demonstrated that these monks are keenly aware of how closely they are watched. As they engage in social and political issues, they must remain especially circumspect to avoid negatively affecting their projects.

Russell Sizemore and Donald Swearer (1990) argue that a dialectical tension within Buddhism has existed between nonattachment and the acquisition of wealth throughout its history. The key to mediating between these values is dana or generosity, as a means of using wealth to display selflessness and gain merit. As Sizemore and Swearer sum up the view of Phra P. A. Payutto,

[M]aterial conditions are important only to the extent that they influence one's ability to cultivate non-attachment. Extreme scarcity will be bad if it stimulates greed and provokes acts of crime; economic sufficiency is good because it is conducive to spiritual growth and more generally to individual and social well-being. (Sizemore and Swearer 1990, 2)

Key to the work of socially engaged monks, Phra Payutto said, "It is not wealth that is praised or blamed, but the way one acquires and uses it" (Sizemore and Swearer 1990, 2).

Fame

Phra Prajak's case consumed considerable attention during the seminar in Prachinburi, not only because of the tensions surrounding the legal issues it raised, but because it aimed a spotlight on the work of all environmental monks. In his case, the attention was negative and critical. Positive attention also creates challenges for environmental monks. As environmental issues became more popular across the nation, people sought heroes and role models. The "Magic Eyes" campaign established in Bangkok by an upper-class woman, Khunying Chodchoy Sophonpanich, rapidly became one of the best-known anti-pollution and environmental education programs in the country (Smith and Piya 2008, 226). Smith and Piya describe its success in a way that provides insight into why the environmental monks who managed to avoid criticism nevertheless became the center of popular attention:

> The success of the [Magic Eyes] programme in promoting personal and community responsibility has, in part, been the result of the campaign tapping into Thai culture—in particular the shame of losing face (*seayah naah*), citizens being embarrassed if they were seen dropping litter, thus linking values to action through citizens coming to understand underlying reasons but also being able to ensure compliance through moral coercion. (Smith and Piya 2008, 226–27)

Through tree ordinations in particular, environmental monks captured the imagination of the Thai public, but also raised the question of morality and values, similar to yet beyond the Magic Eyes campaign. The fact that monks, holding the highest social status in the country, cared about the condition of the forests and waterways and linked this concern to the Buddhist religion pushed them to the forefront of people's interest.

Media coverage contributed to this growing attention. The popular children's television series *Thung Sang da Wan* filmed Phrakhru Pitak teaching village children about the problems of deforestation in 1993. Since then they have produced shows on other monks, including Phrakhru Manas and Phra Somkit. Phra Somkit was later interviewed for another television show on his model integrated agriculture farm behind his temple in Nan. Several national television programs highlighted the work of Phrakhru Manas.

Environmental monks began receiving national awards for their work. The Village Foundation (a national NGO) and Matichon Newspaper awarded Phrakhru Pitak the Model Citizen Award in 1993, at the height of the controversies surrounding activist monks and the sangha as a whole. Both Phrakhru Manas and Phra Somkit received Green Globe awards for environmental work, sponsored by the Petroleum Authority of Thailand (PTT) in 2000 and 2003 respectively. They were among fourteen monks who won the Green Globe award between 1999 and 2008.[14]

People began flocking to visit the more famous environmental monks. Besides reporters, members of NGOs and other activist monks traveled to observe the work of different monks. These observations contributed to the growth of the Buddhist environmental movement, as monks and the NGOs that support them learned various methods and gained inspiration and encouragement. Soon the numbers of lay visitors increased. In 1999, Phra Somkit claimed that he received close to a thousand visitors that year to his model farm. Groups of students came from abroad to spend time volunteering and studying on his farm, including a group from Fresno State University in California and one from a Japanese university.

The challenge for the monks is to maintain focus on their projects despite the outside attention. Some people in Nan Province worried that Phrakhru Pitak's fame distracted him from the actual work with villagers. On one level, the renown of these monks is not unlike the revered monks in numerous glossy national magazines on Thai Buddhism with their photos splashed on the covers. Newsstands are full of these magazines promoting particular monks for their barami, spiritual prowess, or magical powers. The difference for environmental monks is that the fame takes time to handle, as invitations to speak at seminars, be filmed for television, and be interviewed by anthropologists increase accordingly.

Phra Paisal Visalo pointed out to me that for many activist monks, the recognition they get for their work can become their main focus or a "one-man show." "Monks who have been involved in certain projects," he said, "hold onto them, and other monks don't get involved. . . . It becomes a personal affair." The effect is that some monks become more concerned with their reputation for their work than with thinking about the benefits of joint efforts. "Without good coordination," he continued, "monks tend to live and work individually" (interview, 10/6/2006).

Even the growing structure of the Buddhist environmental movement itself contributed to the problems activist monks encountered. Phra Kittisak Kittisophano, former chairman of Sekhiyadhamma, described the impact of Sekhiyadhamma's programs: "It was difficult. Senior monks were already working with existing activities. With more organization, there was more work for them. Networking took too much time. Seminars, meetings, trainings increased their workload. Many monks felt they had no time" (interview, 10/8/2006).

In 2006, Phrakhru Pitak informed me that he no longer spoke at seminars because his ecclesiastical duties left him with no time or energy. Along with his growing popularity among the laity, the sangha hierarchy began to tap his reputation. In the early cases, such as Phra Prajak's or Phra Phothirangsri's, the sangha distanced itself. Later the well-known environmental monks often attracted positive attention from the sangha. Rather than expressing concern about damaging the reputation of the sangha as a whole, the sangha hierarchy seemed to recognize the benefits from supporting and promoting monks like Phrakhru Pitak, Phra Somkit, and numerous other monks across the nation because of the esteem with which the public holds them. The associated challenge for these monks is that as they are promoted and acknowledged for their work, they are given greater responsibilities. Phra Paisal noted that "as monks get older, they are promoted in the hierarchy, and don't have time for activism. . . . Naturally, when one is promoted, it leads to more administrative work, management, paperwork, sangha work" (interview, 10/6/2006). The irony in many cases is that, unlike for Phra Phothirangsri, the environmental projects of some monks brought them the fame and recognition that has made it difficult for them to continue with their activism.

Women

The seminar in Prachinburi occurred in 1992, after a series of scandals involving monks erupted on the national stage. Monks were accused of sexual affairs, mishandling money, fraud, and undertaking rituals and selling sacred amulets for financial and personal gain. Most relevant for the environmental monks were Phra Prajak's arrests and two sexual scandals involving Achan Pongsak Techadhammo of Chiang Mai and Phra Yantra Amaro of Kanchanaburi Province, both popular and well-known environmental monks.

Achan Pongsak had faced numerous obstacles before. The forest conservation methods of the Dhammanaat Foundation, which emphasized removing people, especially upland minorities, from the forests, were controversial. Other environmental monks criticized his approach.[15] The year following Phra Prajak's arrests, challenges to Achan Pongsak hit a low point. He had been accused of communism several times during the 1980s, and even physically threatened, allegedly by a police officer, because of Dhammanaat's work with villagers in Chom Thong District of Chiang Mai Province (interview, 3/18/1993). In 1992, a photograph was given to the media, supposedly documenting Achan Pongsak sitting with a woman's legs over his.[16] Although the photograph was only published in one local paper, despite having been mailed to newspapers nationwide, the scandal threatened both his reputation and his work. Achan Pongsak denied the accusations. His followers pointed to evidence that the photograph had been computer altered, and argued that it had been produced by businessmen whose profits the work of the Dhammanaat Foundation threatened. He nevertheless left the sangha within days of the scandal's outbreak in order to defuse the situation and preserve the reputation of the sangha as a whole.[17]

Shortly thereafter, Phra Yantra Amaro of Kanchanaburi Province was accused of sexual relations with several of his female followers. Although less directly related to his environmental activism (which took the form of preaching more than engaging in specific projects), the scandal surrounding Phra Yantra, the lengthy and public investigation, and his flight to the United States in order to remain a monk after the Thai sangha hierarchy defrocked him, affected public support for other activist monks.[18]

A section of the Prachinburi seminar focused on the issue of women. This discussion was the first and only time during any of my research when monks asked me not to participate because it made them uncomfortable that I was a woman. I do not know the details of what they discussed, and I respect their request. The three topics of money, fame, and women all entail temptations that monks must resist. A significant aspect of Buddhist practice involves facing and resisting *tanhā*, or desire. Forest monks in particular often went to the wilderness in order to challenge themselves through encountering wild animals, charnel grounds and death, spirits, and loneliness (and thus feelings of self) (Kamala 1997). Activist monks, in their close work with the laity and the attention paid to it by the public, face additional temptations and fears, including the need to be especially careful concerning money, fame, and women.

After the scandals surrounding Phra Prajak, Achan Pongsak, and Phra Yantra, environmental monks had to act more carefully as they came under closer public scrutiny. Phrakhru Pitak, for example, found himself under continual observation of his personal behavior because of his activist work. Ironically, early in his work as an environmentalist he had been shot at before he became well known for performing tree ordinations. He believed loggers were most likely behind the attack, although he had no proof. He received a letter threatening him with death if he continued to protect the forests in his home district. As he gained fame, Phrakhru Pitak had to be more circumspect and proper than less well-known monks, although physically he was probably safer because of media attention. Both lay people and other monks looked to him as a moral role model. He was more closely watched and likely to be criticized. He, like all activist monks, had to embody a concept and perception of purity beyond those used to judge most monks.

Pak Mun Dam

Protests against the Pak Mun Dam in the 1990s illustrate several key issues environmental monks address and engage, as well as the way in which larger concerns can envelop the monks. This case shows the sensitivity of both government and business forces to the power of alternative ideas of development, modernity, and spirituality. Monks interested in learning more about the potential impacts of the dam on both nature and the people whose lives depend on the river came under surveillance by government forces, again putting pressure on all environmental monks to move cautiously.

The Mun River runs through several northeastern provinces, providing water and livelihoods for many people. In addition to irrigating farmland, the river contains fish on which many of the poor in the northeast depend. In 1991, the Electrical Generating Authority of Thailand (EGAT) began construction of a dam at the mouth of the river in Ubon Ratchatani Province. Hydroelectric power offers relief to the high energy demands of Thailand's urban centers, especially Bangkok, and promotes the nation's growing industry. Opposition to the dam erupted immediately, coming from national NGOs and local organizations and people. Opponents emphasized environmental damage and the loss of livelihood for local people. The dam threatened the main fish species in the river and would flood large areas of farmland.

In June 1991, TICD and the Project for Ecological Recovery (PER) sponsored a monks' seminar at a temple in Ubon Ratchatani. The seminar brought together more than fifty monks, including Phra Prajak, to share their experiences of applying Buddhist environmental practices and principles. On the third day of the seminar, the organizers planned a study tour of the dam construction site for the monks. They visited some of the villages that would be affected.

The first day of the conference, armed police and military personnel entered the temple grounds. They came at the request of the provincial governor to observe the seminar and determine who attended. On the third day, as they arrived at the dam, the monks were met by more than two hundred armed police and special military units who followed them as they toured the site. Although no direct confrontations occurred, the police continued to follow the monks as they returned to the temple, again carrying their weapons into the temple compound.[19] Given Buddhism's emphasis on nonviolence, bringing guns into a temple compound was highly disrespectful.

Although no serious confrontation occurred, the temple abbot and seminar organizers demanded an apology from the governor, Saisit Phornkaew. A month after the incident, the governor arranged a meeting at the temple. I visited the temple that day with two environmentalist monks who had attended the conference and several NGO workers from TICD and PER. We reached the temple just before the governor arrived. The monks and NGO workers expected an apology and an explanation.

After making a religious offering, the governor explained the government's concerns surrounding the monks' interest in the dam. He claimed that he did not see the monks themselves as a problem and had not ordered the police to carry weapons. He worried that the seminar was a vehicle for negative influences from leftist NGOs and university students from Bangkok and that they were damaging the reputation of the sangha. He stated that he feared influence from Burmese and Sri Lankan monks, who were known to be political activists. These disruptive influences, he argued, could threaten the stability of Thai society and needed to be monitored. Although he admitted that the police and military had acted improperly, he felt that their observation of the seminar was justified to protect both society and Buddhism. He condoned the action, "to protect myself, the society, and the religion" (field notes, 7/15/1991).

The meeting, modestly covered by national media, defused the uproar about the armed police entering the temple compound. The governor left seeming pleased with himself; the monks involved were not pleased. They felt he had further insulted them by trying to placate them and equating their interest in learning about the dam and concerns for the impacts it would have with "disruptive" elements in society. Additionally, there was clearly no connection between the seminar and Burmese monks, who have too many life-threatening issues of their own to interfere in environmental debates in Thailand. Finally, as for involvement by NGOs and students, representatives of both had participated in planning and running the seminar out of the desire to promote social and environmental justice. Yet, while considering themselves opposed to many government policies, these students and NGOs were not like those who after the 1976 protests and crackdown fled violence in the capital to join communist insurgents in the jungle as the governor claimed. In 1991, NGOs and students mostly took the approach of working within the system to bring about social change rather than literally fighting it.[20]

The governor's explanation pushed some monks into firmer opposition to the dam and the larger policies it represented. Some of the monks were adamantly opposed to the dam and critical of the government before the incident. Others had tried to temper their positions, arguing that the sangha stood for the middle path and should model efforts to mediate between conflicting opinions. The monks with whom I spoke after the governor's brief visit—two of whom were from other parts of the country—indicated that the incident had clarified for them the importance of opposing unbridled economic growth.

The monks from the area surrounding the dam remained concerned about extreme positions. Most villagers had no problem denouncing the dam and calling for its cancellation. Some of the monks argued for moderation; they recognized the negative effects of the dam and equated it with the root evils in Buddhism, particularly greed. They agreed with environmentalists who argued for changes in lifestyles in Bangkok so that less electricity would be required, rather than damaging rural areas to support urban demand. They were concerned about the anger displayed in some of the lay protests against the dam. Drawing from Buddhist teachings, they took the middle ground, balancing between conservative and radical positions, representing the local people against the demands of modernity represented by the dam and Bangkok. Yet they realized that trying to stop change was unrealistic.

Ultimately, the Pak Mun Dam was built. Evidence indicates that the environmentalists and villagers were correct: there are fewer fish in the river, and many villagers were relocated from the flooded lands. Livelihoods were damaged, and many people still seek restitution for what they lost. In response to local demands, four months per year the dam is opened, allowing water to flow and villagers to fish. Nevertheless, tensions surrounding this dam and others remain high, and the debates over their impact remain unresolved (Fahn 2003, 89–96). The Pak Mun Dam case served to further the resolve of many environmental monks to find moral and cultural solutions to Thailand's environmental problems. Their approach continues to be one of seeking alternatives to large-scale development and integrating concepts that originated in the West, such as sustainable agriculture and ecological science, into their religious teachings.

The Pak Mun Dam protests eventually led to the creation of the Assembly of the Poor, one of the most powerful and influential people's organizations in Thailand (Missingham 2004). The monks' role in the protests was minor in comparison; few people besides the governor took notice of or criticized the monks' involvement. The focus sat squarely on the farmers and fishers who organized themselves effectively to bring their opposition and their complaints to the national stage.

For environmental monks, especially in the northeast, such issues and seminars pulled them closer together. The governor's response highlighted the urgency of incorporating a moral perspective into development and environmental work. The incident further solidified Buddhist environmentalism as a movement despite—or because of—the risks.

All of these examples—Phra Prajak's arrests, the scandals surrounding Achan Pongsak and Phra Yantra, the attack and death threats against Phrakhru Pitak, and the close public scrutiny of environmentalist monks—indicate an intensification of efforts to discredit or at least challenge the work of activist monks. I do not believe that this intensification emerged from serious concern that such work was inappropriate for monks. After all, the government itself had involved the sangha in social, developmental, and political efforts to expand Bangkok's influence to peripheral areas over the past century. The reaction to environmentalist monks from the government, business, and even the media came more from the threat to industrial and capitalist development that the monks posed. Monks criticized government policies. Their efforts to promote sustainable, environmentally sound projects and to protect forest resources for local people obstructed the profits of businessmen. The influence monks have among lay people, especially in rural areas, increased the perceived threats economic development proponents felt from Buddhist environmental programs, and led to even stronger efforts to diminish their success or stop their work outright.

Dangerous Activism

Far more serious than maintaining purity of mind, dealing with scandals, or efforts to discredit them, environmental monks and lay activists faced violence. Between January 2001 and January 2005, according to the Asian Legal Resource Center, a human rights organization, eighteen human rights activists, many engaged in environmental activities, were killed (Haberkorn 2005). The list did not include Phra Supoj, as his assassination occurred shortly after its publication.[21] Haberkorn's description of the context for these killings mirrors the tensions between environmental monks, the state, and business interests:

> The 18 stories of murdered human rights defenders appeared in the Fa Dieu Kan magazine in late 2004. A brief introduction to the stories made three insightful observations. First, the rise in assassinations of human rights defenders has been concurrent with a broader mobilization of citizens to demand justice. Second, the strategies employed by the human rights defenders, especially those engaged in environmental struggles, have grown increasingly savvy and ingenious. As a result, the opportunities for capitalist investors have markedly decreased. In turn, this may have increased the frequency and types of violence used against them. Finally, the harsh and often inflexible response to various activist and people's groups by the Thai Rak Thai government, especially Prime Minister Thaksin himself, has caused the groups to be branded "enemies of the state." This has caused private investors and other opponents of these struggles to become even more emboldened in their actions. (Haberkorn 2005, n.p.)

The Northern Development Monks Network, to which Phra Supoj belonged, claims that the monk was murdered by "influential people" (Budsarakham 2005, n.p.). "Influential people" (*phu mi itthiphon*) is a euphemism for powerful people with only their own interests at heart. The private investors referred to by Haberkorn would fall under this category in their push for capitalist development and opposition to environmental struggles. The concern in Phra Supoj's case is that Buddhist monks are no longer immune to the violence inflicted on human rights and environmental activists. The journalist, Vasana Chinvarakorn (2005, n.p.), noted that "the conditions that led to the latest killing of Phra Supoj send a signal that from now on whoever stands in the path of the powers-that-be will have to suffer, be they men, women, children or monks."

Phra Maha Boonchuay Siridharo, chair of the Northern Development Monks Network, told me that region of Chiang Mai Province was rife with conflict. "We [members of the Network] frequently discussed the problems in the area. But we didn't think it could turn out that violent. We didn't think they planned to take life" (interview, 10/18/2006). Phra Supoj's death shocked everyone, especially socially engaged monks.

Phra Supoj's case is even more disturbing because of the nature of his involvement in the Buddhist environmental movement. Several monks described him as quiet, good natured, and primarily involved in the movement through maintaining Sekhiyadhamma's Web site. He helped run meditation retreats that spread the teachings of Buddhadasa Bhikkhu. He was not an outspoken activist like many environmentalists or monks such as Phra Prajak or Achan Pongsak who encountered direct opposition.

Phra Supoj and Phra Kittisak Kittisophano moved to Fang District in 1998 to help with plans by Sulak Sivaraksa to build an education center for the Spirit in Education Movement (SEM), one of Sulak's organizations. Both monks worked closely with Sekhiyadhamma, and had participated in the Dhammayatra walks around Songkla Lake in the south. While the site for SEM's center changed, the two monks remained on the land, which had been donated to Sulak. Local people had established much of the land as a community forest, and were trying to conserve the forest there. A few lucrative tangerine plantations thrived nearby, and the owners eyed the protected land for expansion. Although the government and some environmentalists promote fruit trees as appropriate development to reforest upland areas, many monks and lay environmentalists raise concerns about the negative impacts of such plantations. The trees require considerable investment of chemical fertilizers, herbicides, and pesticides. As a cash crop, they contribute to the dependence of local people on the market system rather than encouraging self-sufficiency. The plantations owners often live elsewhere and hire local people (whose livelihoods were lost when land was sold) to maintain the orchards.

The two monks worked with local villagers to protect the land. According to Phra Kittisak (interview, 10/8/2006), they planted trees and tried to prevent businessmen from claiming the land was degraded or unused. The monks brought charges against some businessmen who brought bulldozers to clear land in an attempt to claim it legally. Some of the monks' followers suffered attacks, but the police refused to take on the cases. The monks petitioned the government, which ordered the local police to investigate. Before they announced any conclusions, Phra Supoj was killed.

As in other cases (notably that of Charoen Wat-aksorn, an environmentalist who was murdered one year before Supoj), Phra Supoj's case was referred to the Department of Special Investigations. Phra Maha Boonchuay monitored the lack of progress of the investigation closely, and informed me that "there was still no progress" more than a year later (interview, 10/18/2006) despite his being a monk.

Phra Kittisak continued to speak out against the government and rampant development, even after special witness protection was taken away from him.[22] Phra Maha Boonchuay commented that activist monks are not scared, but "still do their work. Once they decide to do this kind of work, it is not an act of experimentation. . . . They have to do it. Whatever they have to do, they have to be more careful" (interview, 10/18/2006). Phra Paisal echoed this sentiment when he said, he "didn't think it could happen. Very cruel. This will make monks more cautious about their actions when they have to confront influential people" (interview, 10/6/2006).

Appropriation and Expectation

The efforts by "influential people" to undermine the work of environmental monks backfired. The public initially questioned the appropriateness of monks engaged in socioeconomic and political issues when Phra Prajak's case captured the media's attention. The long-term effect of the renown of monks such as Phra Prajak, Phrakhru Pitak, and others, however, led to public acceptance of the work of environmental monks. Environmental monks who were involved as the movement coalesced slowly gained respect and recognition for their work. Phrakhru Pitak and Phrakhru Manas both experienced strong criticisms early in their conservation efforts, and yet both later received national environmental awards.

Environmental monks as a group survived criticism, scandal, arrest, and attack, and continued to work. Together with lay environmentalists, they convinced the sangha administration, the media, the government, and the public of the urgency of protecting the forests, and the value of incorporating

Buddhist principles and symbols into the process. In many places, they have successfully protected forest land and other environmental sites, at least so far.

Yet another kind of challenge came with the positive recognition granted environmental monks. By the mid to late 1990s, tree ordinations in particular became popular. The powers that most environmental monks criticized through their performance of tree ordinations and their environmental projects began to use these same rites to bolster their own image. Government agencies and corporate organizations adopted the symbolic capital of tree ordinations and environmental monks to change their reputations from destroyers of nature and people's livelihoods to supporters of "green" projects. While this shift seemed to be positive evidence of the success of Buddhist environmentalism, it threatened to dilute the deeper meanings of the ritual and the long-term social and spiritual changes the monks sought to enact. Activist monks needed to adjust their methods and criticisms accordingly to maintain the effectiveness and moral imperative of their work.

Conservative Rituals

Within less than a decade after the first performance of a tree ordination, people across the nation took up the rituals as symbolic markers of claims to land, community membership, and even allegiance to the king. As early as 1991, Phrakhru Manas commented that "the whole nation is going crazy for ordaining trees."[23] The previous day, the governor of Chiang Mai Province sponsored the ordination of the large rubber trees that lined the road from Chiang Mai city to Lamphun Province to protect them from being cut for the road's expansion. Phrakhru Manas complained that the ritual was performed without consideration of long-term care of the trees, but rather to make an immediate and superficial political statement.

In 1996–97, tree ordinations reached a new height. The Northern Farmers' Network organized a program to ordain fifty million trees in community forests in honor of King Rama IX's fiftieth year of reign (Brown 2006; Delcore 2004b; Isager and Ivarsson 2002; Tannenbaum 2000). Nicola Tannenbaum notes how, in the process, tree ordinations "have changed from protests led by environmentalist monks to acts that the King supports" (Tannenbaum 2000, 109). She describes how a remote upland Shan village used a tree ordination as part of the king's program to protest against development in their area.[24] At the same time, use of the ritual indicated that the villagers had become connected to larger political, religious, and economic structures on a national level that supported development. More broadly, I argue that as tree ordinations became increasingly popular and used across Thailand for a range of political as well as religious and environmental purposes, they pulled the environmental monks into positions of implicitly supporting the same economic and political structures they initially criticized.

Lotte Isager and Soren Ivarsson point out how since Buddhism entered environmental debates in Thailand, people have used the religion and its symbolic tools—i.e., tree ordinations—"to legitimate highly different positions" (Isager and Ivarsson 2002, 402). Their examples illustrate differences of approach among environmental monks themselves, comparing Achan Pongsak's accusation of highland Hmong people as directly contributing to deforestation with Phra Prajak's criticisms of the government's relocation and reforestation program in the northeast. More to the point are the ways in which the objects of both of these criticisms appropriated the rituals themselves.

Isager and Ivarsson (2002), Tannenbaum (2000), and Hayami (1997) all document minority people's use of tree ordinations to lay claim to community forests surrounding their villages, some as early as 1993. In the process, they tap into the discourse of being members of the national community. As Tannenbaum comments,

> [T]he tree ordination allied the villagers with the King and the national government as well as local and international nongovernmental organizations interested in environmental protection. Tree ordinations, environmentalism, and sustainable development are now part of the rhetoric and practice of Thai intelligentsia, development workers, and politicians. In the past, tree ordinations organized by monks were part of a larger protest against modernization, capitalism, and development that were seen as destroying traditional values and ways of life. (Tannenbaum 2000, 116–17)

Henry Delcore (2004b) emphasizes the ways in which tree ordinations contributed to a process of cultural objectification of rural people by middle-class NGO activists through the generification of the ritual as an aspect of an idealized "local wisdom." Also drawing from tree ordinations done as part of the celebration for the king, he shows that while villagers and environmental monks participated in the planning and performance of the rituals, they were largely controlled by NGO activists. These tree ordinations "had the effect of symbolically bolstering the hierarchical structure of the Thai state and Thai society as a whole—a structure in which local leaders and middle class NGO activists exercise power as arbiters of 'good' and 'bad' culture among rural people" (Delcore 2004b, 1). Unlike in the cases of minority peoples using the tree ordinations to incorporate themselves more fully within the state structure as a means of protecting their cultural identities and building their political power, Delcore describes a process in which rural people lose some of their cultural and political capital. In both cases, the political meaning of the ritual shifted away from the original moral concerns of the environmental monks about deforestation and the suffering it causes.

None of these authors argue that tree ordinations were no longer effective as means of establishing and protecting community forests. Rather, they evolved from serving a focused purpose to becoming entangled in complex ways in ever-changing environmental debates and political struggles. These debates and struggles are reified as the simplified "environmental narratives" Forsyth and Walker (2008) criticize as driving environmental policy in Thailand. Most environmental monks attempt to assess the specifics of the local areas in which they work, but their methods and the symbolic meaning of their rituals have been appropriated and simplified as environmentalism has swept the Thai imagination.

Environmental monks have found themselves embroiled in these debates, and at times used by different players to bolster their positions. The example of the PTT "Green Globe" Awards mentioned above—granted to fourteen monks among many other recipients—highlights how one of the corporations most often criticized for environmental damage has appropriated the environmental movement to change its image.[25] PTT initiated this award shortly after environmental and Buddhist activists, including Sulak Sivaraksa, publicly protested its involvement in building a natural gas pipeline from the Burmese border through a national park in Thailand. For the monks honored by the award, receiving it boosted support for and validated the value of their work. At the same time, PTT used famous environmental monks—and, implicitly, Buddhism itself—to offset criticisms laid against it for its environmental record.[26]

Phrakhru Manas told me that in 2003 the Ministry of Education published a book of people who supported and spread traditional Thai wisdom. The list included both him and Phra Somkit. In the process, the government, much as the middle-class NGO activists discussed by Delcore, defined and reified "Thai wisdom." "The government wants to claim our work," Phrakhru Manas complained (personal communication, 9/30/2006).

Whose Rituals?

The work of environmental monks, in particular the use of tree ordinations, has become a manifestation of a new kind of tension facing socially engaged Buddhists. On the one hand, monks such as Phrakhru Manas and Phrakhru Pitak struggled for years to gain wider acceptance in Thai society. Their criticisms of state-led development and its links with capitalist exploitation of the natural environment needed to be heard in order to be effective. The challenge they now face is that their symbolic rhetoric has been appropriated by numerous actors all laying claim to a Buddhist base for their positions on environmentalist and other political debates.

Duncan McCargo (2004) argues that Thai Buddhism has long served to legitimate state power and foster a nationalist ideology. Several movements challenged this reactionary position, especially over the past century, but have, in McCargo's eyes, failed to fulfill the revolutionary potential of the religion to promote social and political equality and progressive ideas. The case of environmental monks is another example of a Buddhist movement challenging the effects of state policies rather than ignoring or even endorsing them. Yet as tree ordinations rapidly gained popularity to support numerous varied positions, their effectiveness declined as they too became tools of the state and broader social powers.

As governmental and nongovernmental organizations accepted and backed tree ordinations and the work of environmental monks, the issues addressed became less about local community needs and challenging state policies and more about integrating the criticism into a broader rhetoric, what Forsyth and Walker (2008) would call environmental narratives. Many NGOs, themselves critics of state-led development, shifted the ritual's meaning away from relieving the suffering of local peoples through criticizing state-led development to solidifying a generic definition of "local wisdom" (Delcore 2004b). They linked the symbolism of Buddhist ritual to national goals and agents of power in a way that complicated and undermined the monks' support of local people's agency.

When government agents began to participate, the issues became even more complex. On one hand, monks such as Phrakhru Pitak invited the participation of government and military officials, as well as sangha officials and businessmen. Having witnessed the challenges faced by Phra Prajak and Achan Pongsak, Pitak aimed to avoid overt conflict with people in power. Pulling them into the projects got them to demonstrate public acceptance of both the projects and the implicit criticisms of consumerism and capitalist development as underlying causes of environmental destruction. At the same time, their involvement contributed to changing the ways in which the rituals are read publicly. Especially after the fifty-million-trees ordination project in honor of the king, the ritual became a symbol of the state and the monarchy's efforts to care for the people. While the symbolic power of the king brought additional incentives for people to participate and uphold the goals of the project, the connection with the state simultaneously undermined the moral criticisms of economic development policies.

In the process, the concept of using Buddhism for social change has evolved. While the majority of Thai monks do not undertake explicit social projects such as rural development or environmental conservation, Thai society no longer views environmental monks as oddities. Stories abound about the interconnection of humans and the forest, and Buddhist responsibility of people to care for the natural environment. Few debates occur about the authenticity of Buddhist environmentalism. It seems environmental monks have successfully mediated the tension between Buddhist ideals and social action. The problem is that that same tension provided power and impact to the monks' projects.

Environmental monks no longer shock society into thinking about social issues of environmental degradation and poverty through performing tree ordinations. Instead, as several monks told me in 2006, the public expects monks to engage in environmental work and perform these rites, especially if they live near a forested area. According to Phra Kittisak,

> Now it is a normal role for monks to do environmental work. It is expected. Monks have more relevance to politics and have expressed political thoughts more than before. If monks live close to the forest and they do not protect it, not only villagers will raise questions, but the government, too. People and the government expect monks to take on this work. (Interview, 10/8/2006)

Coupled with the increasing number of tree ordinations sponsored by the state or in order to strengthen national sentiments, including the staging of a tree ordination in conjunction with a national beauty contest ("Beauty Contestants Ordain Tree" 2010; Plate 4), the expectations monks face to engage in environmental projects even if they are not so inclined threatens the effectiveness of Buddhist environmentalism. Monks who undertake environmental projects need to be committed to them and the local people, and think deeply about the religious and moral implications of their work. The further danger is that lay people will approach tree ordinations with a perfunctory attitude rather than reflecting about the underlying moral message environmental monks hope to convey. People may spend less time in preparation and education about environmental issues and actions they can take to protect their forests. Without being incorporated into a larger, well-planned project with detailed follow-up, tree ordinations are unlikely to promote the attitude and behavioral changes necessary for genuine conservation.

Continued Moral Challenges

Monks still negotiate their relationship with the state while following their moral conscience to deal with social problems. Phra Somkit Jaranathammo, for example, runs a model integrated agriculture farm in Nan Province. He receives support from both NGOs and, at one point, a government-sponsored project, *Krongkan Luang,* or the Royal Project Foundation. His work, like that of many environmental monks across Thailand, emphasizes both the local needs of villagers to respond to the negative effects of cash cropping and consumerism, and the growing recognition in the nation of the importance of sustainable agriculture. He may articulate a "simplified" environmental narrative that, in the words of Forsythe and Walker (2008, 26), has "underpinned normative visions of both environment and society," thereby supporting the state's policies and agenda. At the same time, Phra Somkit and others like him still challenge state-led development and its accompanying materialist values. They are expanding the duties of monks and the kinds of problems they address. Phra Maha Boonchuay summarized the situation well when asked about the future for monks working with social problems, stating, "In my own ideas, it's the duty of a monk . . . to give back to society" (interview, 10/18/2006). In his position as chair of the Northern Development Monks Network and vice chancellor of Mahachulalongkorn Buddhist University, Boonchuay saw "giving back" as including social engagement.

Environmental monks may be increasingly subject to violence and secular law, as in the cases of Phra Supoj and Phra Prajak. They have to uphold a standard higher than the average monk because they are pushing the boundaries of a monk's duties to include more social issues, including those that challenge the state and big business. They have changed their methods, adjusted their visibility on the national stage, and suffered defamation, death threats, and the loss of their colleague. They work with villagers, NGOs, and government agents, depending on what they determine is most appropriate in a given situation. In spite of obstacles and opposition, they remain a moral compass for the nation. They have challenged the state to rethink its positions on numerous issues, including forest conservation, and to adapt its environmental narratives even as the monks have adjusted theirs.

The future of Thai civic religion is still in flux, and probably always will be. The small strand of radical modern Thai Buddhism in Thai civic religion mentioned by Frank Reynolds (1994, 445) that challenges the status quo and powers that be is largely represented by engaged monks, including environmental monks. While engaged monks and the Thai state continue to negotiate their relationship and the articulation of Buddhist environmental knowledge, the dynamic serves as a check on both parties: Monks are reminded that they are the representatives of the religion and must behave accordingly, including giving back to society. The state is reminded that Buddhism holds a critical place in the discourses of national identity and Thai civic religion, without which it cannot maintain the respect and commitment of its people. All parties involved engage in forms of political performance, staging their positions, pulling the audience of the Thai public into the debate over control of land, meanings of power, and manipulation of spiritual symbols.

8

The Future

The Buddha said the sangha should rely on the laity for food, clothing, medicine, housing. . . . That means we have to give back to society through the ways in which we are skilled. . . . It's a must, something monks ought to do. Because we go bindabat for food from people's offerings.
                    —Phra Maha Boonchuay Siridharo, October 18, 2006

IF WE RECONSIDER the images from the opening of the book, the evolution of Buddhist environmentalism and the meanings and impacts of tree ordinations are now sharper. The progression of meanings reflects the ways in which socially engaged Buddhists have taken on and performed environmental actions and how Thai society has responded to them. From an understated recognition of the cultural sanctity of certain trees through marking them with colored cloths, to the quiet performance of tree ordinations in local communities, through increasingly public performances performed primarily by environmental monks and NGOs, followed by NGO- and state-sponsored performances, especially in honor of the king's fifty-year reign, tree ordinations have become an accepted and expected aspect of Thai popular culture.

This progression has not been uniform; neither is the Buddhist environmental movement itself. Environmental monks do not always agree on methods or priorities, although the majority tend to take similar stances against the direction of state-led economic development and the rise of consumerism in the nation. This progression reflects but does not reveal the underlying struggles accompanying tree ordinations and the work of environmental monks. The risks monks face when they engage in rural development or environmental actions remain hidden in these images. There are no clues here for solving Phra Supoj's murder. What these images do indicate is the power of the symbolism of tree ordinations and other rituals for capturing the Thai imagination and raising social justice issues surrounding land use and economic rights for rural people. The appropriation of the ritual symbol of the tree ordination and the assassination of environmental and social justice activists together demonstrate that these activists have touched a sensitive spot for those with power. The issues engaged monks are addressing through their rural development and environmental projects are real; people are in debt, often manipulated by those who stand to gain from their debt or who covet their land. Tensions surrounding land use and water rights are real. While Buddhism provides only one response to these tensions, the popularity of tree ordination performances shows its effectiveness. Engaged Buddhist monks have influenced, and continue to influence, Thai society. They have brought attention to social problems, and offered solutions.

Buddhist monks depend upon the laity for material support. In return, they provide spiritual guidance in the form of advice, performing rituals, and modeling ethical behavior. The degree to which spiritual guidance intersects with people's daily lives is continually negotiated, and depends on interpretations of the teachings of the Buddha. For engaged Buddhists, this relationship should consider issues of social justice, social ethics, and social responsibility. Development and environmental monks in Thailand interpret their responsibility as focusing on the material as well as spiritual suffering of the people they serve, promoting lifestyles that break cycles of debt and dependence on material goods as a measure of well-being. They emphasize the mutual dependence between people and the natural environment, and how the latter can be used to ensure the well-being of both rather than being destroyed in pursuit of material gain. Despite the challenges these monks face, they remain willing to take risks. They think and act for the future, aiming to reduce the suffering of all through pushing people to consider the effects, intentional and unintentional, of their actions. They do this through continuing to perform tree ordinations and long-life ceremonies for waterways, through exchanging and expanding approaches, and sharing their insights and engaging in dialogue with other Buddhists. The Buddhist environmental movement is far from slowing down; it has become accepted and entrenched, and even appropriated. It is evolving as both society and the issues the monks aim to address evolve.

Phra Somkit "has been well and still does a lot activities apart from the tree preservation," my colleague, Pipop Udomittipong, wrote me in early 2009. "He will have one tree ordination ceremony in which he will invite the

Governor to preside over later this month." Phra Somkit, Phrakhru Pitak, Phrakhru Manas, and others monks continue to perform new tree ordinations and other environmental activities. They return to the sites of previous rituals to perform renewal ceremonies, in some places annually, to keep people invested in the projects. In Phrakhru Pitak's home village, even though villagers no longer regularly conduct annual renewal rites, the consecrated community forest is still standing. They still honor the Buddha image and the spirit shrine on their way to collect sustainable forest products.[1]

The challenge now is how environmental monks can continue to stimulate Thai society to address the environmental crisis and the concomitant suffering seriously, despite attacks on their persons and their reputations, and the appropriation of their symbolic methods by state and corporate powers. The potential lies in their creativity and their ability to hold the respect of the Thai people. While tree ordinations have become mainstream practice rather than radical statements for social reform, often devoid of the educational and moral undertones central to the effectiveness of the larger projects the rites mark, the monks still have influence locally. Working closely with people in specific locales, people with whose problems they are intimately familiar and whose beliefs they understand, environmental monks implement effective, small-scale programs. On the other hand, they inspire expansion beyond Thailand, as activists reach out to the sangha in the neighboring countries of Laos, Cambodia, and Burma. Tree ordinations have even become models of creative thinking farther abroad, as Buddhist groups in the United States, for example, have adopted innovative methods of using rituals and other culturally appropriate means of encouraging more environmentally conscious and less consumptive lifestyles (Darlington 2009).

Environmental monks, like the interpretations of Buddhism that inspire them, are not static in their ideas. They continue to seek creative—and skillful—means to teach villagers and relieve suffering. In the late 1980s, the scholar monk P. A. Payutto (1987, 83) wrote that "belief in sacred objects . . . is losing its effectiveness because the current, modern generation has declared these beliefs foolish and has tried to teach villagers to stop believing in them." Despite Payutto's concern that belief in sacred objects is no longer effective, the tension between modernity and Buddhism is driving a renewal in both the belief in sacred objects and, more importantly, the power of the concepts underlying them to deal with social problems. Environmental monks continue to act in society, initiating new interpretations of their projects, building new alliances with state and NGOs, and engaging new social issues and outreach as society changes.

New Interpretations

Phrakhru Pitak remains open to new approaches and ways of achieving his goals of relieving suffering and preserving the natural environment. When I visited him in September 2006, he insisted that I go see the latest forest he ordained, the site of a tea "plantation" a few kilometers south of Nan city. The villagers in the area had been cutting trees at high altitudes in order to make ends meet, damaging a watershed as a result. They had gone into debt from cash crop farming sponsored by the government agricultural bank and seed companies, as had farmers across the province. Phrakhru Pitak met with the villagers to discuss the reasons they cut the trees and what it would take to get them to preserve the forest and the watershed while meeting their needs. According to a monk associated with Pitak, the villagers raised the idea of growing tea trees to make and market *miang*, popular fermented tea leaves chewed by Northern Thais. Phrakhru Pitak helped the farmers purchase tea trees, which they planted in the lower altitudes of the mountain. The advantage of tea trees is that they grow in shade and do not compete with other plants. The farmers do not need to cut the forest to plant tea, as they do with most other cash crops. In exchange, the villagers agreed to conserve the forest in the watershed. They created a trail and rest areas along small waterfalls to promote tourism in the area as an additional incentive for preservation and another source of income. Phrakhru Pitak conducted a tree ordination to consecrate both the preserved forest at the top and the newly planted tea trees near the base of the mountain.

The innovation of the tea forest project is that Phrakhru Pitak assisted farmers in developing a new cash crop rather than consecrating a community forest and insisting that villagers collect from it primarily for personal use. For years, he had criticized villagers' engagement in the market economy, but in this case, miang seemed to be the best alternative to provide people with a livelihood rather than logging and clear cutting for other crops. Tea is arguably sustainable in that the trees can be planted without destroying the existing forest, and leaves can be harvested without cutting down the trees. Pitak still holds his criticism of consumerism, but recognizes that villagers are part of a capitalist society. He is willing to work with them to change how that engagement affects their lives.

One NGO worker in Nan raised concerns that insufficient research had been done about how the villagers could market their tea leaves, or even how they would produce the miang itself. He worried that the villagers would sell the leaves to middlemen, again leaving them vulnerable to exploitation. The popularity of miang is declining in northern Thailand, and there is no market beyond the region. Instead of producing fermented tea leaves, this NGO worker suggested Hak Muang Nan Foundation, the organization that works closely with Phrakhru Pitak, should research whether they could develop a worldwide market for black tea as some NGOs in Sri Lanka have successfully done.

The tea project represents Phrakhru Pitak's adaptation to help rural villagers. He listens to their concerns and ideas, and seeks ways to assist them both to improve their livelihoods (while still emphasizing basic needs rather than accumulating goods and money) and to preserve the natural environment. He told me that although he was tired because of the administrative requirements of his ecclesiastical position, he maintains his principle that engaging in social issues is part of a monk's responsibility.

By 2010, Phrakhru Pitak had expanded his projects in yet another way. He facilitated the establishment of a meditation center in Nan Province. In addition to monks' residences, the center houses a small integrated agriculture farm. A fish pond sits just beyond the monks' huts, surrounded by fruit trees and other crops (Plate 31). Above the center is a protected forest. While not as explicitly a model farm as that of Phra Somkit, this meditation center promotes concepts of environmentalism among the monks who practice there, subtly encouraging them to undertake responsibility for caring for both the environment and the people who depend on it. It also provides Phrakhru Pitak himself a place to slow down and concentrate on his own practice, something his fast-paced schedule as an activist monk and ecclesiastic leader has not often allowed.

New Alliances

Phra Somkit sees education as the key to helping people help themselves. In addition to completing a Masters in environmental management at Chiang Mai University, writing his thesis on how people use and care for aquatic animals in their livelihoods in Nan Province (Somkit 2005), he undertook a research project on the revival of local weaving using natural materials among the women in his village. He promoted this project to preserve local culture and to complement women's agricultural livelihoods (Somkit and Committee 2002). Besides the weaving project, through which the few women who still held the knowledge of the methods and patterns taught others, Phra Somkit sponsors farmers to learn new methods through his model integrated agriculture farm. In 2006, he began cooperating with Dr. Seri Phongphit of Chulalongkorn University to offer weekend courses through the Life University (*mahawithiyalai chiwit*).

The Community Enterprise Institute and Life University is a project initiated by Seri to provide basic knowledge in areas such as accounting, economics, and politics to rural villagers who tend to have only a primary school education. These fields give them skills to take better care of themselves, improve their livelihoods, and avoid exploitation by outside middlemen.

More recently, the Royal Project Foundation (*Khrongkan Luang*), a government-sponsored organization, selected Phra Somkit's integrated agriculture farm as a site for one of its centers. The Royal Project Foundation (RPF) primarily focuses on developing upland peoples' livelihoods and incorporating them within the Thai state. Phra Somkit's village is high in the mountains of Nan, neighboring several upland minority groups. The monk frequently visits these minority groups, talking with them about conserving the forest they all share. The situation complicates the criticisms of Forsyth and Walker (2008) that Northern Thais usually blame the upland peoples for environmental destruction. Phra Somkit works with all groups living in the highlands, Thais and minorities alike, to solve the environmental and economic problems they all face.

While many environmental monks criticize the government's environmental and economic policies and use their activities to promote alternatives, Phra Somkit chose to work with the Royal Project Foundation and other organizations. Their cooperation allowed him some freedom from the logistical aspects of the work. He recognized the value of the scientific expertise and resources they brought to his work. As Forsyth and Walker point out (2008), combining the scientific knowledge of governmental organizations such as the RPF and many NGOs with the local knowledge and experiences of people familiar with specific locales affords greater potential for success of a project. The challenge is that both scientific knowledge and local knowledge are variable and can be interpreted in different ways to promote particular political agendas (Forsyth and Walker 2008, 11–15). Phra Somkit attempted to define social problems through a moral lens, listening to villagers' needs, and contribute spiritual legitimacy to the efforts, increasing the degree of engagement and commitment from the villagers.

I visited a neighboring Khmu village with Phra Somkit in the mid-1990s, and witnessed the respect these non-Buddhist people had for the monk. We attended their annual guardian spirit ritual to renew and protect the village. Although Phra Somkit could not attend the actual ritual because

it included the sacrifice of a buffalo, he remained interested and supportive of the spiritual aspects of the event. The villagers similarly understood
his reason for not participating in the central rite of the day's ceremonies,
given Buddhist principles of nonviolence. The experience demonstrated the
mutual respect between an activist Buddhist monk and non-Buddhist people
that emerged from his building a relationship with them over time. He took
the time to learn about their ways of life and beliefs, as well as sharing his
own. He worked closely with them to assess the value of the forest and natural resources and think through ways of preserving them while supporting
the villagers' livelihoods. His connections with the Khmu provided the RPF
with legitimacy among the upland people, while the organization's resources
and expertise helped advance the monk's goals of relieving suffering among a
greater number of people.

Phra Somkit's collaboration with the RPF illustrates the adaptability of
environmental monks. Rather than letting government and business agents
determine the meanings and use of the Buddhist environmental movement's
symbolic capital, especially tree ordinations, he looks beyond the affiliations
of any particular organization. He asks whether groups such as the RPF and
the Life University can help the people with whom he works—help them
improve their standard of living without tying them into a cycle of consumption and debt. Throughout these relationships, Somkit does not lose sight
of the Buddhist principles on which he grounds his work. He continually
assesses the values of these collaborations for the local people, remaining flexible if the projects do not serve his broader goals. (His relationship with RPF,
for example, only lasted a few years.)[2] He uses the opportunities to preach
to participants, integrating Buddhist values into the work (Chalerm 2005).
Such collaboration means that the monks do not have to do everything or be
responsible for all the logistical aspects of a project. As Phra Paisal pointed
out, activist monks often get promoted and take on ecclesiastical duties that
interfere with their ability to engage in social projects. Through cooperating with NGOs and government organizations, monks can gain support for
their projects and assistance with the details.

New Issues

Phrakhru Pitak maintains that environmental issues and their impact on
rural people, especially the expansion of debt, are the main problems facing
villagers. Finding continual support and funding for environmental projects,

however, is challenging. As with many other monks, he has expanded his socially engaged work as the interests and concerns of mainstream Thai society have shifted. Besides incorporating more market-oriented aspects of forest conservation, as with the tea tree project, Phrakhru Pitak has moved into HIV/AIDS hospice work. This shift is occurring across Thailand as society changes; people accept the importance of environmental work and even expect it of rural monks. Thai society is also beginning to recognize the scale of HIV/AIDS infection in the country and the urgency of dealing with it. Gradually, people are learning more about the disease, its causes and symptoms, and, even more slowly, the stigma against people with HIV/AIDS is breaking down. Socially engaged monks play a key part in this process, as their assistance for families of people with AIDS and their hospice work have the potential to change the moral judgments often levied at people with HIV/AIDS.

One well-known monk, Dr. Alongkot Dikkapnyo, began dealing with people with AIDS in 1992, establishing a treatment center at his temple, Wat Phra Baht Nam Phu, in Lopburi Province. This monk's approach has generated controversy as he isolates people with AIDS from the rest of society, and his treatment—itself controversial—emphasizes the negative moral behaviors that led to infection. Other engaged Buddhist monks focus on the suffering caused by the disease and dealing with the social issues surrounding it. The Sangha Metta Project, a program that trains monks to deal with people with AIDS, began in 1997 with this approach.[3] Yet only a few monks engage in HIV/AIDS issues because of a negative moral stigma and lack of knowledge surrounding the disease.

Development and environmental monks, such as Phrakhru Pitak, are gradually moving in this direction, especially with support from existing networks of engaged monks. Bodhiyalai, a network of development monks in northern Thailand, has begun to assist monks engaged in HIV/AIDS work. Phra Maha Boonchuay, head of Bodhiyalai and vice chancellor at Mahachulalongkorn Buddhist University's Chiang Mai branch, described the gradual integration of different yet interrelated issues into engaged monks' work, including HIV/AIDS work: "Monks from different areas can visit and learn from each other, so that they get new ideas and expand their work. Some may be working on AIDS exclusively, but once they visit their fellow monks in other places, they may get ideas how to expand work in their local areas" (interview, 10/18/2006). He framed this process in terms of coordinating the efforts of and providing support for monks engaging a variety of issues.

The network's logistical activities are grounded in the basic Buddhist concept of interconnection. Just as environmental projects emerged from the activities of monks undertaking rural development work, incorporating new efforts such as support for people with HIV/AIDS is not surprising. The monks explain the underlying causes in the same way: society is turning away from Buddhist teachings in everyday life, brought on by the causes of suffering taught by the Buddha—desire, anger, and ignorance. Environmental monks such as Phrakhru Pitak may begin doing HIV/AIDS hospice work, especially as that is where the funding for his socially engaged projects is strongest (interview, 9/10/2006), but that doesn't pull him away from environmental work. His focus remains solidly on what he sees as the primary problem facing rural people: debt.

Throughout my research activist monks articulated two main problems facing Thai society: rural debt (Phrakhru Pitak) and moral decline (Phra Paisal). While Pitak and Paisal expressly framed the issues with these words, other environmental monks would agree. These problems are intertwined with environmental issues. Debt emerges from the government's push toward economic growth through export agriculture and cash cropping, leading farmers and developers alike to view land in terms of its economic potential rather than as an integral component of life. Moral decline underlies this process, as people value money, goods, and social status as the markers of a "good life." They compete with each other, weakening community bonds and support as society becomes increasingly individualized. In the process, people are turning away from the religion as a means of coping, and focusing instead on consumption.

Many Thai monks go along with this process, performing the rituals people request and, especially in larger urban areas, charging large sums for them. They meet people's desire for immediate gratification. Development and environmental monks challenge this process and attempt, despite the risks, to reinstate and reinforce Buddhist values in society. In many cases, they are successful, at least in getting people to rethink the implications of their behavior and begin to work to change society and relieve suffering caused by consumption and environmentally destructive behavior.

Beyond Borders

Although most environmental monks focus on local areas, their influence has reached beyond Thailand's borders to neighboring Theravada Buddhist countries. While Cambodia, Laos, and Burma have distinct forms of Buddhism and their own environmental and social issues, Cambodian and Lao (and to a lesser extent, Burmese) sangha and Buddhist organizations have borrowed, adapted, and contributed to aspects of the Buddhist environmental movement. Monks such as Phrakhru Manas, Phrakhru Pitak, and Phra Prajak serve as role models for how the dhamma can be applied to promote positive change and work toward environmental awareness and education. At the same time, monks, activists, and NGOs in these countries develop and interpret Buddhism in ways appropriate for the local settings. They acknowledge the precedents set by the Thai environmental monks, but work to establish forms of Buddhist environmentalism in their own ways. Below I provide a brief overview of the ways in which Buddhist environmentalism is emerging in Cambodia and Laos.[4]

Cambodia

In 1991, I met an activist monk from Cambodia at the annual conference of the International Network of Engaged Buddhists (INEB) in Thailand. This monk was adamant that while Cambodia struggled to rebuild its society, including Buddhism, after the devastating impact of the Khmer Rouge era in the 1970s, they would find their own ways to do so. He was sensitive to the efforts of Thai Buddhists trying to help, concerned that the Cambodians develop their own approaches to their problems. Given long-standing tensions between the Thais and the Cambodians, I was not surprised at his insistence that while they could learn from the Thais, Cambodian Buddhists did not want Thais to control their rebuilding efforts.

The mutual influences between these Buddhist neighbors continue to go in both directions. The senior Cambodian monk, Maha Ghosananda, not only ran the first Dhammayatra in 1992 that served as the model for the walks for Sangkla Lake in southern Thailand (Poethig 2002, 2004), he became a patron of INEB until his death in 2007. He stood as the face of engaged Buddhism in Cambodia, working tirelessly to reestablish Buddhism and peace in the country as the Khmer refugees returned from camps in Thailand. Maha Ghosananda's philosophy, as quoted here in a manual on environmental education for Lao monks, frames environmental issues in terms familiar from the Thai context, but directly relevant for the Cambodian situation:

When we respect the environment, then nature will be good to us. When our hearts are good, then the sky will be good to us. The trees are like our mother and father, they feed us, nourish us, and provide us with everything; the fruit, leaves, the branches, the trunk. They give us food and satisfy many of our needs. So we spread the Dharma (truth) of protecting ourselves and protecting our environment, which is the Dharma of the Buddha. When we accept that we are part of a great human family—that every being has the nature of Buddha—then we will sit, talk, make peace. I pray that this realization will spread throughout our troubled world and bring humankind and the earth to its fullest flowering. I pray that all of us will realize peace in this lifetime and save all beings from suffering.

The suffering of the world has been deep. From this suffering comes great compassion. Great compassion makes a peaceful heart. A peaceful heart makes a peaceful person. A peaceful person makes a peaceful family. A peaceful family makes a peaceful community. A peaceful community makes a peaceful nation. A peaceful nation makes a peaceful world. May all beings live in happiness and peace. (Souphapane et al. 2005, 20)

As Kathryn Poethig argues, even as the Cambodians focused on reviving their society in their own terms, they received help and influence from numerous transnational NGOs and international organizations. Dealing with environmental issues was no exception as indigenous Khmer NGOs emerged alongside initiatives supported by groups such as the United Nations Development Program's Environmental Technical Advisory Programme (UNDP/ETAP) and the Buddhist Perception of Nature Program.

In 1997, a consortium of Cambodian NGOs, supported and funded by UNDP/ETAP and UNESCO, began a program to provide environmental education for Buddhist monks. They were inspired by the Buddhist Perception of Nature's book, *A Cry From the Forest,* written by the Thai academic, Chatsumarn Kabilsingh (1987a). Chatsumarn consulted on the creation of a Cambodian version of the book, originally targeted toward Thai and Tibetan Buddhists (*Cry From the Forest* 1999, 1). The Cambodian version, *Cry From the Forest: A "Buddhism and Ecology" Learning Tool,* was published in 1999.[5]

While the Cambodian book draws primarily from Khmer Buddhist stories and practices, it references a handful of Thai environmental monks as models for the integration of Buddhism and environmentalism. The abbot of Wat Bodharama (Phrakhru Manas Nathiphitak) is credited with performing the first tree ordination, which monks on Dhammayatra introduced to Cambodia in 1998 (*Cry From the Forest* 1999, 30). Another section on local beliefs and customs cites Phrakhru Pitak's awareness of the importance of spirit beliefs for villagers, and the inclusion of a ceremony to request permission from the local guardian spirit before performing a tree ordination in his home village (*Cry From the Forest* 1999, 40). A third Thai example consists of a short mention of the use of pha pa, or giving the forest robes, ritual as a means of fund raising and educating people about community development (*Cry From the Forest* 1999, 28).

Beyond these brief mentions of Thai examples of Buddhist environmental actions, most references to Buddhism and environment in Cambodia emphasize connections between monks and NGOs, occasionally supported by transnational organizations such as UNDP/ETAP. Two Cambodian environmental NGOs, Mlup Baitong ("Green Shade") and Save Cambodian Wildlife, both incorporate environmental education for monks in some of their programs. Mlup Baitong often partners with governmental and international organizations to promote environmental education. Since 1998, Mlup Baitong's Buddhism and Environment Program has worked with hundreds of monks and fifteen pagodas.[6] Their projects focus on water resource management, tree nurseries, vegetable gardens using natural agriculture (comparable to integrated agriculture), and environmental education for monks. While they have sponsored an occasional tree ordination, the Cambodian monks emphasize the use of Dhammayatras, or dhamma walks, to promote social issues, including environmental problems.

Together with the Alliance of Religions and Conservation (ARC) and the World Bank, Mlup Baitong sponsored an environmental conference in Phnom Penh, the capital of Cambodia, in 2004. As an extension of a newly formed Asian Buddhist Network, the conference brought together monks and environmentalists from Cambodia, Laos, Thailand, Burma, and Vietnam to share ideas and information. Phra Kittisak represented the Thai sangha network, Sekhiyadhamma, and presented on the Spirit in Education Movement (SEM, one of Sulak Sivaraksa's organizations) with a spokesman from World Wide Fund for Nature-Thailand. Most of the conference program was in Khmer, and dealt with Cambodian environmental issues. Probably the most significant outcome of the conference was the creation of a new organization of Cambodian monks dedicated to environmental conservation in 2005 known as the Association of Buddhism for the

Environment (ABE) or in Khmer: "*Samakorm Budsasna Dembei Barekthan*" (*Sor Bor Bor*).[7]

Cambodian monks continue to undertake environmental projects in partnership with NGOs more than Thai environmental monks do (Nardi 2005). Recent examples of Buddhist environmentalism in Cambodia include a group of monks working with the NGO Conservation International to conserve the Central Cardamom Mountains. In September 2010, a Cambodian monk, Bun Saluth, won the Equator Prize, an environmental award sponsored by the UNDP ("Cambodian Buddhist Monk" 2010; MacFarquhar 2010, A11). For eight years Bun Saluth headed the Monk's Community Forest to protect an 18,261-hectare forest area in his home province, Oddar Meanchey in northwestern Cambodia. He stood up to poachers and educated villagers on the value of preserving the forest. He helped villagers learn about ways to support their livelihoods without destroying the forest, including gathering mushrooms, ginger, tree resin, and bamboo. One story told when he received the award described him chanting a good luck ritual for a python that he bought from a farmer who was going to sell it for food.[8]

The stories about Cambodian environmental monks sound familiar. Limited academic research has been done on these monks, but newspaper articles and Web sites indicate a movement less developed than that in Thailand, although far more directly connected with the work of environmental NGOs and international agencies. While it is impossible to point to explicit influences from the Thai monks beyond the occasional reference to their projects as models, the precedents of Theravada monks undertaking environmental and development work are there. In Cambodia, as in Laos, the monks and their supporters will develop the connections and projects in their own way.

Laos

Far less is known about the connections between monks and environmental activism in Laos.[9] The socialist government of Lao Democratic People's Republic (Lao PDR) has discouraged Buddhist activities since its inception in 1975. Yet Buddhism has remained influential in people's lives, serving as what Souphapone et al. (2005, 7) refer to as "social capital." Supported by the World Bank and the Alliance of Religions and Conservation, in 2005 a small NGO called Buddhism and Development Laos coordinated the production of an environmental education manual for monks, based on the Cambodian version of *Cry From the Forest.* The project was also influenced by the "Environmental Education Activity Manual" produced in Cambodia by the Food and Agriculture Organization of the United Nations (FAO), Osmose, Mlup Baitong, and Save Cambodia's Wildlife (Souphapone et al. 2005, 2). The Lao manual aimed to give monks and other primary school educators basic information, techniques, and teaching exercises to promote environmental awareness and teach basic ecology from a Buddhist perspective. As the editors state in the introduction, "The book was born out of a growing need in Lao PDR to spread knowledge about the changes in the environment and is the first of its kind in the country" (Souphapone et al. 2005, 3).

The manual presents basic interpretations of Buddhist teachings in light of environmentalism, followed by concrete teaching activities aimed at primary school children. The book indicates how Lao Buddhists are developing a form of engaged Buddhism to deal with contemporary social issues. As one abbot in the capital, Vientiane, stated, "The dhamma in itself does not change, but the world changes. The problems current at the time of the Buddha were essentially different from those we encounter today. Therefore it is necessary to explain the precepts and other teachings again in the context of current society" (Souphapone et al. 2005, 11). This manual and the Buddhism for Development Project (founded in 2003) that produced it attempt to do this in terms of environmentalism.

The Buddhist teachings presented in the manual follow the same basic ideas seen in Thailand, often integrating community development and environmental issues. It covers things such as the Buddha's life story, dependent origination (*pattica samupadda,* Pali), Buddhist precepts, and stories from the Dhammapada and the Jatakas, all illustrating the close relationship between Buddhism and the natural environment. As with the Thai environmental monks, the emphasis lies in relieving suffering through understanding current problems, including poverty, and applying the dhamma to deal with them. In Laos, because of the lack of support for Buddhism after 1975, much of the focus includes reviving the influence of Buddhism and the sangha in society. The project aims to place monks in positions to impact the direction of development in Laos, preserving and promoting Lao culture and religion as guides for the rapid changes the nation is undergoing.

One innovative way in which the Lao sangha have engaged social issues was through the Metta-Dhamma-HIV-Prevention-Project by the Lao Buddhist Fellowship Organisation (LBFO), supported by UNICEF. In Laos, unlike in Thailand, the monks more quickly found support for such activities often deemed inappropriate for monks through collaboration with the governmental Lao Revolutionary Youth Union, which talked about the more explicit sexual aspects of HIV/AIDS. The monks followed up with discussions of Buddhist morality (Souphapane et al. 2005, 15–16).

Similarly, the environmental education manual encourages monks to build understandings of Buddhism together with addressing immediate social problems people face. Monks draw on their position of respect in society to help people think about community development in terms of Buddhist morality while dealing with problems of poverty and social alienation that can lead to misuse of the forest and natural resources. As the authors point out,

> To teach these topics is a great chance for the sangha to combine traditional Buddhist teachings with a new topic. Besides engaging in an activity that is beneficial for society, monks also spread the dhamma to the younger generation in this way, as the learning about prayer and general Buddhist morality has always been a part of the lessons monks give in schools. It is, however, necessary to combine traditional teaching and new topics, as preaching alone is very often not sufficient to change the behaviour of people. In practise this means that the Buddha's teachings and prayer have to be seen in a new perspective and monks and nuns have to learn new techniques of teaching and knowledge transmission. (Souphapane et al. 2005, 17)

The Spirit in Education Movement (SEM), founded in Thailand by Sulak Sivaraksa, supports this process in Laos, as well as Cambodia and Burma. SEM's outreach program provides education and resources to help the sangha in each location identify its own needs and approaches. Generally, the projects supported by SEM focus on community development and education, often with an environmental perspective.

SEM works primarily with the Lao Buddhism for Development (LBFD) project, which sponsored the environmental education manual for monks. Beginning in 2008, LBFD offered training for monks in areas such as socially engaged Buddhism, community and sustainable development, and social leadership and activism. The curriculum emphasized eight aspects of knowledge, ranging from applying Buddhist values for "contemporary community development," inspiring socially engaged Buddhism, and analyzing "complex contemporary social issues locally, regionally and globally" to attaining skills of community organizing, critical thinking, and communication to find solutions for social problems. One of the goals stressed realizing "the importance of ecological system interconnected with all beings and be able to initiate way of life that reduce [*sic*] negative impact toward environment" (SEM 2009, 2).

The projects that highlighted environmental issues integrated community development and environmentalism. These included natural and integrated farming, mushroom growing, and promoting healthy lives through a healthy environment and natural healing. The educational manual mentions tree ordinations, but the emphasis sits more with the community projects than ritual performance. Perhaps because Buddhist rituals occurred less frequently in Laos after the socialist revolution, using such techniques would not be as effective as in Thailand. The projects in Laos emerged from feedback from the participants, mostly young monks recruited by LBFD. These programs are still in early stages, but work closely with the Lao sangha authorities rather than as independently as in Thailand, or as closely with NGOs as in Cambodia. Buddhism is reemerging in Laos, and the sangha seem to be careful to undertake new projects in conjunction with governmental organizations, or to keep low profiles to avoid objections from the socialist government.

In all the Theravada Buddhist countries of Southeast Asia, environmental Buddhism is connected with other forms of engaged Buddhism with an aim to deal with place-specific issues, needs, and understandings. While Buddhist environmentalism has existed longest in Thailand, largely due to its relatively calmer recent history and openness to monks' involvement in social issues, local and national forms are emerging in neighboring countries. This process illustrates the adaptability of Buddhism to changing social circumstances, enabling people to find their own ways of dealing with the impacts of modernity.

Adapting to Modernity

Ramachandra Guha's interpretation of environmentalism in India is reminiscent of the situation in Thailand. He wrote of this interpretation that

[i]t suggests that one does not have to wait for a society to be fully industrialized for an ecological critique to manifest itself. It argues that the relationship between religion and environmentalism follows rather than precedes industrialization. Once the evidence of

environmental degradation becomes widespread, writers and activists seek solace as well as solutions in practices of the past: thus the search for elements of an environmental ethic in the scriptures; thus also the rehabilitation of folk practices of conservation such as sacred groves and community irrigation systems. Over the past few decades much energy and ink has been expended on understanding what religion and custom offer us in countering or moderating the ecological excesses of the present day. The irony is that this return to tradition is itself a product of, indeed is only made possible by, the onset of modernity. (Guha 2006, 8–9)

The Thai Buddhist environmental movement is similarly a response to and a product of modernity. A handful of Thai monks observed the suffering accompanying modernity. Because of their interpretations of Buddhist teachings that emphasize relieving suffering and their closeness with rural people, these monks used creative performance of ritual to enact social justice and encourage environmentally responsible behavior. Tree ordinations grabbed people's attention and engendered villagers' commitment to caring for the forest and its resources. The public and media initially labeled these monks crazy and their actions inappropriate for members of the sangha. Some called for them to derobe from the sangha as a result.

The monks' actions threatened people with power who stood to benefit from exploitation of both villagers and forest. Evidence of the effectiveness of tree ordinations, the creation of community forests, and promotion of integrated agriculture came in three forms: first, villagers' participation in projects and the spread of the movement to other locations; second, social and physical threats and attacks on the monks, apparently aimed at undermining their reputations and their projects; and third, perhaps most telling, the appropriation of tree ordinations by the state for its own agenda. Tannenbaum (2000) argued that using tree ordination for political protest to protect a Shan village's forest in northern Thailand simultaneously incorporated the minority village into the nation-state in ways not possible before. The case demonstrates the complexities surrounding tree ordinations and how and why they are appropriated by the state. Tree ordinations have also become part of popular Thai culture, for example, used in demonstrating the "Thainess" of national beauty contestants. No longer do these rituals evoke shock and cries of outrage. Rather, the public expects monks living near the forest to perform them.

The irony is that the success of tree ordinations threatens their effectiveness. If the rites are performed pro forma, without accompanying efforts of environmental education and the establishment of mechanisms to maintain conservation projects, they could become empty rituals. The Thai sangha have been criticized for emphasizing ritual over philosophical scriptural comprehension or meditation practice. As part of this criticism, environmental monks sought to invest tree ordination rites with deeper meanings, in terms of both practical, urgent aspects of villagers' lives (relieving suffering) and promoting reengagement and commitment in the Buddhist religion through making it relevant for people's lives. As tree ordinations enter popular culture or become commodified, they risk becoming meaningless and contributing to the problem of over-ritualization devoid of deeper significance.

Prompted by a growing multifaceted and vocal environmental movement, Thai society began to recognize the damage its drive for economic growth on all levels had done to the natural environment (Hirsch 1996). While most blame government policies and business, it became popular among the growing middle class to acknowledge the contribution of its consumer lifestyle to the crisis. This contribution was offset the same way many of the sins of people worldwide are countered—through symbolic efforts to atone. For some, these efforts took the form of support for the small number of well-known environmental monks, shown through participation in such rituals as the long-life ceremony for the Nan River. The challenge is in translating such engagement into a genuine change in lifestyle, something for which environmental monks persistently push, each in his own way, responding to immediate needs, threats, and changing circumstances.

The Thai Buddhist environmental movement consists of a variety of methods, interpretations, and approaches: Luang Pu Phuttapoj's emphasis on rural development aimed at reducing economic needs and empowering farmers; Phra Somkit's model farm for integrated agriculture supported by NGOs and GOs; Phra Prajak's explicit political statements embedded in the struggle for rural people's land rights; Achan Pongsak's deep green emphasis on removing Hmong farmers from watershed areas, leading to accusations of racism and hypernationalism; and Phrakhru Pitak's and Phrakhru Manas's use of rituals such as tree ordinations and long-life ceremonies to give meaning to environmental projects such as community forests, preserving waterways, and sustainable livelihoods. Together these monks embody an aspect of what David McMahan calls "late modern Buddhist discourse" (2008, 180) as they respond to current and changing political, social, economic, and environmental circumstances. They are contributing, subtly and gradually, to a rethinking of Thai Buddhist practice. McMahan describes this age-old process through the debate between canonical authenticity and religious innovation:

> The historian of religion, qua historian, should not merely recapitulate sectarian or even canonical rhetorics of authenticity but examine what practitioners *do* with the texts and other elements of the tradition. The reconfiguration of traditional doctrine and practice in response to novel historical circumstances is the norm in the development of religions. Texts and doctrines are never static but are repeatedly reappropriated to deal with changing situations. Certain themes fall away into irrelevance, others emerge as salient, and both are given new meanings that arise in a dialectical relationship with changing political, economic, social, and material realities, as well as other traditions. The text or doctrine, then, is not a static reference point but a dynamic process whose meanings are always being reconstituted. This dynamic process of tradition-in-change establishes what Buddhism *is* empirically. (McMahan 2008, 179)

As an example of this process, environmental monks continue to perform tree ordinations and suep chata rituals for waterways, and seek new methods of incorporating their projects into broader contexts of social justice while promoting Buddhism. This struggle to stay relevant and articulate rural people's perceived needs and problems through performance leads monks to engage in new interpretations, alliances, and directions, keeping the movement creative and ahead of expropriation by those who would co-opt its symbolic rituals—all examples of McMahan's dynamic and dialectical process. The monks adapt and respond, remaining flexible to deal with the changes and challenges thrown their way, enacting upaya, or skillful means. In the process, as they move into the future they hold onto the ultimate goal underlying their actions: relieving suffering.

Notes

Chapter 1. The Framework

1. Quoted in Santikaro 1996:161; from *Buddhasasanik kap Kananurak Dhammajati* (*Buddhists and the Conservation of Nature*) (Bangkok: Komol Kimtong, 1990), 13.
2. Thus the title of Philip Hirsch's (1996) edited book on environmentalism in Thailand, *Seeing Forests for Trees.*
3. For other photographs of the event, see the Web site of Bangkok Broadcasting & T.V. Co., Ltd. (Channel 7), the pageant's sponsor: http://mtu. ch7.com/gallery.aspx?PostId=2850. Accessed 8/22/2011.
4. I deliberately use the term *citizen* here, aware of the debates and inequalities related to ethnic minorities, particularly in the Northern uplands, who do not hold citizenship and usually are not Buddhist. The discourses surrounding both non-Buddhist and Buddhist upland peoples and their relationship with and rights to use forest resources form another significant aspect of all of these debates, but are beyond the immediate scope of this work. For more on these issues, see Forsythe and Walker 2008; Lohmann 1993, 1999, 2000; and Pinkaew 2001.
5. A handful of monks focus their social efforts on issues of urban poverty, but they are less well known than those who work in rural areas.
6. The Eightfold Path defines proper behavior and attitudes that lead to the cessation of dukkha (see Payutto 1985, 251–52).
7. See King (2005) for a detailed consideration of the ethical aspects of engaged Buddhism.

8. The Forum on Religion and Ecology, currently based at the Yale School of Forestry and Environmental Studies, maintains an extensive Web site and database on examples of connections between religion and ecology: http://fore.research.yale.edu. Accessed 8/18/2011.

9. Buddhist environmentalism, as with all forms of environmentalism, is not a single, unified, cohesive movement. Different approaches and groups within Buddhist environmentalism draw on various interpretations of ecology, and have differing degrees of scientific knowledge. Western Buddhists in particular most often draw from deep ecology.

10. Environmentalism in the West is itself complicated and not monolithic. For a good discussion of major trends in the United States, see Cronon, 1996.

11. Phra Prajak was twice arrested in 1991 because of his outspoken position and actions related to environmentalism and social justice. For details on his case, see chapter 7.

12. Forsythe and Walker (2008, 17) define "environmental narratives" as follows: "In environmental studies, the term 'narrative' has been used to describe succinct summaries of environmental cause and effect that are seen as factual within popular debates or policy networks, but which are essentially based on highly selective participation in the problem definition and knowledge production." Their use of the term fits the various ways in which "environmental monks" talk about their work and the problems that they address, although they do not consider the monks' concern over the suffering that results.

13. The main exception to this position is Phra Achan Pongsak Techadhammo. In the early 1990s, the Dhammanaat Foundation, which he founded and ran, called for the removal of Hmong farmers from the uplands in Chom Thong District, Chiang Mai Province, claiming that their agricultural methods damaged the watersheds and threatened the forests and water supply critical for the lowland Thais in the area. For more on this controversy, see chapter 7, as well as Darlington 2005, Forsythe and Walker 2008, 96–99, Lohmann 1999, and Paiboon 2003.

14. I have previously called these monks "ecology monks" (Darlington 1998). I now prefer the term "environmental monks" for the same reasons, as "ecology" implies too much emphasis on the natural world while "environmental" incorporates people and politics with nature.

15. The tree ordination performed as part of the Miss Thailand Universe 2010 contest involved a full ritual, including merit making and reverence

of Buddhist monks. In some ways, the ritual illustrated the degree to which being Buddhist and being concerned for the environment have become part of what it means to be "Thai." Nevertheless, the question remains as to the main purpose of this ritual—to engage in Buddhist environmentalism targeted at relieving suffering, or to promote a beauty contest. For photographs of the ritual event, see Channel 7's Web site: http://mtu.ch7.com/gallery.aspx?PostId=2850 (accessed 8/23/2011).

16. The more general translations of these terms are "tangibles" (*rupatham*; So 1989, 251) and "intangibles" (*namatham*; So 1989, 155).

17. *Achan* means teacher or professor. Used as a title, it denotes respect, and can be used for either lay people or monastics (usually combined with *phra*).

18. *Luang Pu* is a term of respect for an older monk, meaning "revered grand-father." I use this title here because of my reverence for him, and because that it how most Thais refer to him. Phuttapoj Waraporn is his most recent title. Chan Kusalo is his given name, and is included as a way to identify him through title changes. Monks' titles (which are used as their names) change as they progress through the ecclesiastical hierarchy, in response to their educational and ecclesiastical responsibilities. Through-out the book I use the most recent title for monks, unless they are better known by a particular name. I have written about Luang Pu elsewhere under previous titles: Dhammadilok, and Phra Thepkavi. I also referred to him as *Luang Pho,* or "revered father." At the time of his death in 2008, he was ninety-one, and commonly referred to as Luang Pu.

19. To complicate the discussion of female monastics in Thai Buddhism, see Brown 2001 and Lindberg Falk 2007.

20. Buddhist environmentalists such as Sulak Sivaraksa, for example, led the fight against UNOCAL in Thailand where the pipeline cut across Thung Yai Naresuan wildlife reserve. They joined with human rights activists in dealing with the multifaceted issues surrounding Burma.

21. See Hirsch 1996 for a discussion of the complexities of Thai environmentalism.

22. Integrated agriculture involves interplanting different species of plants, such as rice, fruits, and vegetables, and raising animals, including fish, chickens, and pigs, together in the same plot of land. The plants and animals benefit each other: the plants provide food for the animals and nutrients for each other (some kinds of beans, for example, provide needed nitrogen); animals fertilize the plants and stir up the soil. Key

to integrated agriculture is to grow first for consumption, selling only the surplus. For an analytical discussion of a farmer who employs this method in Nan, see Delcore 2004a.

23. Theravada Buddhists consider giving alms to monks a powerful form of accruing religious merit toward a better rebirth or even better conditions in the current life. Monks serve as "fields of merit" because they provide the opportunity for lay people to make merit through their gifts.

Chapter 2. The Forest, the Village, and the Ecology Monk

1. Biography of Achan Sanguan (former name of Phrakhru Pitak Nanthakhun) compiled by the Thai Interreligious Commission for Development (TICD; n.d.[1993], 3); author's translation. Manuscript in the author's possession.

2. The Malbri are the smallest ethnic minority in Thailand. They are a hunting and gathering culture, although today most live in settled villages in remote areas of Nan and Phrae provinces. Only a few hundred of them remain (Sakkarin Na Nan 2006).

3. This figure comes from Wyatt 1994, 1076. Although an old figure, the population of Nan has grown little, and may have even decreased due to migration to Bangkok, over the past couple of decades.

4. In 1993, the village had seventy-five households.

5. "Ui" means grandparent in Northern Thai, used as a title of respect for elders. Ui Lek passed away in the mid-1990s.

6. According to Ui Lek, three families had already settled in the area when he and his brothers arrived, but they did not stay for long. I could not find out anything more about them. Most villagers today cite Ui Lek and his brothers as the original settlers. Ui Lek also told me that he and his two brothers came originally as hired laborers, working to clear farmland. I never understood for whom they supposedly worked or why they were able to stay, building houses and establishing a village. I only heard one other villager refer to this story as part of the founding of the village.

7. The connection with Laos is not surprising given that prior to the Siamese-French war of 1893 the kingdom of Nan stretched north of the Mekong River far into what is present-day Laos (Wyatt 1994, 1084–85).

8. See Stott 1991 for a historical discussion of Thai attitudes towards the "wild" forest.

9. Ui Lek performed a brief ceremony of simple offerings to introduce me to the spirit within two weeks of my arrival to ensure the success of my work and the safety of the village.

10. Pitak is referring to nearby camps for refugees from Laos.

11. The forests of Nan were one of the last holdouts of the Communists when the government amnesty in 1980 significantly reduced their numbers. By the mid-1980s the insurgency was all but over.

12. He claims that he no longer carries any debt since when he stepped down as headman in 2001 he stopped borrowing to grow cash crops. Instead, he is able to support himself selling herbs (personal communication, 9/29/2006).

13. Monks often change their ecclesiastical titles and names as they are promoted within the sangha hierarchy. For the sake of simplicity, I refer to Phrakhru Pitak Nanthakhun by his most recent title and name rather than following the name changes through his lifetime. This life story is based on discussions and interviews with Pitak during my research, hearing him relate stories of his life at various events, and a handful of published accounts and transcripts of interviews with other people. See Arawan 1993; Delcore 2000; Webb 1998.

14. This option seems to be more popular in northern Thailand than in other regions as the number of novices compared with *bhikkhu* (fully ordained monks, who must be over the age of twenty) is higher in the north than elsewhere.

15. Delcore (2000, 171) says Pitak was asked to lie for the headman concerning the missing wood to government soldiers who regularly patrolled the area. Pitak could not uphold the lie, and questions by the soldiers drove the headman away in shame.

16. According to Delcore (2000, 172 n. 8), the term "village forest preserve" (*pa sanguan mu ban*) was used. Later, as the concept of community forestry gained prevalence nationwide, Pitak shifted to using the term "community forest" (*pa chumchon*) instead. By the time he performed a tree ordination in Dok Dang in 1990, this term was used. Community forestry is a popular concept in Thailand, and forms the basis of the controversial Community Forestry Bill, which has been contested for over a decade. See Local Development Institute 1992; Saneh and Yos 1993.

17. Before Dok Dang's tree ordination, Ui Lek, the local spirit medium, conducted a ceremony requesting the village guardian spirit's permission to consecrate the forest and his support in protecting it. Phrakhru Pitak

was criticized by some environmental monks for using spirit beliefs to protect the forest, as they saw it as using fear and superstition rather than reason and Buddhist teachings. Even Buddhadasa criticized spirit beliefs and Brahmanic aspects of Thai religion, and aimed at a purer form of Buddhist practice (Jackson 2003). On the spirit ceremony in Dok Dang, see Darlington 2003c.

18. In 2011 the government widened the road that ran through the village, moving all the houses and clearing the forest on one side of the road. Traveling through the village now, one can see for miles due to the height of the village and the lack of trees. Despite this outside factor contributing to deforestation there, the villagers have maintained the main section of the consecrated community forest on the other side of the road.

Chapter 3. The Rituals

1. Although Mahayana Buddhism emphasizes this approach more than Theravada as a mode of religious teaching, engaged Buddhists across schools of thought adapt and use the idea of skillful or expedient means to connect social, moral, and religious ideas in their efforts to achieve social justice.

2. There are many more individual rituals performed as well, but these tend to hold less significance in villages as a whole. On the differences that can occur between monks and villagers in interpreting the function of rituals and merit making, and their relationship with community, see Darlington 1990, 111–41.

3. The *bhikkhuni* order was reintroduced in Sri Lanka in 1998 (Mrozik 2009, 361). Although a handful of Thai women ordained in Sri Lanka, their ordination as bhikkhuni is still controversial in Thailand.

4. Swearer (2004, 301) defines *sai sincana,* or sacred cord, as "the string used in rituals to transfer power from Buddha images and monks to material objects; used especially in making holy water (Thai, *nam mon*)." Suep chata rites use the same sacred thread, even though there is no Buddha image involved.

5. On the Buddha image ceremony, see Swearer 2004.

6. Forest monks in Theravada Buddhism traditionally emphasize meditation and austere practices in isolation from society. While many forest monks in Thailand are concerned about the state of the forests, they are

not the same as environmental monks. For more on forest monks, see Kamala 1997; Tambiah 1984; and J. Taylor 1993a.

7. Phrakhru Pitak may be a rare monk in that he works with and respects non-Buddhist minorities in his region. Even as he teaches them Buddhist principles, believing that Buddhist practice can improve their lives and futures, he does not exclude them from his projects if they do not convert. The complex issue of relations between Buddhist monks and ethnic, non-Buddhist minorities in northern Thailand is important, but beyond the scope of this work.

8. Economic enterprises that destroy natural forests include the creation of eucalyptus plantations and logging hardwood trees such as teak. The former is occurring primarily in the northeast legally, and at a rapid rate (Lohmann 1991), while the latter continues throughout the country despite a national ban passed in 1989. The widespread belief is that both frequently occur with the backing of factions within local, regional, and national governments and the military (Pinkaew and Rajesh 1992).

9. Thongchai Winichakul and Robert Bickner first pointed out to me the multiple meanings of the term as used on the sign.

10. I borrow the term *indigenous NGO* from Delcore (2000) to refer to organizations that emerged locally rather than from outside (nonlocal or non-provincial) influences.

11. The network called its support of village-based conservation projects across northern Thailand "*khrongkan pa chomchon,*" or the Community Forest Project. At the meeting I attended on July 1, 1991, the participants drafted a statement of their definition of community forestry. This occurred amid the national debates about the Community Forestry Bill, which ultimately was included in the 1997 Constitution. The 1997 Constitution, the "People's Constitution," was overthrown after a coup d'état in 2006, leaving the issue of community forestry hanging once again.

12. At this network meeting the participants discussed how they could lend support to a range of projects. In particular, they examined specific initiatives in Chiang Rai, Lamphun, Phayao, Mae Hong Son, and Chiang Mai provinces, as well as the project in Nan.

13. As far as I am aware, the World Wildlife Fund never expanded the project to include other major religions. They published a book in 1987 entitled *Tree of Life, Buddhism and Protection of Nature,* with a "Declaration On Environmental Ethics" by His Holiness the Dalai Lama, that was published in English, Tibetan, and Thai.

14. Most of the seminars for environmental monks held during my main research period, 1991–93, were sponsored and organized by TICD. Sometimes they partnered with other organizations, such as WFT. Many were held under the banner of Sekhiyadhamma, an activist monk network facilitated and initially run by TICD.

15. Most of Chatsumarn's attention focused on the rights of women within Buddhism, particularly the right to full ordination. No official *bhikkhuni* (ordained nun) line exists in Theravada Buddhism, which leads the sangha in Thailand to deny full ordination to women. Her mother became the first Thai woman to be ordained as a bhikkhuni through a Taiwanese preceptor. Later, Chatsumarn formally ordained in Sri Lanka. Both bhikkhuni live and practice in Thailand, still promoting gender equality in Theravada Buddhism. On Buddhist women in Thailand, see Brown 2001 and Lindberg Falk 2007. On female ordination in Buddhism more generally, see Mzorik 2009.

16. The term *radical conservatism* is borrowed from the title of a book in honor of Buddhadasa Bhikkhu. The late Buddhadasa is recognized as the leading Thai Buddhist philosopher who advocated a return to the basic teachings of the Buddha in terms relevant for contemporary society (Thai Interreligious Commission for Development 1990). I take the term farther, using it here to describe the use of essential religious concepts, including elements of spirit beliefs as well as basic Buddhist principles, in new contexts and articulations in order to promote social change.

Chapter 4. The Precedents

1. Luang Pu Phuttapoj Waraporn frequently repeated this phrase (*setthakit kap chitchai tong kae panha phromkan*) over the two years I conducted fieldwork on his nongovernmental organization, the Foundation for Education and Development of Rural Areas (FEDRA), from 1986–88. When I visited him in 2006, one of the first things he mentioned to me was this phrase, which he asked me to write in English in his guest book.

2. Buddhists believe that the accumulation of their actions, good and bad, result in merit, which affects both the quality of their current lives and their future rebirths. The balance of merit can be affected through "merit-making," including donations to the sangha.

3. I use the term *development monks* for monks engaged in independent development work, as opposed to those members of the sangha who participate in or promote government development schemes.

4. See the case of Phrakhru Sakorn Sangvorakit, recounted in Seri (1988, 44–53).
5. Between the fall of Ayutthaya and the establishment of the Chakri dynasty, King Taksin began the reconstruction of the kingdom that the Siamese needed to pull themselves out of the crisis of defeat to the Burmese and begin again (Wyatt 1984, 139–45).
6. While the exact date of the *Traiphum* is debated, and the text itself was reconstructed in the late eighteenth century, the essential details of how the world worked laid out in the *Traiphum* remain influential even today. See Reynolds and Reynolds 1982, 5; C. Reynolds 1976, 204–11; Thongchai 1994, 20.
7. See Thongchai 1994, 20–36 on the sacred topographies within Siam prior to the nineteenth century.
8. For the details of Mongkut's religious reform movement and its impact on Siamese society, religion, and politics, see Kamala 1997, 5–9 (in which she connects the reform movement with the development of "modern state Buddhism"); Keyes 1989a; Jackson 1989, 43–46; C. Reynolds 1976; Swearer 1995, 131; Tambiah 1976, 208–19. Johnson (1997, 233) critiques most Western biographies of Mongkut as imposing a Western definition of "rationality" onto Mongkut, stating, "Against the simplicity of this kind of portrait, I argue that the 'rationality' of Mongkut was a unique and complex negotiation among many competing ideologies, of which the West's was only one."
9. For a detailed discussion of the left-wing "political" monks during this period, see Somboon 1982, 100–31.
10. In 1988, Seri (1988, 150) reported that a survey conducted by Maha Chulalongkorn University and the Thai Interreligious Commission for Development listed more than one hundred monks who engaged in community development work.
11. It should be noted, however, that there is often a gap between the goals of many of these development monks and those of the villagers. See Darlington 1990 for a discussion of the differing motivations, perceived needs, and social and cultural value systems enacted in development projects of monks, development workers, and villagers.
12. Development monks primarily, although not exclusively, work in rural areas.
13. Although this group is interreligious, it predominantly follows Buddhist principles and works with monks. This is not surprising, as Thailand is over 95 percent Buddhist. See Bobilin 1988, 77–98.
14. This section is based primarily on discussions with and observations of

Luang Pu Phuttapoj done while I was in the field, and on some of his extensive writings (Thepkavi n.d., 1988) and pamphlets and articles about his work (for example, FEDRA 1985). See Darlington 1990.

15. See also Khantipalo 1986, 2.

16. In interviews conducted in a village in Chiang Mai in the late 1980s, most villagers emphasized making merit to improve this life. Few mentioned concerns about their next lives, except in the contexts of funerals.

17. Phuttapoj visited Sarvodaya Shramadana in February 1988 as part of an exchange that brought two Sri Lankan monks to Wat Pa Dharabhirom in April 1988.

18. See Haas 1964, 75 and So 1985, 54–55 for definitions of *khrong* as "control," although Luang Pu Phuttapoj interprets the word somewhat differently than the standard usage.

19. Similarly, the philosophy of development behind Sri Lanka's Sarvodaya Movement is based on "a 'waking up' on every level—personal, spiritual, cultural, economic" (Macy 1988, 174). This involves the interdependent development of the individual at the root level, up through the community (village), regional, and national levels of society.

20. Sherry Ortner describes the line of questioning in practice theory, which is considered here, as trying

> to understand something the people did or do or believe, by trying to locate the point of reference in social practice from which the beliefs or actions emerge. This is not just a question of locating the actor's point of view, although that is a part of it. It is a question of seeking the configuration of cultural forms, social relations, and historical processes that move people to act in ways that produce the effects in question. (Ortner 1989, 12)

21. Lanna is the name of the ancient Northern Thai kingdom. People in the north frequently still refer to themselves as the people of Lanna. The first chairman of the Lanna Development Monks Group's was Phrakhru Saokham, the abbot in the village in Chiang Mai where I conducted my research on the work of FEDRA.

22. *Barami* involves ten perfections: generosity, morality, renunciation, wisdom, effort, tolerance, truthfulness, resolution, loving-kindness, and equanimity (Payutto 1985, 284). In lay terms, the concept is more general, embodying the idea of spiritual perfection of highly spiritual and revered monks.

23. Weber describes the rejection of "all rational economic conduct" (1946, 247) as a critical aspect of charismatic authority. The merit donations to

Phuttapoj can be seen as fitting this aspect as well; while much of the funding for his development work comes from a formal funding agency, the more important part, which provides it legitimacy in the eyes of the Thai Buddhists who both give to and receive from FEDRA, is that which is derived from merit donations to Phuttapoj.

24. For the version presented by FEDRA, see FEDRA 1985, 10. Other versions come from various perspectives, such as the development workers and the villagers.
25. Bunnag (1973) and Chai (1985) found similar responses among the rural Central Thai, and Spiro (1982) among the Burmese.
26. Spiro (1982, 94) demonstrates the same concept of merit among the Burmese. He also shows how these three ways are derived from the scriptures: the *Sangiti Suttanta* of the *Digha Nikaya* III, 1, 218, in *Dialogues of the Buddha,* Pt. III, 211.
27. Several anthropologists have dealt with the issue of how meritorious acts are ranked by rural Thai, resulting in slightly different orders. See Kaufman (1960, 133–34) and Tambiah (1970, 146–47).
28. Luang Pu Phuttapoj has been criticized by members of other NGOs for just giving to the villagers, thereby threatening their self-esteem and dignity. Giving them donations from the rich denies them the opportunity to earn a living on their own, and makes them feel inferior to those who gave the money. Even some of the development workers of Phuttapoj's organization, FEDRA, are concerned about the impact of the donations given as charity.
29. The five basic precepts in Buddhism are not to take life, steal, lie, commit sexual offenses, or take intoxicants.

Chapter 5. The Grassroots

1. Phrakhru Manas's story comes from an interview, 9/30/2006, and various personal documents he shared with me.
2. Some scholars, such as Anthony Walker, challenge the accepted notion in northern Thailand of "the importance of forests in maintaining the hydrological health of local and national river systems" (2002, 4) and raise concerns about the political implications and decisions based on what they see as misinformed knowledge. It is not my goal to address this debate from a scientific perspective. Whichever view of the link between forests and water supply is ultimately proven correct, monks such as

Phrakhru Manas and Phrakhru Pitak and the villagers with whom they work accept the causal relationship.

3. See Williams (1997) for a discussion of the politics of Buddhists' ritually releasing animals in medieval Japan.

4. In 2006, the Love Nan Province Foundation, which oversees most of Phrakhru Pitak's projects, did not have a count of the number of fish sanctuaries established.

5. Several bird sanctuaries established by environmental monks in the 1980s and 1990s can be defined as Buddhist environmental projects. The difference between these projects and the stork sanctuary described above is that the monks consciously use the former to educate people, particularly children in some places, such as the "Children Love Birds Association" at Tha Mafaiwan Village in the northeast (Sanitsuda 1994, 78).

6. Even though thudong monks isolated themselves for their religious practice, they remained under the control of the sangha authority in Bangkok. As monks returned periodically to Bangkok, occasionally recalled by the sangha authority, they were given instructions on how to relate to remote villagers and to encourage connections with the Bangkok state. For more information, see Kamala 1997; J. Taylor 1993a.

7. Several prominent forest monks did become central to the Buddhist environmental movement, especially in Isan, including Luang Pho Khamkhien Suwanno, discussed for his development work in chapter 4.

8. Often transcribed in English as *Khor Jor Kor*.

9. For details on his work that won the award, see the PTT Green Globe Web site: http://pttinternet.pttplc.com/greenglobe/2547/personal-06.html. Accessed 7/15/2008; in Thai.

10. This parallels Taylor's 1991 discussion of forest monks in the northeast engaging in small-scale conservation. Achan Pongsak's work goes much further in scale, impact, and controversy.

11. Some other environmental monks and environmentalists disagreed with Achan Pongsak that the Hmong needed to be moved in order to conserve the area.

Chapter 6. The Movement

1. Purdue (2007, 7) describes most social movements as mutually defining who is included and who the adversaries are. While environmental monks do the former, they tend to target programs, policies, and behaviors rather than specific other people or groups. Even as some criticize

the state, most of them work to include government officials in their projects or the rituals that establish projects in order to avoid direct confrontations.

2. In the introduction to his translation of P.A. Payutto's essay, "Monks and the Forest," Swearer describes the monk's qualifications as follows:

Acknowledged as an outstanding scholar, Dhammapitaka's [P.A. Payutto's former ecclesiastic title] published work includes two Pali dictionaries and a highly regarded, systematic interpretation of Buddhist doctrine. He has also written extensively on a variety of topics including Buddhist education, Buddhism and science, Buddhist economics, and Buddhist ethics as well as numerous topical, doctrinal treatises. From the mid-1960s to the mid-1970s he was actively involved in institutional leadership roles as the abbot of Phra Phirain Monastery in Bangkok and served as the deputy secretary-general of Mahachulalongkorn University for Buddhist monks. He has been awarded several honorary doctorates and in 1994 received the UNESCO Peace Education Prize. (Swearer 1999, 459)

3. Somboon Suksamran (1977, 1982, 1988) wrote extensively and critically about the "political" monks who worked with the government in its projects to develop the nation and incorporate remote areas within Bangkok's political power. In his later work (1988), he praised the alternative approach of "development" monks who worked independently of government programs.

4. Khruba Sriwichai could be seen as one of the first development monks, undertaking such a project independently of government control several decades before those I categorize as development monks. The difference is that Khruba Sriwichai had people build the road primarily for religious reasons rather than to improve their livelihoods.

5. On the ecological effects of the cable car, see Banziger 1992.

6. Chayant (1998, 267) notes that the project is periodically revived, but to date, it has not gone farther than occasional discussion.

7. Phra Phothirangsi was later promoted, well after concern about the cable car had abated.

8. Pinkaew (2001) notes some "deep green" conservation NGOs side with the RFD in calling for the removal of people, especially minority groups, from the forest in order to prevent deforestation. On community forestry, see Saneh and Yos 1993; Yos 2003, 169–94.

9. On the invention of community forest and the community forestry movement in Thailand, see Pinkaew 2001, 161–66.

10. On the rise of the Thai environmental movement and its diversity, see Hirsch 1996.

11. Such coalitions have failed in other cases, notably against the construction of the Pak Mun Dam. Ironically, even the government has since admitted to many problems caused by building the dam that opposition questioned during their protests, especially the loss of fish species and decrease in fishers' livelihoods. See Fahn 2003, 91–92.

12. On "framing as an act of cultural appropriation" and a means of promoting action among individuals used by social movements, see McAdam 1994, 37–38.

13. Hirsch (1996, 25) lists personnel differences between urban-based NGOs, staffed primarily by university graduates, and rural or local NGOs, led by community leaders such as monks, teachers, etc.

14. The bot at this temple, Wat Suan Kaew, was modeled after the main assembly building at Buddhadasa Bhikkhu's meditation retreat, Suan Mokh.

15. At that time, he had been arrested only once. His second arrest later that year occurred during a farmers' protest against a government program to relocate them off of "denuded" land, which was then rejuvenated, often through economic plantations. Questions and curiosity surrounding Phra Prajak's arrests fueled national awareness and debate about environmental monks.

16. Whether the broader members of the sangha supported him is unclear, as no formal study was done. Since most monks only knew what they got from media coverage, they probably questioned the appropriateness of his actions for a monk.

17. Lanna was the name of the largest kingdom in northern Thailand before it became fully incorporated into Siam. Many Northern Thais identify the region with Lanna.

18. See Poething (2004) for details on the Dhammayatra in Cambodia. Poething notes that the original idea for a peace walk across Cambodia emerged during discussions among a couple of Americans, who requested the support and leadership of Maha Ghosananda while he was attending the annual conference of the International Network of Engaged Buddhists in Thailand (Poething 2004, 200).

19. For in-depth examination of the problems in southern Thailand, see McCargo (2008).

Chapter 7. The Challenges

1. As noted in chapter 6, individual monks engaged conservation issues, usually in conjunction with alternative development projects, before the cable car protests. Their critiques of the state and economic powers remained on a local level, though, drawing little attention.
2. On the album *World: Folk Zen,* released 1991.
3. On the rhetorical arguments made for and against Phra Prajak, see F. Reynolds 1994, 443 et seq.
4. F. Reynolds (1994, 444 n. 14) notes that legally monks come under the jurisdiction of secular authorities only after being defrocked.
5. Jim Taylor argues that Phra Prajak's case was as much about localized disputes concerning power and influence as a challenge to national policies and state power. He points out the complexities of the governmental apparatus, and the drive of local officials to exercise their power (1993b, 1997, 39).
6. On Kho Cho Ko and the politics of eucalyptus plantations, see Lohmann 1990, 1991.
7. Technically, thudong is specific to forest monks, involving thirteen ascetic practices, including not sleeping in shelters. Phra Prajak used the practice for lay people to push their spiritual progress and to think about their relationship with the forest.
8. Hundreds of thousands of people filled the forests surrounding Achan Cha's original forest temple on the occasion of his funeral in 1993 (Saowarop 1993, 21). For more on Achan Cha and other forest monks, see Kamala 1997, Tambiah 1984, and J. Taylor 1993a.
9. This concept is borrowed from Seri 1988, 157, who discusses the secularization of the concepts of barami and charisma in relation to development monks.
10. Sulak Sivaraksa was one of the few people who continued to support Phra Prajak throughout the cases, and continues to do so today.
11. Mae chi are female ascetics who wear white robes and practice eight precepts. Their status is ambiguous in Buddhism. They consider themselves as ordained, but they are not admitted to the Thai sangha, who view them as devout lay women. For a full discussion of the Thai mae chi and gender issues in Thailand, see Brown 2001 and Lindberg Falk 2007.
12. Luangta Maha Bua Yanasampanno passed away in January 2011. His fund to help the nation's foreign reserves continued until shortly after his cremation in March. According to Parista and Yuttapong (2011), the

fund totalled 967 gold bars and U.S.$10 million since it began in July 1998 until his death. Even at his death, he bequeathed all his personal property and donations made for his cremation to be added to the fund (Sawai 2011; see also "Luangta Maha Bua" 2011).

13. In the late 2000s, HMN moved its office to a building just outside of Wat Aranyawat, further distancing it from Phrakhru Pitak's direct influence.

14. Green Globe Award Winners can be found at http://pttinternet.pttplc. com/greenglobe/eng/winner.html (in English); http://pttinternet. pttplc.com/greenglobe/winner.html (in Thai). Accessed 7/13/2009. For details on Phra Somkit's work that won the award, see the PTT Green Globe Web site: http://pttinternet.pttplc.com/greenglobe/2547/personal-06.html. Accessed 7/15/2009; in Thai.

15. For discussions of the racialization of environmentalism of the Dhammanaat Foundation, the organization founded by Achan Phongsak, see Forsyth and Walker 2008, 96–99, Lohmann 1999, 2000, and Pinkaew 2001, 111–20.

16. In order to preserve their purity, Theravada monks are not allowed to come into any physical contact with women.

17. After leaving the sangha, Achan Pongsak continued to wear the white robes of a devout lay person and retreated to his meditation site in Chom Thong. Dhammanaat Foundation continued its work in Chom Thong with less direct input from Achan Pongsak, gradually moving away from its identification as his NGO.

18. Information on Phra Yantra's case comes from numerous newspaper accounts, including "Crisis of faith" 1995; McGirk 1995.

19. A month after the seminar I saw a video of this event, including the tour of the dam site and affected villages. The video was shown to demonstrate solidarity with the monks involved at another seminar for environmental monks of Isan sponsored by TICD. It showed armed police and military personnel entering the temple during the first two days of the seminar, before the monks toured the dam site. The fact the police and military were monitoring the conference before the monks showed any public interest in the dam implied that the government was concerned about all the activities of environmental monks, not just those that touched on controversial issues.

20. This incident occurred before the protests of May 1992, which were again put down violently, an event often referred to as "Bloody May."

21. As recently as July 28, 2011, a vocal opponent of coal mining in Samutsakorn Province was assassinated, demonstrating the continued threats to

human rights and environmental activists.

22. By 2009 Kittisak again had police protection. See Harris 2010.
23. Comment made at seminar, "Mountain Peoples' Ecological Conservation Attitudes and Adaptations," in Chiang Mai, 8/4/1991.
24. The Shan are an upland minority people closely related to ethnic Tai people. They are predominantly Buddhist.
25. PTT Public Company Limited was formerly known as the Petroleum Authority of Thailand. On the awards, see the PTT Green Globe Web site: http://pttinternet.pttplc.com/greenglobe/eng/history.html. Accessed 7/16/2009.
26. It is interesting to note that members of the judging panel for the award include a wide range of public figures, including a representative of the royal family, members of the Thai Environment Institute, which is a leading research institution, several academics, a member of the RFD, and a leader of one of the best-known hill tribe NGOs (Judging Committee, http://pttinternet.pttplc.com/greenglobe/eng/history_referrence.html. Accessed 7/16/2009).

Chapter 8. The Future

1. According to the former headman (personal communication, 9/29/2006), a renewal ritual was performed annually until he stepped down as headman in 2001. Since then, only a couple of ceremonies have been performed. Yet I witnessed villagers still paying respect to both the Buddha image at the base of the ordained tree and the spirit shrine as they passed on their way to collect mushrooms in the community forest. In 2011, the government widened the road through the village, moving all the buildings and cutting down the forest on one side of the road. Despite this, most of the protected community forest still stands.
2. When I visited Phra Somkit in 2011, his collaboration with the RPF had ended, although the foundation maintained an office at his model farm. It was not clear to me how often staff members came there, or why the relationship had ended. Meanwhile, Somkit was developing new collaborations with other organizations.
3. See the program's Web site at http://www.buddhanet.net/sangha-metta/project.html. Accessed 6/17/2011.
4. While there is some evidence of Buddhist monks engaging in environmental issues in Burma (Nardi 2005), given the political and human

rights situation there the sangha primarily focus on other issues. I have found little concrete evidence of Buddhist environmentalism beyond what a couple of monks told me in 1991. These monks were living with a group of displaced, primarily Karen, people near the Thai border, in an area that has since fallen to the Burmese military. I do not know what has happened to either the monks or their small environmental projects since.

5. An English-language version of the Cambodian book is available online through the Cambodian Research Centre for Development: *Cry from the forest* 1999 (http://www.camdev.org/_publications/Cry-English-Revised-for-printing.pdf. Accessed 5/23/2011).

6. On the history and programs of Mlup Baitong, see the organization's Web site (www.mlup.org) and its 2005 Annual Report (available online at http://www.mlup.org/userimages/report/MB%202005%20Annual%20Report%20%28complete%20draft%29.pdf. Accessed 5/23/2011).

7. On the Phnom Penh environmental conference, see the Alliance of Religions and Conservation Web site (http://www.arcworld.org/projects.asp?projectID=229 and http://www.arcworld.org/news.asp?pageID=68. Accessed 5/23/2011).

8. On Bun Saluth's Equator Prize, see MacFarquhar 2010, the UNDP Cambodia Web site (http://www.un.org.kh/undp/pressroom/cambodian-buddhist-monk-wins-undp-environmental-award. Accessed 5/23/2011), and the Alliance of Religions and Conservation website (http://www.arcworld.org/news.asp?pageID=412. Accessed 8/23/2011).

9. Little academic work has been written on engaged Buddhism in Laos, with even less focused on Buddhist environmentalism. I am grateful to Patrice Ladwig for sharing a copy of the book he helped produce on environmental education (see Souphapone et al. 2005). The Spirit in Education Movement (SEM) in Thailand also supplied me with some information about their outreach programs to Laos and Burma (Spirit in Education Movement 2009).

References

Anan Ganjanapan. 2000. *Local control of land and forest: Cultural dimensions of resource management in northern Thailand.* Chiang Mai: Regional Center for Social Science and Sustainable Development (RCSD), Faculty of Social Sciences, Chiang Mai University.

Arawan Karitbunyarit, ed. 1993. *Rak Nam Nan: Chiwit lae Ngan khong Phrakhru Pitak Nanthakhun (Sanguan Jaruwanno)* [*Love the Nan River: The life and work of Phrakhru Pitak Nanthakhun (Sanguan Jaruwanno)*]. In Thai. Nan: Sekhiyadhamma, The Committee for Religion in Society, Communities Love the Forest Program, and The Committee to Work for Community Forests, Northern Region.

Banziger, Hans. 1992. Biodiversity, Buddhism, and bulldozers in Thailand's Doi Suthep Sanctuary. *Proceedings of the second Princess Chulabhorn Science Congress: Environment, Science, and Technology,* 673–86. Bangkok: Chulabhorn Research Institute.

"Beauty contestants ordain tree." 2010, March 17. *Daily News [khao sot rai wan]* 7048, 11. http://www.khaosod.co.th/view_news.php?newsid=TUROd01ERXlNREUzTURNMU13PT0=&sectionid=TURNd. Accessed 4/3/2010.

Blum, Mark L. 2009. The transcendental ghost in ecoBuddhism. In *Trans-Buddhism: Transmission, translation, and transformation,* ed. Abraham Zablocki, Jay Garfield, and Nalini Bhushan, 209–38. Amherst: University of Massachusetts Press.

Bobilin, Robert. 1988. *Revolution from below: Buddhist and Christian movements for justice in Asia. Four case studies from Thailand and Sri Lanka.* Lanham, MD: University Press of America.

Bowie, Katherine A. 1991. Introduction. In *Voices from the Thai Country-side: The Short Stories of Samruam Singh,* Monograph 6, ed. and trans. Katherine A. Bowie, 1–41. Madison: Center for Southeast Asian Studies, University of Wisconsin.

———. 1997. *Rituals of national loyalty: An anthropology of the state and the village scout movement in Thailand.* New York: Columbia University Press.

Brown, Kevin. 2006. Spectacle as resistance: Performing tree ordinations in Thailand. *Journal of Religion and Theatre* 5, no. 2: 91–103. http://www.rtjournal.org/vol_5/no_2/brown.html.

Brown, Sid. 2001. *The journey of one Buddhist nun: Even against the wind.* Albany: State University of New York Press.

Buddhadasa Bhikkhu. 1989. *Me and mine: Selected essays of Bhikkhu Buddhadasa.* Ed. Donald K. Swearer. Albany: State University of New York Press.

Bunnag, Jane. 1973. *Buddhist monk, Buddhist layman: A study of urban monastic organization in central Thailand.* Cambridge: Cambridge University Press.

Budsarakham Sinlapalavan. 2005, June 24. Lost protectors of human rights: "Misguided policies" blamed for killings. *The Nation.* http://www.nationmultimedia.com/home /LOST-PROTECTORS-OF-HUMAN-RIGHTS-Misguided-policies-117475.html. Accessed 2/26/2011.

"Cambodian Buddhist monk wins UNDP environmental award." 2010. United Nations Development Programme Cambodia. http://www.un.org.kh/undp/pressroom/cambodian-buddhist-monk-wins-undp-environmental-award. Accessed 5/23/2011.

Chai Podhisitra. 1985. Buddhism and Thai world view. In *Traditional and changing Thai world view,* ed. Chulalongkorn University Social Research Institute/Southeast Asian Studies Program, 25–53. Singapore: Institute of Southeast Asian Studies.

Chalerm Bungmek, Phrapalad. 2005. *Chao Adhikam Somkid Caranadhammo* (Chan-On)'s application of Buddhadhama to the forest preservation. Unpublished Master of Arts (Buddhist Studies) thesis, Chiang Mai University.

Chatsumarn Kabilsingh. 1987a. *A cry from the forest: Buddhist perception of nature, a new perspective for conservation education.* Bangkok: Wildlife Fund Thailand.

———. 1987b. How Buddhism can help protect nature. In *Tree of life: Buddhism and protection of nature,* ed. Shann Davies, 7–16. Hong Kong: Buddhist Perception of Nature Project.

————. 1998. *Buddhism and nature conservation.* Bangkok: Thammasat University Press.

Chayant Pholpoke. 1998. The Chiang Mai cable-car project: Local controversy over cultural and eco-tourism. In *The Politics of Environment in Southeast Asia: Resources and Resistance,* ed. Philip Hirsch and Carol Warren, 262–77. London: Routledge.

Clippard, Seth Devere. 2011. The Lorax wears saffron: Towards a Buddhist environmentalism. *Journal of Buddhist Ethics* 11: 212–48. http://blogs.dickinson.edu/buddhistethics/. Accessed 8/15/2011.

Cronon, William. 1996. The trouble with wilderness; or, getting back to the wrong nature. In *Uncommon ground: Rethinking the human place in nature.* New York and London: W. W. Norton.

Cry from the Forest: A "Buddhist and ecology" community learning tool. 1999. Phnom Penh: the Buddhist Institute in cooperation with the NGO Working Ground for Non-formal Environmental Education Project (MEEP) and UNDP-ETAP. http://www.camdev.org/_publications/Cry-English-Revised-for-printing.pdf. Accessed 5/23/2011.

Darlington, Susan M. 1990. Buddhism, morality, and change: The local response to development in Thailand. PhD dissertation, University of Michigan.

————. 1993. Monks and environmental conservation: A case study in Nan Province. *Seeds of Peace* 9, no. 1: 7–10.

————. 1997. Not only preaching—The work of the ecology monk Phrakhru Pitak Nanthakhun of Thailand. *Forest, Trees and People Newsletter* 34: 17–20.

————. 1998. The ordination of a tree: The Buddhist ecology movement in Thailand. *Ethnology* 37 no. 1: 1–15.

————. 2003a. Buddhism and development: The ecology monks of Thailand. In *Action dharma: New studies in engaged Buddhism,* ed. Christopher Queen, Charles Prebish, and Damien Keown, 96–109. London: RoutledgeCurzon Press.

————. 2003b. Practical spirituality and community forests: Monks, ritual, and radical conservatism in Thailand. In *Nature in the global South: Environmental projects in South and Southeast Asia,* ed. Paul Greenough and Anna L. Tsing, 347–66. Durham and London: Duke University Press.

————. 2003c. The spirit(s) of conservation in Buddhist Thailand. In *Nature across cultures,* ed. Helaine Selin, 129–45. Dordrecht: Kluwer Academic Publishers.

———. 2007. The good Buddha and the fierce spirits: Protecting the northern Thai forest. *Contemporary Buddhism* 8, no. 2: 169–85.

———. 2009. Translating modernity: Buddhist response to the Thai environmental crisis. In *TransBuddhism: Transmission, translation, and transformation,* ed. Abraham Zablocki, Jay Garfield, and Nalini Bhushan, 183–208. Amherst: University of Massachusetts Press.

Davies, Shann, ed. 1987. *Tree of life: Buddhism and protection of nature.* Hong Kong: Buddhist Perception of Nature.

Delcore, Henry D. 2000. Localizing development: Environment, agriculture, and memory in northern Thailand. PhD dissertation, University of Wisconsin at Madison.

———. 2004a. Development and the life story of a Thai farmer leader. *Ethnology* 43, no. 1:33–50.

———. 2004b. Symbolic politics or generification? The ambivalent implications of tree ordinations in the Thai environmental movement. *Journal of Political Ecology* 11, no. 1: 1–30.

———. 2005. Buddhist environmentalism in Thailand: Ideals and interests. Paper presented at the 104th Annual Meeting of the American Anthropological Association, Washington, DC.

Demaine, Harvey. 1986. Kanpatthana: Thai views of development. In *Context, meaning, and power in Southeast Asia,* ed. M. Hobart and R. Taylor, 93–114. Ithaca: Southeast Asia Program, Cornell University.

Devall, Bill. 2000. Deep ecology and political activism. In *Dharma rain: Sources of Buddhist environmentalism,* ed. Stephanie Kaza and Kenneth Kraft, 379–92. Boston: Shambhala.

Dhammanaat Foundation for Conservation and Rural Development. 1990. An outline of the Dhammanaat Foundation solution for the problem of deforestation in Thailand, with particular reference to the Mae Soi Valley project. Ms in author's files.

England, Philippa. 1996. UNCED and the implementation of forest policy in Thailand. In *Seeing forests for trees: Environment and environmentalism in Thailand,* ed. Philip Hirsch, 53–71. Chiang Mai: Silkworm Books.

Fahn, James David. 2003. *A land on fire: The environmental consequences of the Southeast Asian boom.* Boulder: Westview.

Forsythe, Tim, and Andrew Walker. 2008. *Forest guardians, forest destroyers: The politics of environmental knowledge in northern Thailand.* Seattle and London: University of Washington Press.

Foundation for Education and Development of Rural Areas (FEDRA). 1985. *Raingan Pracham pi 2528 [Annual Report 1985].* In Thai. Unpublished.

Fox, R. G. 1991. For a nearly new culture history. In *Recapturing anthropology: Working in the present,* ed. R. G. Fox, 93–113. Santa Fe: School of American Research Press.

Geertz, Clifford. 1966. Religion as a cultural system. In *Anthropological approaches to the study of religion,* ed. M. Banton, 1–46. New York: Praeger.

Guha, Ramachandra. 2006. *How much should a person consume? Environmentalism in India and the United States.* Berkeley: University of California Press.

Gusfield, Joseph R. 1994. The reflexivity of social movements: Collective behavior and mass society theory revisited. In *New social movements: From ideology to identity,* ed. Enrique Laraña, Hank Johnston, and Joseph R. Gusfield, 58–78. Philadelphia: Temple University Press.

Haas, Mary R. 1964. *Thai-English student's dictionary.* Stanford: Stanford University Press.

Haberkorn, Tyrell. 2005. Appendix I: Collusion and influence behind the assassinations of human rights defenders in Thailand. In *Special report: Rule of law vs. rule of lords in Thailand, Article 2,* 4, no. 2. http://www.article2.org/mainfile.php/0402/188/.

Halifax, Joan. 1990. The third body: Buddhism, Shamanism, and deep ecology. In *Dharma Gaia: A harvest of essays in Buddhism and ecology,* ed. Allan Hunt Badiner, 20–38. Berkeley: Parallax Press.

Harris, Ian. 1991. How environmentalist is Buddhism? *Religion* 21: 101–14.

———. 1994. Causation and *Telos*: The problem of Buddhist environmental ethics. *Journal of Buddhist Ethics* 1: 45–57.

———. 1995. Getting to grips with Buddhist environmentalism: A provisional typology. *Journal of Buddhist Ethics* 2: 173–90.

———. 1997. Buddhism and the discourse of environmental concern: Some methodological problems considered. In *Buddhism and ecology: The interconnection of dharma and deeds,* ed. Mary Evelyn Tucker and Duncan Ryuken Williams, 377–402. Cambridge: Harvard University Center for the Study of World Religions Publications.

Harris, Trent. 2010, January 15. Forest monks. *Religion and Ethics Newsweekly.* Public Broadcasting Service. http://www.pbs.org/wnet/religion-andethics/episodes/january-15-2010/forest-monks/5472/. Accessed 8/8/2011.

Hayami, Yoko. 1997. Internal and external discourse of community, tradition, and environment: Minority claims on forest in the northern hills of Thailand. *Tonan Ajia Kenkyu (Southeast Asian Studies)* 35, no. 3: 558–79.

Hirsch, Philip. 1996. Environment and environmentalism in Thailand: Material and ideological bases. In *Seeing forests for trees: Environment and environmentalism in Thailand,* ed. Philip Hirsch, 15–36. Chiang Mai: Silkworm Books.

———, ed. 1996. *Seeing forests for trees: Environment and environmentalism in Thailand.* Chiang Mai: Silkworm Books.

Holder, John J. 2007. A suffering (but not irreparable) nature: Environmental ethics from the perspective of early Buddhism. *Contemporary Buddhism* 8, no. 2: 113–30.

Isager, Lotte, and Søren Ivarsson. 2002. Contesting landscapes in Thailand: Tree ordination as counter-terriorialization. *Critical Asian Studies* 34, no. 3: 395–417.

Ishii, Yoneo. 1968. Church and state in Thailand. *Asian Survey* 8, no. 10: 864–71.

———. 1975. A note on Buddhistic millenarian revolts in northeastern Siam. *Journal of Southeast Asian Studies* 6, no. 2: 121–26.

———. 1986. *Sangha, state, and society: Thai Buddhism in history.* Trans. Peter Hawkes. Kyoto: Monographs of the Center for Southeast Asian Studies, Kyoto University; Honolulu: University of Hawai'i Press.

Jackson, Peter A. 1989. *Buddhism, legitimation, and conflict: The political functions of urban Thai Buddhism.* Singapore: Institute of Southeast Asian Studies.

———. 2003 [1987]. *Buddhadâsa: Theravada Buddhism and modernist reform in Thailand.* Chiang Mai: Silkworm Books.

Johnson, Paul Christopher. 1997. "Rationality" in the biography of a Buddhist king: Mongkut, King of Siam (r. 1851–1968). In *Sacred biography in the Buddhist traditions of South and Southeast Asia,* ed. Juliane Schober, 232–55. Honolulu: University of Hawai'i Press.

Kamala Tiyavanich. 1997. *Forest recollections: Wandering monks in twentieth-century Thailand.* Honolulu: University of Hawai'i Press.

Kamolthip Bai-Ngern. 1998, May 26. RAD bid to curb temple overcharging. *The Nation.* http://www.highbeam.com/doc/1P1-6986668.html. Accessed 8/19/2011.

Kaufmann, Howard K. 1960. *Banghuad: A community study in Thailand.* Locust Valley, NY: J. J. Augustin.

Kaza, Stephanie, and Kenneth Kraft, eds. 2000. *Dharma rain: Sources of Buddhist environmentalism.* Boston: Shambhala.

Keyes, Charles F. 1975. Buddhist pilgrimage centers and the twelve-year cycle: Northern Thai moral orders in space and time. *History of Religions* 15, no. 1: 71–89.

————. 1977. Millennialism, Theravāda Buddhism, and Thai society. *Journal of Asian Studies* 36, no. 2: 283–302.

————. 1989a. Buddhist politics and their revolutionary origins in Thailand. *International Political Science Review* 10, no. 2: 121–42.

————. 1989b. *Thailand: Buddhist kingdom as modern nation-state.* Bangkok: Editions Duang Kamol.

Khantipalo, Bhikkhu. 1986. *Buddhism explained.* Bangkok: Mahamkut Rajavidyalaya Press.

King, Sallie B. 2002. From is to ought: Natural law in Buddhadasa Bhikkhu and Phra Prayudh Payutto. *Journal of Religious Ethics* 30, no. 2: 275–93.

————. 2005. *Being benevolence: The social ethics of engaged Buddhism.* Honolulu: University of Hawai'i Press.

Kirsch, A. Thomas. 1977. Complexity in the Thai religious system: An interpretation. *Journal of Asian Studies* 36, no. 2: 241–66.

Laird, John. 2000. *Money politics, globalisation, and crisis: The case of Thailand.* Singapore: Graham Brash Pte.

Lee, Yok-shiu F., and Alvin Y. So. 1999b. Environmental movements in Thailand. In *Asia's environmental movements: Comparative perspectives,* ed. Yok-shiu F. Lee and Alvin Y. So, 120–42. Armonk, NY, and London: M. E. Sharpe.

Lindberg Falk, Monica. 2007. *Making fields of merit: Buddhist female ascetics and gendered orders in Thailand.* Seattle: University of Washington Press.

Ling, Trevor. 1973. *The Buddha: Buddhist civilization in India and Ceylon.* London: Temple Smith.

Local Development Institute. 1992. *Community forestry: Declaration of the customary rights of local communities. Thai democracy at the grassroots.* Bangkok: Local Development Institute.

Lohmann, Larry. 1990. Commercial tree plantations in Thailand: Deforestation by any other name. *The Ecologist* 20, no. 1: 9–17.

————. 1991. Peasants, plantations, and pulp: The politics of eucalyptus in Thailand. *Bulletin of Concerned Asian Scholars* 23, no. 4: 3–17.

————. 1993. Thailand: Land, power, and forest colonization. In *The struggle for land and the fate of the forests,* ed. Marcus Colchester and Larry Lohmann, 198–227. London: Zed Books.

————. 1999. Forest cleansing: Racial oppression in scientific nature conservation. *Corner House Briefing 13.* http://www.thecornerhouse.org.uk/item.shtml?x=51969. Accessed 10/10/2005.

————. 2000. For reasons of nature: Ethnic discrimination and conservation in Thailand. *The Corner House.* http://www.thecornerhouse.org.uk/item.shtml?x=52023. Accessed 10/10/2005.

Luangta Maha Bua. 2011, February 1. *The Telegraph.* http://www.telegraph. co.uk/news/obituaries/religion-obituaries/8296853/Luangta-Maha-Bua. html. Accessed 8/8/ 2011.

MacFarquhar, Neil. 2010, September 30. Trying to lace together a consensus on biodiversity across a global landscape. *New York Times,* A11.

Macy, Joanna. 1985 [1983]. *Dharma and development: Religion as resource in the Sarvodaya self-help movement.* West Hartford, CT: Kumarian Press.

———. 1988. In Indra's net: Sarvodaya and our mutual efforts for peace. In *The path of compassion,* ed. Fred Eppsteiner, 170–81. Berkeley: Parallax Press.

———. 2000. The third turning of the wheel. In *Dharma rain: Sources of Buddhist environmentalism,* ed. Stephanie Kaza and Kenneth Kraft, 150–60. Boston: Shambhala.

Magagnini, Steve. 1994, Summer. If a tree falls . . . A monk's blessing for Thailand's forest. *The Amicus Journal:* 12–14.

Maina, Wachira. 1998. Kenya: The State, donors, and the politics of democratization. In *Civil society and the aid industry,* ed. Alison Van Rooy, 136–67. London: Carthsean Publications.

Mayer, Theodore. 1996. Thailand's New Buddhist movements in historical and political context. In Brian Hunsaker, Theodore Mayer, Barbara Griffiths, and Robert Dayley, *Loggers, monks, students, and entrepreneurs: Four essays on Thailand,* 33–66. DeKalb, IL: Center for Southeast Asian Studies, Northern Illinois University.

McAdam, Doug. 1994. Culture and social movements. In *New social movements: From ideology to identity,* ed. Enrique Laraña, Hank Johnston, and Joseph R. Gusfield, 36–57. Philadelphia: Temple University Press.

McCargo, Duncan. 2004. Buddhism, democracy, and identity in Thailand. *Democratization* 11, no. 4: 155–70.

———. 2008. *Tearing apart the land: Islam and legitimacy in southern Thailand.* Ithaca: Cornell University Press.

McGirk, Tim. 1995, November 12. All kinds of monky business. *The Independent (London),* 18.

McGurty, Eileen. 2009. *Transforming environmentalism: Warren County, PCBs, and the origins of environmental justice.* New Brunswick, NJ, and London: Rutgers University Press.

McMahan, David. 2008. *The making of Buddhist modernism.* Oxford: Oxford University Press.

Missingham, Bruce D. 2004. *The assembly of the poor in Thailand: From local struggles to national protest movement.* Seattle: University of Washington Press.

Mlup Baitong. 2005. *2005 annual report.* http://www.mlup.org/userimages/report/MB%202005%20Annual%20Report%20%28complete%20draft%29.pdf. Accessed 5/23/2011.

Moore, Donald S. 1999. The crucible of cultural politics: Reworking "development" in Zimbabwe's Eastern Highlands. *American Ethnologist* 26, no. 3: 654–89.

Mrozik, Susanne. 2009. A robed revolution: The contemporary Buddhist nun's movement. *Religion Compass* 4, no. 3: 360–78.

Nardi, Dominic J., Jr. 2005. Green ideas and saffron robes: The ecology monks of Thailand, Cambodia, and Burma analyzed and contrasted by political culture and ecological variables. Unpublished honors thesis, Georgetown University.

Nash, Nancy. 1987. The Buddhist Perception of Nature project. In *Buddhist perception of nature,* ed. Shann Davies, 31–33. Hong Kong: Buddhist Perception of Nature.

Nelson, Rod G. 1990. The Dhammanaat Foundation. *MekongInfo.* http://www.mekonginfo.org/mrc/rdf-odi/english/papers/rdfn/10e-ii.pdf. Accessed 10/10/2005.

Olson, Grant. 1991. Cries over spilt holy water. *Journal of Southeast Asian Studies* 22: 75–85.

———. 1995. Introduction. In Payutto, P. A. [Phra Prayudh Payutto], *Buddhadhamma: Natural laws and values for life,* trans. Grant A. Oson, 1–33. Albany: State University of New York Press.

Ortner, Sherry B. 1989. *High religion: A cultural and political history of Sherpa Buddhism.* Princeton: Princeton University Press.

Paiboon Hengsuwan. 2003, July 11–14. Contradictions on the struggles over resources and contesting terrain of ethnic groups on the hill in Protected Area, Chom Thong, Chiang Mai. Presented at the International Conference, *Politics of the commons: Articulating development and strengthening local practices,* organized by the Regional Center for Social Science and Sustainable Development (RCSD), Faculty of Social Sciences, Chiang Mai University, Chiang Mai, Thailand.

Parista Yuthamanop and Yuttapong Kumanodnae. 2011, February 2. Abbot leaves multi-million baht legacy. *Bangkok Post.*

Pasuk Phongpaichit and Chris Baker. 1998. *Thailand's boom and bust.* Chiang Mai: Silkworm Books.

Payutto, P. A. [Phra Rajavaramuni]. 1984. *Thai Buddhism in the Buddhist world. A survey of the Buddhist situation against a historical background.* Bangkok: Mahachulalongkorn Buddhist University.

———. 1985. *Photcananukrom Phutthasasat (Dictionary of Buddhism).* In Thai and English. Bangkok: Mahachulalongkornrajavidyalaya.

———. 1987. *Looking to America to solve Thailand's problems.* Trans. Grant A. Olson. Bangkok: Sathirakoses-Nagapradipa Foundation.

Pearmsak Makarabhirom. 2002. Constraints on people's participation in forest management in Thailand. *Kyoto Review of Southeast Asia* 2. Kyoto: Center for Southeast Asian Studies. http://kyotoreview.cseas.kyoto-u.ac.jp/issue/issue1/index.html. Accessed 12/11/2002.

Pedersen, Poul. 1995. Nature, religion, and cultural identity: The religious environmentalist paradigm. In *Asian perceptions of nature,* ed. Ole Bruun and Arne Kalland, 258–76. Surrey, UK: Curzon Press.

Petroleum Authority of Thailand. 2000. Green Globe Award winners: Phrakhru Manas Natheephitak. http://pttinternet.pttplc.com/greenglobe/2543/personal-01.html. Accessed 7/15/ 2008. In Thai.

———. 2004. Green Globe Award winners: Phra Somkit Jaranathammo. http://pttinternet.pttplc.com/greenglobe/2547/personal-06.html. Accessed 7/15/2008. In Thai.

Phra Prajak Khuttajitto. 2007. *Seeds of Peace* 23, no. 2: 25.

Pinkaew Laungaramsri. 2001. *Redefining nature: Karen ecological knowledge and the challenge to the modern conservation paradigm.* Chennai: Earthworm Books.

———. 2002. On the politics of nature conservation in Thailand. *Kyoto Review of Southeast Asia* 2. Kyoto: Center for Southeast Asian Studies. http://kyotoreview.cseas.kyoto-u.ac.jp/issue/issue1/index.html. Accessed 12/11/2002.

———, and Noel Rajesh, eds. 1992. *The future of people and forests in Thailand after the logging ban.* Bangkok: Project for Ecological Recovery.

Poethig, Kathryn. 2002. Movable peace: Engaging the transnational in Cambodia's Dhammayietra. *Journal for the Scientific Study of Religion* 41, no. 1: 19–28.

———. 2004. Locating the transnational in Cambodia's Dhammayatra. In *History, Buddhism, and new religious movements in Cambodia,* ed. John Marston and Elizabeth Guthrie, 197–212. Honolulu: University of Hawai'i Press.

Pongsak Techadhammo Bhikkhu. 1990, October 27. Buddhists and forest conservation. Summary translation of a talk given at a seminar held for monks at Wat Palat. Ms in author's files.

———. 1991a. Hilltribes and the destruction of watershed forests in northern Thailand: An interview with Ajahn Pongsak on 3 December 1991. Translated ms by Project for Ecological Recovery, in author's files.

———. 1991b. *Phutthasatsana kap Kananuraksa Pamai* [*Buddhism and Forest Conservation*]. In Thai. Bangkok: Phitakschiwitmatuphumi Group.

———. 1991c. Meeting of Monks' Association for the Conservation and Protection of the Environment. Translated ms in author's files.

———. n.d. How can Buddhist principles be applied to conservation? Translated ms in author's files.

Purdue, Derrick. 2007. Introduction: Dimensions of civil society. In *Civil societies and social movements: Potentials and problems,* ed. Derrick Purduc, 1–16. London and New York: Routledge.

Rappaport, Roy A. 1979. The obvious aspects of ritual. In *Ecology, meaning, and religion.* Berkeley: North Atlantic Books.

Renard, Ronald D. 1994. The monk, the Hmong, the forest, the cabbage, fire, and water: Incongruities in northern Thailand opium replacement. *Law and Society Review* 28, no. 3: 657–64.

Reynolds, Craig J. 1976. Buddhist cosmography in Thai history, with special reference to nineteenth-century culture change. *The Journal of Asian Studies* 35, no. 2: 203–20.

Reynolds, Frank E. 1977. Civic religion and national community in Thailand. *Journal of Asian Studies* 36, no. 2: 267–82.

———. 1994. Dhamma in dispute: The interactions of religion and law in Thailand. *Law and Society Review* 28, no. 3: 433–52.

———, and Mani B. Reynolds, trans. 1982. *Three worlds according to King Ruang: A Thai Buddhist cosmology.* Berkeley Buddhist Studies Series 4. Berkeley: Asian Humanities Press/Motilal Banarsidass.

Rigg, Jonathan. 1995. Counting the costs: Economic growth and environmental change in Thailand. In *Counting the costs: Economic growth and environmental change in Thailand,* ed. Jonathan Rigg, 3–24. Singapore: Institute of Southeast Asian Studies.

———, and Philip Stott. 1998. Forest tales: Politics, policy making, and the environment in Thailand. In *Ecological policy and politics in developing countries: Economic growth, democracy, and environment,* ed. Uday Desai, 87–120. Albany: State University of New York Press.

Roth, Robin. 2004. Spatial organization of environmental knowledge:

Conservation conflicts in the inhabited forest of northern Thailand. *Ecology and Society* 9, no. 3: 5. http://www.ecologyandsociety.org/vol9/iss3/art5. Accessed 4/25/2007.

Rolex Awards for Enterprise. 1997. Nancy Lee Nash. http://www.rolex-awards.com/laureates/laureate-41-nash.html#top. Accessed 7/14/2008.

Sakkarin Na Nan. 2006, January 12–15. The resource contestation between hunter-gatherer and farmer society: Revisiting the Mlabri and the Hmong community in northern Thailand. Paper presented at the World Archaeological Congress (WAC) Inter-Congress, Osaka, Japan.

Saneh Chamrik and Yos Santasombat, eds. 1993. *Pa Chumchon nai Prathetthai: Naewthang kan Phatthana [Community forests in Thailand: The direction for development]*. In Thai. Vols. 1, 2, 3. Bangkok: Local Development Institute.

Sanitsuda Ekachai. 1994. *Seeds of hope: Local initiatives in Thailand*. Bangkok: Thai Development Support Committee (TDSC).

Santikaro Bhikkhu. 1996. Buddhadasa Bhikkhu: Life and society through the natural eyes of voidness. In *Engaged Buddhism: Buddhist liberation movements in Asia,* ed. Christopher S. Queen and Sallie B. King, 147–93. Albany: State University of New York Press.

———. 2000. Dhamma walk around Songkhla Lake. In *Dharma rain: Sources of Buddhist environmentalism,* ed. Stephanie Kaza and Kenneth Kraft, 206–15. Boston: Shambhala.

Santita Ganjanapan. 1996. A comparative study of indigenous and scientific concepts in land and forest classification in northern Thailand. In *Seeing forests for trees: Environment and environmentalism in Thailand,* ed. Philip Hirsch, 247–67. Chiang Mai: Silkworm Books.

Saowarop Panyacheewin. 1993, January 16. Gathering to pay respects to Acharn Chah. *Bangkok Post,* 21, 28.

Sawai Boonma. 2011, February 2. Luangta Maha Bua—doing good even in death. *Bangkok Post.* http://www.bangkokpost.com/opinion/opinion/219417/luangta-maha-bua-doing-good-even-in-death. Accessed 8/8/2011.

Schmithausen, Lambert. 1997. The early Buddhist tradition and ecological ethics. *Journal of Buddhist Ethics* 4.

Scott, James C. 1990. *Domination and the arts of resistance: Hidden transcripts.* New Haven and London: Yale University Press.

Scott, Sir Peter. 1987. Introduction. In *Buddhist perception of nature,* ed. Shann Davies, 2–4. Hong Kong: Buddhist Perception of Nature.

Scott, Rachelle M. 2009. *Nirvana for sale? Buddhism, wealth, and the*

Dhammakāya Temple in contemporary Thailand. Albany: State University of New York Press.

Seri Phongphit. 1988. *Religion in a changing society: Buddhism, reform, and the role of monks in community development in Thailand.* Hong Kong: Arena Press.

———, ed. 1986. *Back to the roots: Village and self-reliance in a Thai context.* Culture and Development Series 1. Bangkok: Rural Development Documentation Centre.

Shalardchai Ramitanondh. 1984. *Phi Chaonai* [*The Spirit Lords*]. In Thai. University Monograph Project, Monograph Series No. 18. Chiang Mai: The Library of Chiang Mai University.

Sizemore, Russell F., and Donald K. Swearer. 1990. Introduction. In *Ethics, wealth, and salvation: A study in Buddhist social ethics,* ed. Russell F. Sizemore and Donald K. Swearer, 1–24. Columbia: University of South Carolina Press.

Smith, Mark J., and Piya Pangsapa. 2008. *Environment and citizenship: Integrating justice, responsibility, and civic engagement.* London/New York: Zed Books.

So Sethaputra. 1989. *New model Thai-English dictionary.* Bangkok: Thai Wathanaaphanich.

Somboon Suksamran. 1977. *Political Buddhism in Southeast Asia: The role of the sangha in the modernization of Thailand.* New York: St. Martins Press; London: C. Hurst.

———. 1982. *Buddhism and politics in Thailand.* Singapore: Institute of Southeast Asian Studies.

———. 1988. A Buddhist approach to development: The case of "development monks" in Thailand. In *Reflections on development in Southeast Asia,* ed. Lim Teck Ghee, 26–48. Singapore: ASEAN Economic Research Unit, Institute of Southeast Asian Studies.

Somkit Jun-On (Phra). 2005. *Kansueaksa botbat watnatham chumchon thi songphon to khwamsamret khong ongkon khueakhai onurak phan satnam ban hat pha khon kingamphoe Phu Phiang, Changwat Nan* [*The study of community cultural roles affecting the success of the Aquatic Animal Conservation Network organization, Ban Hat Pha Khon, King Amphoe Phu Phiang, Changwat Nan*]. In Thai. Unpublished Masters thesis, Chiang Mai University.

———, and Committee. 2002. *Krabuankanphatthana phafaiyom sithamachat klum satri tho phayom sithamachat ban phonkham amphoe Santisuk changwat Nan.* [*The advancement of natural dyed cotton and the women's natural dye weaving group, Ban Pong Kham, Amphoe Santisuk, Nan Province*]. In Thai. Unpublished research report. Thailand Research Fund.

Souphapone Lee, Patrice Ladwig, and Mirjami Tran Minh, eds. 2005. *Environmental education activity manual for monks and educators teaching at primary schools in Lao PDR.* Vientiane, Lao PDR: Alliance of Religions and Conservation and the World Bank.

Spirit in Education Movement (SEM). 2009. Grassroots leadership training for the Lao Buddhist community: Mid-year report 1st April – 31st August 2009. Unpublished progress report. Bangkok: Spirit in Education Movement (SEM) Under the Sathirakoses-Nagapradipa Foundation (SNF), 1–20.

Spiro, Melford E. 1982 [1970]. *Buddhism and society: A great tradition and its Burmese vicissitudes.* 2nd ed. Berkeley: University of California Press.

Stott, Philip. 1991. *Mu'ang* and *pa*: Elite views of nature in a changing Thailand. In *Thai constructions of knowledge,* ed. Manas Chitakasem and Andrew Turton, 142–54. London: School of Oriental and African Studies, University of London.

Sulak Sivaraksa. 1986. *A Buddhist vision for renewing society.* Bangkok: Tienwan Publishing House.

———. 1987 [1976]. *Religion and development.* Bangkok: Thai Inter-Religious Commission for Development.

———. 1992. *Seeds of peace: A Buddhist vision for renewing society.* Ed. Tom Ginsburg. Berkeley: Parallax Press and Bangkok: International Network of Engaged Buddhists, Sathirakoses-Nagapradipa Foundation.

———. 2000 [1992]. The religion of consumerism. In *Dharma rain: Sources of Buddhist environmentalism,* ed. Stephanie Kaza and Kenneth Kraft, 178–182. Boston: Shambhala.

Suphaphan Na Bangchang. 1991. *"Raksa Pa Khue Raksa Tham": Phra Achan Phongsak* [*"Caring for the forest is caring for dhamma": Phra Achan Phongsak*]. In *Khon kap Pa* [*People and the forest*], 45–60. In Thai. Bangkok: MILD.

Swearer, Donald K. 1995. *The Buddhist world of Southeast Asia.* Albany: State University of New York Press.

———. 1997. The hermeneutics of Buddhist ecology in contemporary Thailand: Buddhadasa and Dhammapitaka. In *Buddhism and ecology: The interconnection of dharma and deeds,* ed. Mary Evelyn Tucker and Duncan Ryuken Williams, 21–44. Cambridge: Harvard University Center for the Study of World Religions Publications.

———. 1999. Dhammapitaka on monks and the forest. In *Socially engaged*

Buddhism for the new millennium: Essays in honor of The Ven. Phra Dhammapitaka Bhikkhu (P.A. Payutto) on his 60ᵗʰ birthday anniversary, ed. Pipob Udomittipong and Chris Walker, 459–69. Bangkok: Sathirakoses-Nagapradipa Foundation and Foundation for Children.

———. 2004. *Becoming the Buddha: The ritual of image consecration in Thailand.* Princeton: Princeton University Press.

———, Sommai Premchit, Phaithoon Dokbuakaew. 2004. *Sacred mountains of northern Thailand and their legends.* Chiang Mai: Silkworm Books.

Tambiah, Stanley J. 1970. *Buddhism and the spirit cults in north-east Thailand.* Cambridge: Cambridge University Press.

———. 1976. *World conqueror and world renouncer: A study of Buddhism and polity in Thailand against a historical background.* Cambridge: Cambridge University Press.

———. 1978. Sangha and polity in modern Thailand: An overview. In *Religion and legitimation of power in Thailand, Laos, and Burma,* ed. Bardwell L. Smith, 111–33. Chambersburg, PA: AMINA Books.

———. 1984. *The Buddhist saints of the forest and the cult of amulets.* Cambridge: Cambridge University Press.

Tannenbaum, Nicola. 2000. Protest, tree ordination, and the changing context of political ritual. *Ethnology* 39, no. 2: 109–27.

Taylor, Diana. 2002. "You are here": The DNA of performance. *TDR: The Drama Review* 46, no. 1: 149–69.

———. 2006. Performance and/as history. *TDR: The Drama Review* 50, no. 1: 67–86.

———. 2009. Performing Ruins. In *Telling ruins in Latin America,* ed. Lazzara and Unruh, 13-21. New York: Palgrave Macmillan.

Taylor, J. L. 1991. Living on the rim: Ecology and forest monks in northeast Thailand. *Sojourn* 6, no. 1: 106–25.

Taylor, Jim. 1993a. *Forest monks and the nation-state: An anthropological and historical study in northeastern Thailand.* Singapore: Institute for Southeast Asian Studies.

———. 1993b. Social activism and resistance on the Thai frontier: The case of Phra Prajak Khuttajitto. *Bulletin of Concerned Asian Scholars* 25, no. 2: 3–16.

———. 1994. *A social, political, and ethnoecological study of community forests and rural leadership in northeastern Thailand.* IOCPS Occasional Paper No. 36. Nedlands, W. Australia: The Indian Ocean Centre for Peace Studies.

———. 1996. "*Thamma-chaat*": Activist monks and competing discourses of nature and nation in northeastern Thailand. In *Seeing forests for trees: Environment and environmentalism in Thailand,* ed. Philip Hirsch, 37–52. Chiang Mai: Silkworm Books.

Tegbaru, Amare. 1998. Local environmentalism in northeast Thailand. In *Environmental movements in Asia,* ed. Arne Kalland and Gerard Persoon, 151–78. Nordic Institute of Asian Studies Man & Nature in Asia Series, No. 4. Surrey, England: Curzon Press.

Thai Inter-religious Commission for Development (TICD). 1981. *Tha Mafaiwan village (Rice Phapa ceremony).* Bangkok: Thai Inter-religious Commission for Development.

————. n.d. [1993]. *Phrasong kap kananurak singwaetlaum: karani suksa Phra Palat Sanguan Jaruwanno, Wat Aranyawat, T. Naiwiang, J. Nan [Monks and Environmental Conservation: Case Study of Phra Palat Sanguan Jaruwanno, Wat Aranyawat, T. Naiwiang, Nan Province].* In Thai. N.p.

Thai Inter-Religious Commission for Development and the International Network of Engaged Buddhists, ed. *Radical conservatism: Buddhism in the contemporary world.* Bangkok: The Sathirakoses-Nagapradipa Foundation.

Thepkavi, Phra. 1988. *Wisdom of Ven. Pra Thepkavi.* Chiang Mai: Glangvieng Printing.

————. n.d. *Kan phatthana chonabot [Rural Development].* In Thai. Chiang Mai: Ratanapon Printing.

Thongchai Winichakul. 1994. *Siam mapped: A history of the geo-body of a nation.* Honolulu: University of Hawai'i Press.

Tucker, Mary Evelyn, and Duncan Ryuken Williams, eds. 1997. *Buddhism and ecology: The interconnection of dharma and deeds.* Cambridge: Harvard University Center for the Study of World Religions Publications.

Vasana Chinvarakorn. 2005, June 29. Dead—for doing the right thing. *Bangkok Post.* http://archives.mybangkokpost.com/bkkarchives/front-store/news_detail.html?aid=169818&textcat=General%20News&type=a&key=Phra%20Supoj&year=2005&click_page=1&search_cat=text&from=text_search. Accessed 2/26/2011.

Walker, Andrew. 2002. Forests and water in northern Thailand. Resource Management in Asia-Pacific Working Paper No. 37. Canberra: Resource Management in Asia-Pacific Program, Research School of Pacific and Asian Studies, The Australian National University.

Webb, Benjamin. 1998. Reviving ritual, conservation, and community in Thailand: Pra Kru Pitak Nanthakun. In *Fugitive faith: Conversations on spiritual, environmental, and community renewal,* ed. Benjamin Webb, 206–13. Maryknoll, NY: Orbis Books.

Weber, Max. 1946. *From Max Weber: Essays in sociology,* ed. and trans. H. H. Gerth and C. Wright Mills. New York: Oxford University Press.

Wells, Kenneth E. 1975. *Thai Buddhism and its rites and activities.* Bangkok: Suriyabun Publishers.

Wilaiwan Lekkaew, trans. 1996. The biography of a dedicated Buddhist monk: Pra Kru Manas Nathee Phitak and his pioneered project of tree ordination for forest conservation. Unpublished paper, Maechaiwittayakom School, Phayao, Thailand. Manuscript in author's possession.

Williams, Duncan Ryûken. 1997. Animal liberation, death, and the state: Rites to release animals in medieval Japan. In *Buddhism and ecology: The interconnection of dharma and deeds,* ed. Mary Evelyn Tucker and Duncan Ryuken Williams, 149–57. Cambridge: Harvard University Press.

Williams, Martin. 1992/1993. Wanted: A place to breed. *Birds illustrated.* http://www.drmartinwilliams.com/openbills/openbills.html. Accessed 7/14/2008.

Worsley, Peter. 1986. *The trumpet shall sound: A study of cargo cults in Melanesia.* Berlin: Schocken Books.

Wyatt, David K. 1984. *Thailand: A short history.* New Haven and London: Yale University Press.

———. 1994. Presidential address: Five voices from Southeast Asia's past. *Journal of Asian Studies* 53, no. 4: 1076–91.

Yos Santasombat. 2003. *Biodiversity: Local knowledge and sustainable development.* Chiang Mai: Regional Center for Social Science and Sustainable Development (RCSD), Faculty of Social Sciences, Chiang Mai University.

Index

285

merit-making (*continued*)
and releasing small animals, 139, 140
military involvement:
and deforestation, 36, 154, 255n8
monitoring of a sangha seminar at Ubon
Ratchatani, 216–217, 264n19
and the policy of *Kho Cho Ko*, 144–145,
201–202
suep chata ritual held on military land by
Phrakhru Pitak (1993), 190
modernity:
and Buddhadasa's concern with the social
relevance of Buddhism, 170–173
and engaged Buddhism in Thailand, 23,
28, 172, 177, 179, 245–247
P.A. Payutto on, 171–172, 177, 179
money:
and the dialectical tension between nonattachment and the acquisition of wealth
in Buddhism, 210–211, 237
precepts against monks handing money,
208
scrutiny of the sangha after the economic
crisis (1997–98), 208–210
and *tanha* (selfish desire), 115–116, 123,
173–175
See also consumerism/consumption; fund-
raising; livelihood issues; merit-making
Mongkut (Rama IV), 97–100, 123–124,
257n8
monks, *bhikkhu*:
and *barami* (spiritual perfection),
124–125, 127, 204–205, 207
ecclesiatical titles and name changes of,
xvii, 61, 125, 251nn17–18, 253n13
as "fields of merit," 27, 169, 252
and gender prerequisites for achieving
enlightenment, 57, 128
high number of novices in northern
Thailand, 253n14
moral authority of, 15, 198
and physical contact with women, 45,
208, 264n16
removal from secular life as the ideal
image of in Thai society, 122–123
role in political debates as controversial,

121, 179, 202
scholar monks, *phra nangsue*, 169–170
See also development monks; environmental monks; sangha (community of
monks)
morality:
the moral authority of monks, 15, 198,
207
rituals used to transform abstract moral
concepts into concrete actions, 54
and spiritual development (*kanphatthana
chitchai*), 116–117
See also silatham

Nan (Phrakhru Phiphitprachanat), Luang
Pho (development monk in Surin
Province), 43, 112–113, 122–123
Nan Province:
compared with Chiang Mai, 29–30
deforestation in, 31, 152–153, plate 6
Dok Dang Village, 30
the forests of Nan as a holdout for Com-
munist insurgency, 36, 253n11
"Green Nan" program, 44–45, 145
and the Hak Muang Nan Foundation
(HMN, "Love Nan Province Foundation"), 85, 86–89, 121, 210, 233
Love the Nan River Project, 49, 85,
86–89, plate 16
Nan River, 84–85
See also Dok Dang Village; Pitak
Nanthakhun, Phrakhru; Ui Lek; Wat
Aranyawat
Nancy Nash, and the Buddhist Perception
of Nature Project, 80–81, 138, 186
National Forest Reserve Land (NFRL):
displacement of villagers living unofficially in, 44
and the human-and-forest debate, 46–47
illegal monastic residences in, 146–147,
189, 201, 206–207
and the 1964 National Forest Reserve
Land Act, 46
and Royal Forestry Department permits:
for commercial tree plantations, 47,
146; for logging, 46, 146, 153

the natural and social environments, 159–161, 164

See also Chiang Mai Province; environmental monks; forest monks

Prajak Khuttajitto, Phra (forest monk in Isan), plate 30

arrests of, 16, 201–203

author's participation in "Dhamma Walk" with, 204

barami of, 204–206

fame/folk hero status of, 201, 205

and the Pak Mun Dam project sangha seminar, 216

updated interpretation of the dhamma by, 205, 263n7

See also environmental monks; forest monks

Prawase Wasi, Dr., 105, 189

public awareness:

and the anti-cable car movement, 25, 168, 180–182, 184–185, 199–200, 263n1

and the Dhammayatra for Songkla Lake, 192–196

and the work of engaged monks, 195–196

Puey Ungphakorn (economist), 105

radical conservatism:

of Achan Pongsak Techadhammo, 161

defined, 90–91, 356n16

and Phrakhru Pitak, 50

of tree ordination, 1, 27, 58

Rajavaramuni, Phra. *See* Payutto, P.A.

religious-temporal relations:

and the Department of Religious Affairs, 43, 209–210

and opposition to economic forests, 44

and the political nature of tree ordinations, 11, 22–23, 75–76, 202, 225, plate 14

and the religious reforms of Mongkut (Rama IV), 97–100, 123–124, 257n8

and the role of monks in political debates, 202

and the state-imposed decentralized

organizational structure for the sangha, 101–102

See also civic religion; state authority

Reynolds, Craig J., on *The Three Worlds According to King Ruang* (*Triphum Phra Ruang*), 98, 257n6

Reynolds, Frank:

on engaged Buddhism in Thailand, 8–9

translation of *The Three Worlds According to King Ruang* (*Triphum Phra Ruang*), 66, 98, 257n6

rice banks:

initiated by Luang Pu Phuttapoj, 111

pha pa rituals used to raised funds for, 131

and the Thai Interreligious Commission on Development (TICD), 113, 129

right wing faction of the sangha, and Kittiwuttho Bhikkhu, 108

rituals:

Buddha image consecration ceremony (*buat phraphutta rup*) adapted for tree ordination, 61, 62, 63, 67, 74–75, 87, 231, 265n1, plates 9, 13

and difficulties in maintaining the original intention behind, 12

and fund-raising, 208, 237

oral/aural and visual experience of, 63–64, plate 9

and performance, 22, 55

and radical conservatism, 90–91

ritualization and profiteering, 208–210

and the transformation of abstract moral concepts into concrete actions, 54

and the transmission of knowledge, 54–55

Royal Forestry Department (RFD):

economic forests supported by, 46–47, 146

establishment of (1896), 142

and illegal monastic residences on National Forest Reserve Land, 206–207

and logging, 61, 142, 153

and the removal of forest-dwellers to prevent deforestation, 261n8